USB Complete

Everything You Need
to Develop Custom USB Peripherals

Jan Axelson

Lakeview Research
Madison, WI 53704

Lakeview Research   Phone: 608-241-5824
2209 Winnebago St.   Fax: 608-241-5848
Madison, WI 53704   Email: info@lvr.com
USA   Web: http://www.lvr.com

14 13 12 11 10 9 8 7 6 5 4 3 2

ISBN 0-9650819-3-1   Manufactured in the United States of America

Table of Contents

Introduction

How can I access USB peripherals from the applications I write?

What's involved in designing the hardware for a USB peripheral?

Over the past couple of years these have been two of the most frequently asked questions in my email. Every new PC has a couple of USB ports. The Universal Serial Bus, or USB, is a fast and flexible interface for connecting all kinds of peripherals. But practical advice about designing and accessing USB peripherals has been scarce.

My previous books, *Parallel Port Complete* and *Serial Port Complete*, showed how to use the PC's original ports. So USB was a natural choice for the next book.

When I began to look into what USB was all about, one of the first things I learned was that it's designed from the ground up to be easy to use. No more manual configuring, no more running out expansion slots or interrupt lines. Plus, USB is suitable for all but the fastest peripherals. And there's just one interface to master, not something different for every peripheral type. In a word, it sounded great.

But as I began to look deeper into what was involved in designing and communicating with a USB peripheral, something else became evident: the price of simplicity for users was increased complexity for developers. The interface itself is more complicated than earlier interfaces, and because it's new, the documentation is often incomplete or just plain not there.

Two things were clear, however:

- USB was going to succeed because the computer and peripheral manufacturers were supporting it. All PCs were shipping with USB ports, and peripheral manufacturers were putting USB ports on their products.

- Programmers were looking for a simple way to communicate with USB peripherals. If USB could be implemented without a long learning curve, developers were ready to use it for projects large and small.

So I set out to discover what was involved in getting a USB peripheral design up and running. I found that it is indeed possible to design USB devices and communicate with them without having to be a guru of device-driver writing, a master embedded programming, or an expert in other arcania. This book documents what I learned.

I won't say that USB is a piece of cake. It isn't. The complexity of the interface, combined with its newness and the evolving support in Windows, will present you with challenges no matter what your background. But by reading this book, you can take advantage of what I learned and skip some of the digging around and trial and error.

Who should read this book?

This book is for you if you want to know how to design a USB peripheral, or if you want to know how to communicate with USB peripherals from applications. These are some of questions the book answers:

- What is USB and how do peripherals use it to communicate with PCs? There's a lot to the USB interface. Learning about it can be daunting at first. I try to make it as simple as possible by breaking topics into manageable chunks and showing how they fit together. I haven't skimped on the details, though. Details are essential when you're designing from the ground up.

- How can I decide if my project should use a USB interface? Maybe your design isn't suited for USB at all. I'll show you how to decide whether it is. If the answer is yes, I'll help you decide which of USB's speeds and transfer types to use.

- How do I choose a USB controller chip for my peripheral design? There are dozens of controller chips designed for use in USB peripherals. I'll compare some of the popular chip families and offer tips on how to decide, based on both your project's needs and your own background and preferences.

- How do Visual-Basic applications communicate with USB peripherals? To communicate with a USB peripheral, a PC needs two things: a device driver that knows how to communicate with the PC's USB drivers, and an application that knows how to talk to the device driver. Some peripherals can use drivers that are built into Windows. Others may use a generic driver or require a custom driver. This book will show you when you can use Windows' built-in drivers and how to use the drivers to send and receive data from Visual-Basic applications. You'll also find out what's involved in writing a device driver and what tools can help to speed up the process.

- What code do USB peripherals need to communicate with Windows applications? USB peripherals require program code that enables them to communicate with PCs. I show how to write the code that enables Windows to identify the device and load the appropriate device driver, as well as the code required for exchanging data with applications. The examples in the book use Cypress Semiconductor's CY7C63000 series of controller chips, which are some of the simplest.

- How do I decide whether my peripheral can use bus power, or whether it needs its own supply? A big advantage to USB is that many peripherals can be powered entirely from the bus. Find out how to ensure that your design can use this feature.

To understand the material in the book, it's helpful to have basic knowledge in a few areas. I assume you have some experience with digital logic, application programming for PCs and writing embedded code for peripherals. You don't have to know anything at all about USB.

Is this book really complete?

Although the title is *USB Complete*, please don't expect this book to contain every possible fact about USB. That would take a library. The *Complete* in the title means that this book will guide you from knowing nothing about USB to developing all of the code required to get a USB peripheral up and communicating with a PC.

There are many other worthy topics related to USB, but limitations of time and space prevent me from including them all.

My focus is on communicating with Windows 98 PCs. For the most part, the material also applies to Windows 2000. Althought the basic principles are the same, I don't include details about how to communicate with peripherals on a Macintosh or a PC running Linux, DOS, or Windows NT.

I cover the basics of the device driver's responsibilities and what's involved in writing a driver, but the details can easily fill a book (and in fact there are several lengthy books on this topic). Instead of describing how to write a device driver from scratch, I show how to use existing drivers, including those provided with Windows, with your devices.

My examples use Visual Basic. Although the process is similar for other languages, this book doesn't include examples in C, C++, Delphi, or other languages. I do try, however, to include enough commentary to enable you to translate to another language as easily as possible.

How did you learn all this?

Some books about technologies such as USB are written by experts, the people who have been involved with developing the chips and software that bring the technology to life, or in writing the specifications that define the technology itself. These books can offer valuable insider information. The downside is that the authors have been so immersed in the technology for so long that they may find it hard to remember what it is that new users need to know.

I came to USB with a background in interfaces and microcontrollers, but very little knowledge about USB. My focus was on finding quick and simple ways to do USB communications. I looked at every product I could find, from every vendor I could find, then took some of the best and tried them out. I also spent considerable time learning about USB itself.

This book is the product of fifteen months of researching and experimenting. I've tried to show not only what I learned but also why it's important and how you can use it. The trials and tribulations (and there were some) were fresh in my mind as I wrote.

Corrections and Updates

In spite of my best efforts, I know from experience that errors will slip through. As they come to light, I'll document them and make a list available at Lakeview Research's website at *http://www.lvr.com*. If you find an error in the book, let me know at *jan@lvr.com*, and I'll add it. The website is also the place to find updates and code examples that weren't available when the book was printed, as well as links to vendors and information and tools from other sources.

Thanks!

USB is too complicated to cover without help. I have many people to thank.

I owe an enormous thank you to my technical reviewers, who generously read my rough and rocky drafts and provided feedback that has improved the book enormously. (With that said, every error in this book is mine and mine alone.)

First and foremost is Paul E. Berg of PEB Consulting, for reading my drafts multiple times, finding and pointing out errors throughout, offering copious tips and insights, and providing encouragement and support from the first.

My other reviewers also provided valuable advice and encouragement, each from a unique perspective. I thank:

Joshua Buergel of BlueWater Systems Inc.

Gary Crowell of Micron Technology

Dave Dowler

Mike Fahrion and the engineers at B&B Electronics

John M. Goodman, author of *Hard Disk Secrets, Peter Norton's Inside the PC, Memory Management for All of Us,* and other books

Lane Hauck, Bijan Kamran, and Dave Wright of Cypress Semiconductor

John Hyde, USB enthusiast and author of *USB Design by Example*

David James of 1Zero1 Technologies

Christer Johansson of High Tech Horizon

Kosta Koeman of Intel Corporation

Robert Severson of J. Gordon Electronic Design, Inc.

Craig R. Smith of Ford Motor Company, R&VT department

Others I want to thank for their help in my researching and writing this book are Walter Banks of Byte Craft; Jason Bock; Brad Markisohn of INDesign LLC; Pete Fowler, Joseph McCarthy, and Don Parkman of Cypress Semiconductor; Tawnee McMullen of Belkin Components; Dave Navarro of PowerBasic; and Amar Rajan, Product Manager of USB Products at QualityLogic and Founder of American Concepts Consulting.

I hope you find the book useful. Comments invited!

Jan Axelson
jan@lvr.com
November 1999

1

A Fresh Start

Computer hardware doesn't often get a chance to start fresh. Anything new has to remain compatible with whatever came before it. This is true of the computers themselves as well as the peripherals they connect to. Even the most revolutionary new peripheral has to use an interface supported by the computers it connects to.

But what if you had the chance to design a peripheral interface from scratch? What qualities and features would you include? It's likely that your wish list would include these:

- **Easy to use**, so there's no need to worry about configuration and setup details.

- **Fast**, so the interface doesn't become a bottleneck of slow communications.

- **Reliable**, so that errors are rare, with automatic correction of errors that do occur.

- **Flexible**, so many kinds of peripherals can use the interface.

- **Inexpensive**, so users (and the manufacturers who will build the interface into their products) don't balk at the price.
- **Power-conserving**, to save battery power on portable computers.
- **Supported by the operating system**, so developers don't have to struggle with writing low-level drivers for the peripherals that use the interface.

The good news is that you don't have to create this ideal interface, because the developers of the Universal Serial Bus (USB) have done it for you. USB was designed from the ground up to be a simple and efficient way to communicate with many types of peripherals, without the limitations and frustrations of existing interfaces.

Every new PC has a couple of USB ports that you can connect to a keyboard, mouse, scanner, external disk drive, printer, and standard and custom hardware of all kinds. Inexpensive hubs enable you to add more ports and peripherals as needed.

But one result of USB's ambitious goals has been challenges for the developers who design and program USB peripherals. USB is more complicated than the interfaces it replaces. Plus, the interface is new, and by necessity, the hardware, software drivers, and development tools couldn't begin to be designed until there was a specification to follow. This means that early developers of USB products face difficulties that will disappear over time.

But even early on, the advantages offered by a USB peripheral outweigh the difficulties. This book will show you ways to get a USB peripheral up and running as simply and quickly as possible by making the best possible use of the tools available now.

This chapter introduces USB, including its advantages and drawbacks, a look at what's involved in designing and programming a device with a USB interface, and a bit of the history behind USB.

What USB Can Do

USB is a likely solution any time you want to use a computer to communicate with devices outside the computer. The interface is suitable for one-of-kind and small-scale designs as well as mass-produced, standard peripherals.

To be successful, an interface has to please two audiences: the users who run applications that access the peripherals, and the developers who design the hardware and write the code that communicates with the interface. USB has features to please both.

User Benefits

From the user's perspective, the benefits to USB are ease of use, fast and reliable data transfers, flexibility, low cost, and power conservation. Table 1-1 compares USB with other popular interfaces.

Ease of Use

Ease of use was a major design goal for USB, and the result is an interface that's a pleasure to use for many reasons:

One interface for many devices. USB is versatile enough to be usable with many kinds of peripherals. Instead of having a different connector and protocols for each peripheral, one interface serves many.

Automatic configuration. When a user connects a USB peripheral to a powered system, Windows automatically detects the peripheral and loads the appropriate software driver. The first time the peripheral connects, Windows may prompt the user to insert a disk with driver software, but other than that, installation is automatic. There's no need to locate and run a setup program or restart the system before using the peripheral.

No user settings. USB peripherals don't have user-selectable settings such as port addresses and interrupt-request (IRQ) lines. Available IRQ lines are in short supply on PCs, and not having to allocate one for a new peripheral is often reason enough to use USB.

Table 1-1: Comparison of popular computer interfaces. Where a standard doesn't specify a maximum, typical maximums are listed.

Interface	Format	Number of Devices (maximum)	Length (maximum, feet)	Speed (maximum, bits/sec.)	Typical Use
USB	asynchronous serial	127	16 (or up to 96 ft. with 5 hubs)	1.5M, 12M (480M in v. 2.0)	Mouse, keyboard, disk drive, modem
RS-232 (EIA/TIA-232)	asynchronous serial	2	50-100	20k (115k with some drivers)	Modem, mouse, instrumentation
RS-485 (TIA/EIA-485)	asynchronous serial	32 unit loads	4000	10M	Data acquisition and control systems
IrDA Data	asynchronous serial infrared	2	6	115k	Printers
Microwire	synchronous serial	8	10	2M	Microcotroller communications
SPI	synchronous serial	8	10	2.1M	Microcotroller communications
I²C	synchronous serial	40	18	400k	Microcotroller communications
IEEE-1394 (FireWire)	serial	64	15	400M	Video
IEEE-488 (GPIB)	parallel	15	60	8M	Instrumentation
Ethernet	serial	1024	1600	10M/100M/1G	Networked PC
MIDI	serial current loop	2	50	31.5k	Music, show control
Parallel Printer Port	parallel	2, or 8 with daisy-chain support	10–30	8M	Printers, scanners, disk drives

Frees hardware resources for other devices. Using USB for as many peripherals as possible frees up IRQ lines for the peripherals that do require them. The PC does dedicate a series of port addresses and one inter-

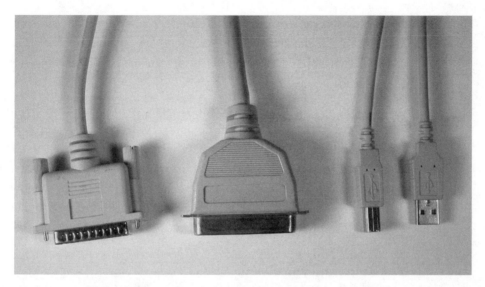

Figure 1-1: The two USB connectors (right) are smaller and slimmer than typical RS-232 serial (left) and Centronics parallel (second from left) connectors.

rupt-request (IRQ) line to the interface, but beyond this, individual peripherals don't require additional resources. In contrast, each non-USB peripheral requires dedicated port addresses, often an IRQ line, and sometimes an expansion slot (for a parallel-port card, for example).

Easy to connect. With USB, there's no need to open the computer's enclosure to add an expansion card for each peripheral. A typical PC has two USB ports. You can expand the number of ports by connecting a USB hub to an existing port. Each hub has additional ports for attaching more peripherals or hubs.

Simple cables. The USB's cable connectors are keyed so you can't plug them in wrong, and cables can be as long as 5 meters. With hubs, a link can extend as far as 30 meters. Figure 1-1 shows that the USB connectors are slim, in contrast to typical RS-232 and parallel connectors. To ensure reliable operation, the specification includes detailed requirements that all cables and connectors must meet.

Hot pluggable. You can connect and disconnect a peripheral whenever you want, whether or not the system and peripheral are powered, without damaging the PC or peripheral. The operating system detects when a device is attached and readies it for use.

No power supply required (sometimes). The USB interface includes power-supply and ground lines that provide +5V from the computer's or hub's supply. A peripheral with moderate power needs (up to 500 milliamperes) can draw all of its power from the bus instead of having its own supply. In contrast most peripherals that use other interfaces have to choose between including a power supply in the device or using a bulky and inconvenient external supply.

Speed

A full-speed USB interface communicates at 12 Megabits per second. The actual rate of data transfer is less than this because the bus must carry status, control, and error-checking signals as well as data, and because all peripherals must share the bus. With just one device communicating, the theoretical maximum rate of data transfer is about 9.6 Megabits/second, or 1.2 Megabytes/second.

If this isn't fast enough, the proposed USB 2.0 specification allows communications at 480 Megabits per second. This will make USB even more attractive for printers and other peripherals that need to transfer large amounts of data quickly

USB also supports a low-speed option of 1.5 Megabits per second. Low-speed peripherals can often be built more cheaply. Plus, their cables can be more flexible (important a mouse), because shielding isn't required.

Reliability

The reliability of USB results from both the hardware design and the data-transfer protocols. The hardware specifications for USB drivers, receivers, and cables eliminate most noise that could otherwise cause data errors. In addition, the USB protocol enables detecting of data errors and notifying the sender so it can retransmit. The detecting, notifying, and retransmitting are typically done in hardware and don't require any programming.

Low Cost

Even though USB is more complex than earlier interfaces, its components and cables are inexpensive. A device with a USB interface is likely to cost the same or less than its equivalent with an older interface. For very low-cost peripherals, the low-speed option has less stringent hardware requirements that may further reduce the cost.

Low Power Consumption

Power-saving circuits and code automatically power down USB peripherals when not in use, yet keep them ready to respond when needed. In addition to the environmental benefits of reduced power consumption, this feature is especially useful on battery-powered computers where every milliamp counts.

Developer Advantages

The above advantages for users are also important to hardware designers and programmers. The advantages make users eager to use USB peripherals, so there's no need to fear wasting time developing for an unpopular interface. And many of the user advantages also make things easier for developers. For example, USB's defined cable standards and automatic error checking mean that developers don't have to worry about specifying cable characteristics or providing error checking in software.

In addition, USB has advantages that specifically benefit developers, including the hardware designers who select components and design the circuits, the PC programmers who write the software that communicates with USB peripherals, and the peripheral programmers who write the code that resides inside USB peripherals.

The benefits to developers result from the flexibility built into the USB protocol, the support in the controller chips and operating system, and the fact that the interface isn't controlled by a single vendor. Although users aren't likely to be aware of these benefits, they'll enjoy the result, which is inexpensive, trouble-free, and feature-rich peripherals.

Flexibility

The USB's four transfer types and two speeds (three with version 2.0) make it feasible for many types of peripherals. There are transfer types suited for exchanging large and small blocks of data, with and without time constraints. For data that can't tolerate delays, USB can guarantee a transfer rate or maximum time between transfers. These abilities are especially welcome under Windows, where accessing peripherals in real time is often a challenge.

Unlike other interfaces, the USB doesn't assign specific functions to signals or make other assumptions about how the interface will be used. For example, the status and control lines on the PC's parallel port were defined with the intention of communicating with line printers. The interface has five input lines, each with an assigned function such as indicating a busy or paper-out condition. When developers began using the port for scanners and other peripherals that send large amounts of data to the PC, the limitation of having just five inputs was an obstacle. (Eventually the interface was expanded to allow 8 bits of input.)

For communicating with common device types such as printers and modems, USB supports classes with defined device requirements and protocols. This saves developers from having to re-invent these for each peripheral.

Operating System Support

Windows 98 was the first Windows operating system to reliably support USB, and its successors such as Windows 2000 support USB as well. This book focuses on Windows 98 programming for PCs, but other computers and operating systems also have USB support. On Apple's iMac, the only peripheral connectors are USB. Other Macintoshes also support USB, and support is in progress for Linux, NetBSD, and FreeBSD.

However, a claim of operating system support can mean many things. The level of support can vary! At the most fundamental level, an operating system that supports USB must do three things:

- Detect when a device is attached to or removed from the system.

- Communicate with newly attached devices to find out how to exchange data with them.

- Provide a mechanism that enables software drivers to communicate with the computer's USB hardware and with the applications that access USB peripherals.

At a higher level, operating system support may also mean the inclusion of software device drivers that enable application programmers to access devices by calling functions supported by the operating system. If the operating system doesn't include these drivers, the peripheral vendors have to provide them.

One of the first classes of USB peripherals with application-level support in Windows is human interface devices (HIDs). Application programmers can access HID-class devices using Windows API (application programmer's interface) functions or DirectX components.

The HID class can include any device that sends or receives data at moderate rates, including devices that define a maximum time between transfers. Classic examples of HIDs are mice, keyboards, and joysticks, where a human's action, such as pressing a key or moving a mouse or joystick, sends information to the PC. But the category isn't limited to these, and an HID doesn't have to have a human interface at all. Other possibilities include data-acquisition devices and control circuits.

Windows 98 also supports audio devices (speakers and microphones). Windows 98 SE, released in June 1999, added a generic modem driver with USB support, and Windows 2000 adds mass-storage and printer drivers.

In the future, Windows will likely include support for other device classes. In the meantime, some controller-chip vendors provide drivers that developers can use with their chips, either as-is or with minimal modifications. If a driver is available for a general device type, such as a modem or printer, the vendor can provide a mini-driver to support additional features and abilities.

Under Windows 98, the USB's bus and device drivers use the new Win32 Driver Model (WDM), which defines an architecture for drivers that runs under both Windows 98 and 2000. This makes it possible for developers to support both with a single driver.

Peripheral Support

On the peripheral side, each USB device's hardware must include a controller chip that handles the details of USB communications. Some controllers are complete microcomputers that include a CPU and memory that stores the code that runs inside the peripheral. Others handle only USB-specific tasks, with a data bus that connects to another microcontroller that performs non-USB related functions and communicates with the USB controller as needed.

The peripheral is responsible for responding to requests to send and receive configuration data, and for reading and writing other data when requested. In some chips, some of the functions are microcoded in hardware and don't need to be programmed.

Many USB controllers are based on popular architectures such as Intel's 8051, with added circuits and machine codes to support USB. If you're already familiar with a chip architecture that has a USB-capable variant, there's no need to learn an entirely new chip architecture in order to use USB.

Most peripheral manufacturers provide sample code for their chips. Using this code as a starting point for your own developing can give you a quick start.

Minimal Fees

Unlike some interfaces, the USB specification and related documents are available free online. Anyone can develop USB software without paying a licensing fee.

However, anyone who sells a device with a USB interface must sign an Adopter's Agreement and pay a fee for a Vendor ID. Both of these are available from the USB Implementers Forum (*www.usb.org*), the organization that sponsors the specification's development and other USB-related activities. In the Adopter's Agreement, which is free, you promise to build a device that complies with the specification. The administrative fee for obtaining a Vendor ID is $200, or you can receive it as one of many benefits of becoming a Forum member at $2500/year.

It's Not Perfect...

All of USB's advantages mean that it's a good candidate for use with many peripherals. But one interface can't do it all.

User Challenges

From the user's perspective, the downside to USB includes lack of support in older hardware and operating systems, speed and distance limits that make USB impractical for some uses, and problems with some products due to difficulties experienced by the developers of early USB products.

Lack of Support for Legacy Hardware

Older ("legacy") computers and peripherals don't have USB ports. If you want to connect a non-USB peripheral to a USB port, a solution is a converter that translates between USB and the older interface. B&B Electronics and other sources have converters for use with peripherals with RS-232, RS-485, and Centronics-type parallel ports.

However, the converter solution is useful only for peripherals that communicate using conventional protocols. Some parallel-port peripherals use custom protocols that converters don't know how to handle. Even standard parallel-port modes such as Nibble, PS/2 (Byte), EPP, and ECP aren't supported by all converters.

If you want to use a USB peripheral with a PC that doesn't support USB, the solution is to add USB capabilities to the PC. This requires two things:

the USB host-controller hardware and an operating system that supports USB. The hardware is available on expansion cards that plug into a PCI slot (or a replacement motherboard). The version of Windows must be Windows 98 or later. Some peripherals have drivers for use with later releases of Windows 95, but it's best not to count on these being available. If the hardware doesn't meet Windows 98's minimum requirements, it will need upgrades. The upgrades may end up costing more than a new system with USB.

If upgrading the PC to support USB isn't feasible, what about using a converter to translate the peripheral's USB interface to the PC's RS-232, parallel, or other interface? Interface converters are generally designed for use only for use between a USB port on a PC and a peripheral with a legacy interface. A converter for the other direction would be much more complicated, because the peripheral would have to contain the host-controller hardware and code that normally resides in the PC. So a converter isn't normally an option when the PC has the legacy interface.

Even on new systems, users may occasionally run applications on older operating systems such as MS-DOS. But the software drivers that Windows 98 applications use to communicate with USB devices are specific to Windows 98 (and Windows 2000). Without a driver, there's no way to access a USB peripheral. Although it's possible to write a USB device driver for DOS, the reality is that few peripheral developers will do so.

However, for the mouse and keyboard, which are standard, essential peripherals, the system's BIOS is likely to include support to ensure that the peripheral is usable any time, including from within DOS, the BIOS screens that you can view on bootup, and Windows' Safe mode (used in system troubleshooting). If there is no BIOS or other support, the system will need to have an old-style keyboard interface and a spare keyboard for these uses.

Speed Limits

USB is versatile, but it's not designed to do everything. Peripherals such as video devices, which need to transfer a lot of data very quickly, will likely use IEEE-1394, which is more complex and expensive than USB but over 30 times faster. USB's proposed 2.0 standard will make USB more suitable for peripherals that need speed.

Distance Limits

USB was designed as a desktop bus, with the expectation that peripherals would be relatively close at hand. A cable segment can be as long as 5 meters. Other interfaces, such as RS-232, RS-485, and Ethernet, allow much longer cables. But you can increase the length of a USB link to as much as 30 meters by using cables that link five hubs and a device, using 6 cable segments of 5 meters each. Another option is to use a USB interface on the PC, but convert to RS-485 or another interface for the long-distance cabling and peripheral interface.

Products that Don't Work

When USB works, it's great. But the reality is that some USB products just plain don't work as well as they should. When something misbehaves, the result can be an inability to communicate with a peripheral or an application or system crash. The source of the problem may be in hardware or software, in the PC or in the peripheral. The reason for these problems is a combination of USB's complexity, newness, and in some cases, inadequate testing.

But there are plenty of products that do perform exactly as advertised. Users buying USB peripherals will have fewer headaches if they follow these steps:

1. Check the Implementer's Forum's list of devices that have passed a series of tests. The tests aren't required, and there's no guarantee that the list is complete and up to date, but it's a good sign if the peripheral you're interested in is listed.

2. Be sure that any USB product you buy is returnable.

3. If you can't get a product to work properly, check the manufacturer's website for advice or updated drivers.

4. If this doesn't help, return the product and try something else.

In time, as USB becomes better supported by operating systems and developers become more familiar with USB, these problems will diminish.

Developer Challenges

From the developer's perspective, the main downside to USB is the increased complexity of the programming. Hardware bugs in both the peripheral's and some PCs' USB components can also slow project development and cause problems after a product is released. However, these will also be less of a problem in time, as the operating-system support increases, more chips and tools are available, and everyone gains more experience.

Protocol Complexity

In order to program a USB peripheral, you need to know a fair amount about the USB's protocols (the rules for exchanging data on the bus). The controller chips handle much of the communications automatically, but they still must be programmed, and this requires tools and knowledge. Different chips vary in how much support they require in performing USB communications. On the PC side, the device driver insulates application programmers from having to know many of the details, but device-driver writers need to be familiar with USB protocols and the driver's responsibilities.

In contrast, some older interfaces can connect to very simple circuits with very basic protocols. For example, the PC's original parallel printer port is just a series of digital inputs and outputs. You can connect to basic input and output circuits such as relays, switches, and analog-to-digital converters, with no computer intelligence required on the peripheral side and no device driver required on the PC (just direct port reads and writes).

Evolving Support in the Operating System

Windows 98 includes drivers that enable applications to communicate with some devices. But these drivers may not include the support your device requires. However, in many cases you can use or adapt a driver provided by the controller-chip vendor, so you don't have write a driver from scratch.

Hardware Bugs

Some early host-controller hardware wasn't bugfree, and some peripheral chips have had problems as well. In most cases, the manufacturers make fixes available in the form of new drivers or coding workarounds. The way to keep on top of these problems is to choose your hardware carefully and make a habit of visiting manufacturers' websites for the latest information and fixes.

History

To understand what USB is all about, it helps to know a little history. The main reason that new interfaces don't come around very often is that existing interfaces have the irresistible pull of all of the existing peripherals that users don't want to scrap. Also, using an existing interface saves the time and expense of designing something new. This is why the designers of the original IBM PC chose compatibility with the existing Centronics parallel interface and the RS-232 serial-port interface—to speed up the design process and enable users to connect to printers and modems already on the market. These interfaces proved serviceable for close to two decades. But as computer power and the number of peripherals have increased, the older interfaces have became a bottleneck of slow communications, with limited options for expansion.

The Motivation for Change

A break with tradition is justified when the pull of possible enhancements overshadows the inconvenience and expense of changing. This is the situation that prompted the development of USB. The result is a versatile interface that can replace existing interfaces to low- to moderate-speed standard and custom peripheral types on computers of all types.

In the past, development of a new interface was often the work of a single company. Hewlett Packard developed the HP Interface Bus (HPIB), which came to be known as the GPIB (general-purpose interface bus) for lab equipment, and the Centronics Data Computer Corporation popularized a printer interface that is still referred to as the Centronics interface.

But an interface controlled by a single company isn't ideal. The company may forbid others from using the interface, or charge licensing fees. Even if the interface is freely available, a company may be reluctant to commit its products to an interface controlled by another company, who may be a competitor and may change the interface without warning.

For these reasons, more recent interfaces are often the product of a collaboration of manufacturers who share a common interest. In some cases, an organization like the IEEE (Institute of Electrical and Electronics Engineers) or TIA (Telecommunications Industry Association) sponsors committees to develop specifications and publishes the results. In fact, many of the older manufacturers' standards have been taken over by these organizations. The IEEE-1284 standard evolved from the Centronics interface, and the GPIB was the basis for IEEE-488.

In other cases, the developers of the standard form a new organization to release the standard and handle other development issues. This is the approach used for USB. The copyright on the USB 1.1 specification is assigned jointly to four corporations, all heavily involved with PC hardware and software: Compaq, Intel, Microsoft, and NEC. All have agreed to make the specification available for use by anyone without charge (which is a refreshing change from the standards published by other organizations). The USB Implementers Forum's website has the latest versions of all USB specifications and other information for both developers and end users.

The Specification's Release

Release 1.0 of the USB specification in January 1996 followed several years of development and preliminary releases. The 1.1 release, which fixed problems identified in release 1.0, is dated September 1998.

USB capability first became available on PCs with the release of Windows 95's OEM Service Release 2. There were two editions of this release, OSR 2.1 and 2.5. Neither was available directly to retail customers. They were sold only to vendors who installed Windows 95 on the PCs they sold. The

USB support in these versions still had bugs, and there weren't a lot of USB peripherals available, so the use of USB was still limited during this era.

Things improved with the release of Windows 98 in June 1998. By this time, many more vendors had USB peripherals available, and USB began to take hold as a popular interface. Windows 98 Second Edition (SE) fixed some bugs and further enhanced the USB support. The original version of Windows 98 is now called Windows 98 Gold, to distinguish it from SE.

This book concentrates on PCs running Windows 98 and later. Windows NT4 doesn't have USB support built in, but its successor, Windows 2000, will. In this book, the term *PC* includes all of the various computers that share the common ancestor of the original IBM PC and are running Windows 98 or later.

USB 2.0

The next step in USB's evolution is version 2.0, whose main promise is *much* faster transfers. The original hope was a 20-times speed increase, but studies and tests showed that this estimate was low, and that a 40-times increase was feasible, resulting in transfer rates of 480 Megabits per second. This makes USB much more attractive for peripherals such as printers, scanners, and drives.

USB 2.0 is backwards compatible with USB 1.1. Version 2.0 peripherals will use the same connectors and cables. To use the new, higher speed, peripherals will need to connect to a Version-2.0 compliant host or hub, which will still be able to communicate with version 1.1 (and 1.0) peripherals. A 2.0-compliant hub that connects to a slower peripheral will translate received data at the new rate to the peripheral's slower rate. This increases the hub's complexity but eliminates the need for different types of hubs for the different speeds.

The leaders of the 2.0 initiative include the four companies who own the copyright to version 1.1, plus Hewlett Packard, Lucent, and Philips. The draft specification for version 2.0 was released to members of the USB Implementers Forum in October, 1999. The release version of the specification was scheduled for release in the first quarter of 2000, with products expected to be available in the second half of that year.

USB and IEEE-1394

The other major interface choice for new peripherals is IEEE-1394. Apple Computer's implementation of the interface is called Firewire. USB and IEEE-1394 take complimentary approaches, with IEEE-1394 being faster and more flexible, but more expensive. IEEE-1394 is best suited for video and other high-speed links, with USB best suited for low- to moderate-speed peripherals such as keyboards, printers, scanners, and disk drives.

With USB, a single host controls communications with many peripherals. The host handles most of the complexity, so the peripherals' electronics can be relatively simple and inexpensive. IEEE-1394 uses a peer-to-peer model, where peripherals can communicate with each other directly. A single communication can also be directed to multiple receivers. The result is a more flexible interface, but the peripherals' electronics are more complex and expensive.

IEEE-1394's 400 Megabits per second is more than 30 times faster than USB 1.1's 12 Megabits per second. As USB is getting faster with version 2.0, IEEE-1394 is getting faster with the proposed IEEE-1394.b. Its speed is 3.2 Gigabits per second, more than six times faster than USB 2.0's 480 Megabits per second.

2

Is USB Right for My Project?

Before you can decide if USB is suitable for a project, you need to know a little more about how USB works and what it can do. This chapter presents some fast facts about USB, with the focus on what's relevant when deciding whether or not USB is a good choice for a project. There's also a look at the steps in developing a USB peripheral.

Fast Facts

Some of the first questions you might have relating to whether or not USB is suitable for a project are these:

- What are the minimum requirements that a PC must meet in order to use USB peripherals?
- How do devices connect to the PC?
- In real-world terms, how fast can a peripheral exchange data with a PC?

- How do applications communicate with the peripheral?
- What are the responsibilities of the code inside the peripheral?

This section answers these questions.

Minimum PC Requirements

Before you decide to design a USB peripheral, it makes sense to be sure that the PCs that will use the peripheral can use the interface. To use USB peripherals, a PC needs two things: a USB controller that connects to one or more USB ports and an operating system with USB support.

The Controller

An interface won't succeed if PC manufacturers don't support it. Fortunately, manufacturers are enthusiastically supporting USB. Just about any new PC will have a USB controller and at least two port connectors. PCs as old as 1997 are likely to have USB support as well. Microsoft and Intel's PC 99 guidelines for new PCs recommend having two USB ports and using USB for the keyboard and other peripherals. The USB Implementers Forum has a *usbready* utility that will examine a PC's resources and report whether or not the PC supports USB.

If a computer doesn't have a USB controller built into its motherboard, you can add one on an expansion card that plugs into a slot on the PCI bus.

The Operating System

The other side of USB support is in the operating system. Your developing will be much easier if you require users to be running Windows 98 or later (including Windows 2000). Windows 95 had some USB support, but the support was greatly improved and enhanced in Windows 98. Windows 95 and Windows 98 can't use the same device drivers. Windows NT 4 doesn't support USB. However, if you're developing a peripheral that needs to run under NT, there are third-party products that you can use to create a device driver that enables the peripheral to be used under NT. DOS and Windows 3.x also have no USB support, though again, third-party products may be available.

The Components

The physical components of the Universal Serial Bus consist of the circuits, connectors, and cables between a host and one or more devices.

The host is a PC or other computer that contains two components: a host controller and a root hub. These work together to enable the operating system to communicate with the devices on the bus. The host controller formats data for transmitting on the bus and translates received data to a format that operating-system components can understand. The host controller also performs other functions related to managing communications on the bus. The root hub has one or more connectors for attaching devices. The root hub detects the attachment and removal of devices, carries out requests from the host controller, and passes data between devices and the host controller.

The devices are the peripherals and additional hubs that connect to the bus. A hub has one or more ports for connecting devices. Each device must contain circuits and code that know how to communicate with the host.

Bus Topology

The topology, or arrangement of connections, on the bus is a tiered star (Figure 2-2). At the center of each star is a hub. Each point on a star is a device that connects to one of the hub's ports. The devices may be additional hubs or other peripherals. The number of points on each star can vary, with a typical hub having two, four, or seven ports. When there are multiple hubs in series, you can think of them as connecting in a tier, or series, one above the next.

The tiered star describes only the physical connections. In programming, all that matters is the logical connection. In communicating with a USB device, neither the host or the device knows or cares how many hubs a communication must pass through. The hubs manage this automatically.

All of the devices on a bus share one data path to the host computer. Only one device can communicate with the host at a time. If you need more

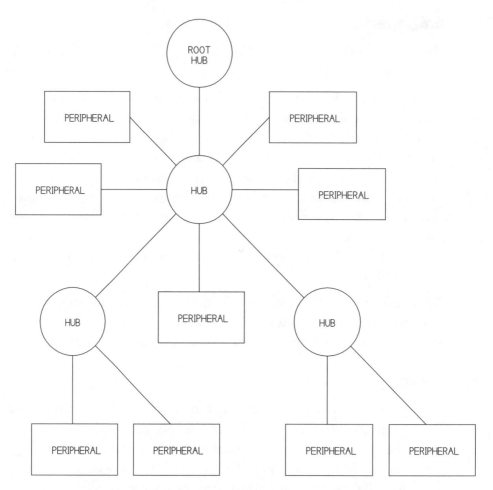

Figure 2-1: USB uses a tiered star topology, where each hub is the center of a star that can connect to peripherals or additional hubs.

bandwidth, you can add a second data path to the host by installing an expansion card with another host controller and root hub.

Figure 2-2 shows a few of the possible configurations for a PC with a root hub that has two USB connectors. If you have just two USB peripherals, you can plug one into each port on the PC. If you have up to five peripherals, you can plug one peripheral into one of the PC's ports and attach a hub with four downstream connectors to the other. You can then connect the

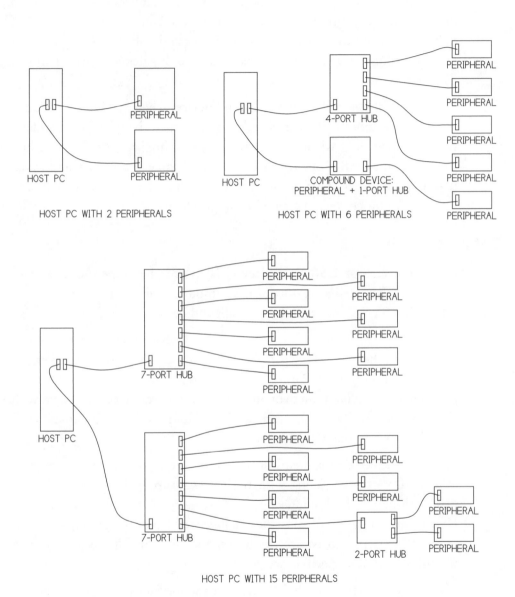

Figure 2-2: There are many possible configurations for connecting USB devices to a host PC.

remaining four peripherals to the hub. Some peripherals are compound devices that contain both a peripheral and a hub. You can cascade up to five hubs in series, up to a total of 127 peripherals and hubs (including the root hub). Of course, it may be impractical to have this many devices sharing a data path.

In some cases, especially with compound devices where the hubs are hidden inside the peripheral, the peripherals may appear to be using a daisy-chain type of connection, where each new peripheral hooks to the last one in a chain. But the USB's topology is both more flexible and more complicated than this. Each peripheral must connect to a hub, and the peripherals and hubs aren't limited to connecting in a single chain.

Defining Terms

In the universe of USB, several everyday words have specific meanings. Along with *host*, defined earlier as the computer that controls the interface, three other such terms are function, hub, and device.

The USB specification defines a *function* as a device that provides a single capability to the host. Many peripherals, such as a mouse, set of speakers, or data-acquisition unit, perform a single function. But it's also possible for a peripheral to contain more than one function. For example, a keyboard with an embedded trackball has both keyboard and trackball functions, even though it has just one USB connector.

A *hub* is a device that contains one or more connectors or internal connections to USB devices along with the hardware to enable communicating with each device. Each connector is a USB port. The hub repeats received USB traffic and also contains the intelligence to manage power, send and respond to status and control messages, and prevent full-speed data from transmitting to low-speed devices.

A *device* is a function or a hub, except for the special case of the compound device, which contains both a hub and one or more functions. Each device has a unique address on the bus, except again for a compound device, whose hub and functions have unique addresses. A peripheral with multiple functions is a composite device. In most cases, the terms peripheral and device are interchangeable.

Ports

This is also a good time to clarify the meaning of the word *port* in relation to USB. A USB port is different in some ways from the traditional serial and parallel ports on a PC.

In a general sense, a computer port is an addressable location that is available for attaching additional circuits. Usually the circuits terminate at a connector that enables attaching a cable to a peripheral such as a keyboard, display, or printer. In some cases, the peripheral circuits are hard-wired to the port. The computer's software monitors and controls the port circuits by reading and writing to the port's address or addresses. Memory addresses are also addressable locations, but they're accessed with a different set of machine instructions. On PCs, most memory addresses connect only to the system's data bus, not to other peripheral circuits.

USB ports differ from many other ports because all ports on the bus share a single path to the host. With the RS-232 serial interface, each port is independent from the others. If you have two RS-232 ports, each has its own data path, and each cable carries its own data and no one else's. The two ports can send and receive data at the same time.

USB uses a different approach. A typical PC has two USB connectors that share a host controller and a data path. Each connector represents a USB port, but unlike RS-232 ports, all devices share the available time. If additional hubs and other devices connect to the root hub, these must share as well. So even though there are multiple ports, each with its own connector and cable, there is only one data path. Only one device, or the host, can transmit at a time. Other interfaces that share a data path include Firewire and SCSI.

The Host's Duties

The host PC is in charge of the bus. The host has to know what devices are on the bus and the capabilities of each. The host must also do its best to ensure that all devices on the bus can send and receive data as needed. A bus may have many devices, each with different requirements, and all wanting to transfer data at the same time. The host's job is not trivial!

Fortunately, the host controller's hardware and the USB support in Windows do much of the work of managing the bus. Each USB device attached to the host must have a device driver, which is a software component that enables applications to communicate with the device. Some peripherals can use device drivers included with Windows, while others require custom drivers. Other system-level software components manage communications between the device driver and the host controller.

Applications don't have to worry about the details of USB communications. All they have to do is send and receive data using standard operating-system functions that are accessible from just about all programming languages.

These are tasks that the host performs with little or no support required from applications:

Detect Devices

On power-up, the hubs make the host aware of all attached USB devices. In a process called enumeration, the host assigns an address and requests additional information from each device. After power-up, whenever a device is removed or attached, the host learns of the event and enumerates any newly attached device and removes any detached device from the devices available to applications.

Manage Data Flow

The host manages the flow of data on the bus. Multiple peripherals may want to transfer data at the same time. The host controller handles this by dividing the data path into 1-millisecond frames and giving each transmission a portion of each frame.

Transfers that must occur at specific rate are guaranteed to have the amount of time they need in each frame. During enumeration, a device's driver requests the bandwidth it will need for transfers that must have guaranteed timing. If the bandwidth isn't available, the host doesn't allow communications with the device. The driver can then request a smaller portion of the bandwidth, or wait until the requested bandwidth is available. Transfers that have no guaranteed rate use the remaining portion of the frames, and may have to wait.

Error Checking

The host also has error-checking duties. It adds error-checking bits to the data it sends. When a device receives data, it can perform calculations on the data and compare the results with the received error-checking bits. If the results don't match, the device doesn't acknowledge receiving the data and the host knows that it should retransmit. (USB also supports one transfer type that doesn't allow re-transmitting, in the interest of maintaining a constant transfer rate.) In a similar way, the host may error-check the data it receives from devices.

The host may receive other error indicators that indicate that a device can't send or receive data. The host can then inform the device's driver of the problem, and the driver can notify the application so it can take appropriate action.

Provide Power

In addition to its two signal wires, a USB cable has +5V and ground wires. Some peripherals can draw all of their power from these lines. The host provides power to all devices on power-up or attachment, and works with the devices to conserve power when possible. Each full-power, bus-powered device can draw up to 500 milliamperes. The ports on some battery-powered PCs and hubs support only low-power devices, which are limited to 100 milliamperes. A device may have its own power supply, using bus power only during the initial communications with the host.

Exchange Data with Peripherals

All of the above tasks support the host's main job, which is to exchange data with peripherals. In some cases, a device driver requests the host to poll a peripheral continuously at a requested rate, while in others the host communicates only when an application or other software component requests it. The device driver reports any problems to the appropriate application.

The Peripheral's Duties

In many ways, the peripheral's, or device's, duties are a mirror image of the host's. When the host initiates communications, the peripheral must respond. However, the peripheral also has duties that are unique.

A device can't begin USB communications on its own. Instead, it must wait and respond to a communication from the host. (An exception is the remote wakeup feature, which enables a device to request a communication from the host.)

The USB controller in the device handles many of the USB's duties automatically. The amount of support required in the device's program code varies with the chip.

Detect Communications Directed to the Chip

Each device monitors the device address in each communication on the bus. If the address doesn't match the device's stored address, the device knows it should ignore the communication. If the address does match, the device stores the data in its receive buffer and generates an interrupt to signal that data has arrived. In almost all chips, this is automatic; it's built into the hardware. The device's program code doesn't have to take action or make decisions until the chip has detected a communication containing its address.

Respond to Standard Requests

On power-up, or when the device attaches to a powered system, the device must respond to the requests made by the host in the enumeration process.

All USB devices must respond to the eleven standard request codes that query the capabilities and status of the device and select a configuration. On receiving a request, the device places the information to send in response in its transmit buffer. In some cases, such as setting an address or configuration, the device takes other action in addition to responding with information.

The device doesn't have to carry out every request, however; it just has to respond to the request in an understandable way. For example, when the host requests to use a configuration that the device doesn't support, the device responds with an indicator that the request is unsupported.

Error Check

Like the host, the device adds error-checking bits to the data it sends. On receiving data that includes error-checking bits, the device does the error-checking calculations and (with some exceptions) may request a retransmit if it detects an error. These functions built into the hardware and don't need to be programmed. When appropriate, the device also detects the acknowledgements that the host sends in reply to data it has received.

Manage Power

If the device isn't bus-powered, it must have its own power supply. When there is no bus activity, the device must enter its low-power Suspend state, while continuing to monitor the bus, exiting the Suspend state when bus activity resumes.

When the host enters a low-power state, such as Windows 98's Standby state, all communications on the bus cease, including the timing markers the host normally sends each millisecond. When the devices that connect to the bus detect the absence of bus activity for three milliseconds, they must enter the Suspend state and limit the current they draw from the bus. A host may also request to suspend communications with a specific device. When bus activity resumes, the device must exit its Suspend state.

Devices that don't support the remote-wakeup feature can consume no more than 500 microamperes from the bus in the Suspend state. With the remote-wakeup feature available and enabled by the host, the limit is 2.5 milliamperes. These are average values over a 1 second; the peak current can be greater.

Exchange Data with the Host

All of the above tasks support the main job of the device's USB port, which is to exchange data with the host. After the device is configured, it must respond to requests to send and receive data.

The host may poll the device at regular intervals or only when an application requests to communicate with it. The device's configuration, the host's device driver, and the applications that use the device together determine what type of requests the host makes and how often it makes them.

For most transfer types, the device must respond to each poll by sending an acknowledge code (ACK) that indicates that it received the data, or a negative acknowledge (NAK) to indicate that it's too busy to handle the data. The device's hardware sends the appropriate response automatically. Some transfers don't use acknowledgements and the host just assumes that the device has received all transmitted data.

The controller chip's hardware handles the details of formatting the data for the bus. This includes adding error-checking bits to data to transmit, checking for errors in received data, and sending and receiving the individual bits on the bus.

Of course, the device must also do anything else it's responsible for. For example, a mouse must always be ready to detect movement and mouse clicks, a data-acquisition unit has to read the data from its sensors, and a printer must translate received data into images on paper.

Speed

A controller chip may be specified as low speed or full speed. Both low- and full-speed peripherals can connect to any USB hub. Users can be completely unaware of whether a device is low- or full-speed, because there are no user settings or configurations to worry about.

The actual rate of data transfer between a peripheral and host is less than the bus speed and isn't always predictable. Some of the transmitted bits are used for identifying, synchronizing, and error-checking rather than data, and the data rate also depends on the type of transfer and how busy the bus is with other transfers.

For time-sensitive data, USB supports transfer types that have a guaranteed rate or guaranteed maximum latency. Isochronous transfers have a guaranteed rate, where the host can request a specific number of bytes (up to 1023) to transfer to or from a peripheral in each 1-millisecond frame. (The term *isochronous* means having a guaranteed delivery rate.) Interrupt transfers have a guaranteed maximum latency, which means that the precise rate isn't guaranteed, but the time between requested transfers will be no greater than a specified amount, ranging from 1 to 255 milliseconds for full-speed devices and from 10 to 255 milliseconds for low-speed devices.

Because the bus is shared, there's no guarantee that a particular rate or maximum latency will be available to a device. If the bus is too busy to allow a requested rate or latency, the host will refuse to complete the configuration process that enables the transfers to occur.

At full speed, the fastest transfers on an otherwise idle bus are bulk transfers, with a theoretical maximum of 1.216 Megabytes per second. The host controller's driver may limit a single bulk transfer to a slower rate, however. The fastest guaranteed rate is isochronous transfers' 1.023 Megabytes per second.

Although the low-speed bus speed is 1.5 Megabits per second, the fastest guaranteed delivery for a single transfer is 8 bytes in 10 milliseconds, or 800 bytes per second. Low speed has uses, however, because the cables are cheaper and circuit-board layout is simpler. Low-speed controller chips may be cheaper as well, though this isn't guaranteed.

The Development Process

After you've made the decision to use a USB interface with your peripheral, what's next? Designing a USB product involves both getting the peripheral up and running and developing the PC software to communicate with the peripheral.

Elements in the Link

A USB peripheral needs all of the following:

- A controller chip with a USB interface.
- Code in the peripheral to carry out the USB communications.
- Whatever hardware and code the peripheral needs to carry out its other functions (processing data, reading inputs, writing to outputs).
- A host that supports USB.
- Driver software on the host to communicate with the peripheral.
- If the peripheral isn't a standard type already supported by the operating system, the host must have application software to enable users to access the peripheral. For standard peripheral types such as a mouse, keyboard, and disk drive, you don't need custom application software (though you may want to write a test application).

Tools

To develop a USB peripheral, you need the following tools:

- An assembler or compiler to create the firmware (the code that runs inside the device's controller chip). If you use assembly code, you'll need a cross assembler that runs on a PC and translates your source code into the machine code the controller understands. If you use C or another high-level language, you'll need a compiler that can generate the machine code for your controller.
- A device programmer to store the assembled or compiled code in the controller's program memory.
- A programming language and environment on the host for developing the host software. The host software may include a device driver or mini-driver and/or application code. To create a device driver, you'll need Visual C++, which is capable of compiling the WDM (Win32 Driver Model) drivers required for USB devices.
- A monitor program, protocol analyzer, or other debugging tools for use in developing your firmware.

Steps in Developing a Project

For a project of any size, you'll want to create the project in modules, a piece at a time, and get each working before moving on to the next. In writing the firmware, you can begin by writing just enough code to enable Windows to detect and enumerate the device. When that's working, you can move on to exchanging simple blocks of data with applications. From there you can add specific code for your application. The steps in project development include the areas of initial decisions, enumerating, and exchanging data:

Initial decisions

Before you begin the developing, you need to gather data and make some decisions:

1. Specify the requirements of your device. For the USB interface, how much data does it need to transfer, and how fast? What else does the device need to do?

2. Using the answer to #1, specify the requirements of the controller chip. If you have a preferred chip family, specify it.

3. Using your requirements, decide whether the PC will communicate with the peripheral using Windows' built-in USB drivers, a generic device driver, or a custom driver.

4. Select a controller chip that matches your requirements.

Enumerating

Here's what you need to do in order to get Windows to enumerate your device:

1. Write the code the controller chip needs in order to be enumerated by its host. The details vary with the chip, but every chip must be able access a series of descriptors, which are data structures that describe the chip's USB capabilities and how they'll be used. The chip must also have program code or hardware that recognizes and responds to the request codes that the host sends when it enumerates the device. Chip vendors generally provide example code that you can use with very few modifications.

2. Create or obtain an INF file so that Windows can identify the device when it enumerates it. The INF file is a text file that you can create with any text editor. The INF file names the driver that the device will use. At this point, you can use any generic driver supported by the chip's descriptors. Again, chip vendors often provide sample INF files and drivers.

3. If necessary, design and build a circuit to connect the chip to the host. In most cases, however, you'll initially use a development board provided by the chip's vendor.

4. Load the code into the device and plug the device into the host's bus. Windows should enumerate the device, adding it to the Control Panel and identifying it correctly.

5. Debug and repeat as needed!

Exchanging Data

These are the steps related to getting the device to perform its intended functions:

1. Add abilities to the device by adding code to the controller chip's firmware and components that connect to the chip.

2. If you're using a custom driver, write the driver code to communicate with the device.

3. If needed, write application code to communicate with the USB device. If you're designing a mouse, keyboard, or other standard device, you can access the device from any application.

4. Debug and repeat as needed.

5. When the code is debugged, you're ready to program the code into the chip and test on your final hardware.

But before you begin with any of this, it's useful to know a more about how the host enumerates and transfers data with devices, so you can make the right choices about controller chips and drivers. This is the purpose of the next four chapters.

3

Inside USB Transfers

In order to design and program a USB device, you need to know a certain amount about the inner workings of the interface. This is true even though the hardware and system software handle many of the details automatically.

This and the next three chapters are a tutorial on how USB transfers data. This chapter has the essentials that apply to all transfers. The following chapters cover the four transfer types supported by USB, the enumeration process, and the standard requests used in control transfers.

USB is complicated, and much of what you need to know is intertwined with everything else. This makes it hard to know where to start. In general, I try to begin with the big picture and work down to the details. Unavoidably, some of the things I refer to won't be explained in detail until later. And some things are repeated because they're important and relevant in more than one place.

The information in these chapters is dense. If you don't have a background in USB, you won't absorb it all in one reading. You should, however, get a feel for how USB works, and will know where to look later when you need to check the details.

You don't need to know every bit of this information in order to get a project up and running, but I've found that understanding something about how the transfers work helps in deciding which transfer types to use, in writing the firmware for the controller chip, and in tracking down the inevitable bugs that will occur when you try out your circuits and code.

The ultimate authority on the USB interface is the specification published by its sponsoring members. The specification document, *Universal Serial Bus Specification,* is available on the USB Implementers Forum's website. However, by design, the specification omits information and tips that are unique to any operating system or controller chip, and this type of information is essential when you're designing a product for the real world.

Transfer Basics

You can divide USB communications into two types, depending on whether they're used in initial configuration or in applications. In configuration communications, the host learns about the device and prepares it for exchanging data. Most of these communications take place when the host enumerates the device on power up or attachment. Application communications occur when applications on the host exchange data with an enumerated device. These are the communications that carry out the device's purpose. For example, for a keyboard, the application communications are the sending of keypress data to the host, to tell an application to display a character or perform other actions.

Configuration Communications

During enumeration, the device's firmware responds to a series of standard requests from the host. The device must identify each request, return the requested information, and take other actions specified by the requests.

On PCs, Windows performs the enumeration, so there's no user programming involved. However, to complete the enumeration, Windows must have two files available: an INF file that identifies the filename and location of the device's driver, and the device driver itself.

Depending on the device and how it will be used, the device driver may be one that's included with Windows or provided by the chip or peripheral vendor. The INF file is a text file that you can usually adapt from an example provided by the driver's provider. Chapter 11 has more details about device drivers and INF files.

Application Communications

After the host has exchanged enumeration information with the device and a device driver has been assigned and loaded, the application phase can be fairly straightforward. At the host, applications can use standard Windows API functions to read and write to the device. At the device, transferring data typically requires placing data to send in the USB controller's transmit buffer, reading received data from the receive buffer when a hardware interrupt signals that data has arrived, and on completing a transfer, ensuring the device is ready for the next transfer. Most devices also require some additional support for handling errors and other events.

Each data transfer on the bus uses one of four transfer types: control, interrupt, bulk, or isochronous. Each has a format and protocol suited for particular uses.

Managing Data on the Bus

The USB's two signal lines carry data to and from all of the devices on the bus. The wires form a single transmission path that all of the devices must share. Unlike RS-232, which has a TX line to carry data in one direction and an RX line for the other direction, USB's pair of wires carries a single differential signal, with the directions taking turns.

The host is in charge of seeing that all transfers occur as quickly as possible. It manages the traffic by dividing time into 1-millisecond frames and giving each transfer a part of each frame (Figure 3-1).

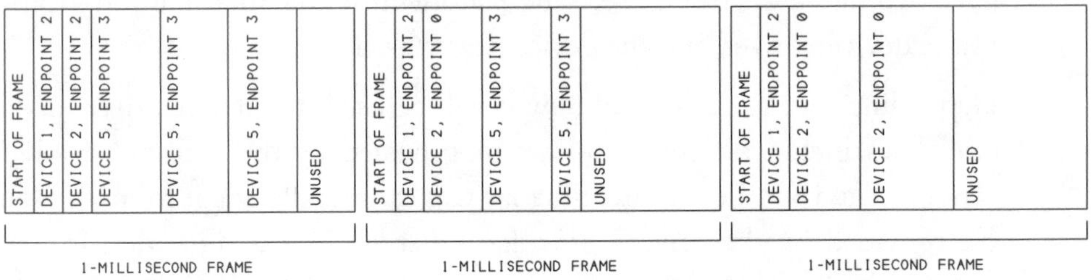

Figure 3-1: The host schedules transactions within 1-millisecond frames. Each frame begins with a Start-of-Frame packet, followed by transactions that transfer data to or from device endpoints. The host may schedule transactions anywhere it wants within a frame.

Each transfer consists of one or more transactions. Control transfers must use multiple transactions because they have separate Setup, (optional) Data, and Status stages. Other transfers use multiple transactions when they have more data than fits in one transaction. Depending on how the host schedules the transactions and the speed of a device's response, a transfer's transactions may all be in a single frame, or they may use multiple frames.

Because all of the transfers share one data path, each transaction must include the address of the transaction's source or destination. Every device has a unique address assigned by the host, and all data travels to or from the host. Each transaction begins with the host's sending a block of information that includes the address of the receiving device as well as a specific location, called an endpoint, within the device. Everything a device sends is in response to receiving a request from the host to send either data or status information in response to received data.

PC-to-PC Communications

The USB doesn't allow peripherals to exchange data directly. All communications must go through a host. And there's no way for two hosts to send data to each other without going through a peripheral. There is, however, a way to enable two PCs to communicate using their USB ports. Cypress Semiconductor's EZ-Link contains two USB peripheral controllers that share a buffer. Each controller connects to a different PC and uses the shared buffer to exchange data. Similar products are available from other vendors.

Elements of a Transfer

Understanding USB transfers requires looking inside several levels deep. Each transfer is made up of transactions. Each transaction is made up of packets. And each packet contains information. To understand transactions, packets, and their contents, you also need to know about endpoints and pipes.

Device Endpoints

All transmissions travel to or from a device endpoint. The endpoint is a buffer that stores multiple bytes. Typically it's a block of data memory or a register in the controller chip. The data stored at an endpoint may be received data, or data waiting to transmit. The host has buffers for received data and data ready to transmit, but the host doesn't have endpoints. Instead, it serves as the starting point for communicating with the device endpoints.

The specification defines a device endpoint as "a uniquely addressable portion of a USB device that is the source or sink of information in a communication flow between the host and device." This suggests that an endpoint carries data in one direction only. However, as I'll explain, a control endpoint is a special case that is bidirectional.

The unique address required for each endpoint consists of an endpoint number and direction. The number may range from 00h to 0Fh. The direction is from the host's perspective: IN is toward the host and OUT is away from the host. An endpoint configured to do control transfers must transfer data in both directions, so a control endpoint actually consists of a pair of IN and OUT endpoints that share an endpoint number.

Every device must have Endpoint 0 configured as a control endpoint. There's rarely, if ever, a need for additional control endpoints.

The other transfer types transfer data in one direction only (though status and control information may flow in the opposite direction). A single endpoint number may support both IN and OUT endpoint addresses. For example, Endpoint 1 on a device might support an IN endpoint address for transfers to the host as well as an OUT endpoint address for transfers from the host.

In addition to Endpoint 0, a full-speed device can have up to 30 additional endpoints (1 through 15, with each supporting both IN and OUT). A low-speed device is limited to two additional endpoints (for example Endpoint 1 IN and Endpoint 2 OUT).

Every transaction on the bus specifies an endpoint number and a code that indicates the direction of data flow and whether or not the transaction is initiating a control transfer. The codes are IN, OUT, and Setup:

Transaction Type	Source of Data	Types of Transfers that Use this Transaction Type	Contents
IN	device	all	generic data
OUT	host	all	generic data
Setup	host	control	a request

As with the endpoint directions, the naming convention for IN and OUT transactions is from the perspective of the host. In an IN transaction, data travels from the peripheral to the host. In an OUT transaction, data travels from the host to the peripheral. In a Setup transaction, data also travels from the host to the peripheral, but a Setup transaction is a special case because it initiates a control transfer. Devices need to identify Setup transactions so they know how to interpret the data they contain. Setup transactions are also the only type that devices must always accept. Any transfer may use IN or OUT transactions, but only control transfers use Setup transactions.

Each transaction contains a device address and an endpoint address. When a device receives an OUT or Setup transaction containing its address, the hardware stores the received data in the appropriate location for the endpoint and typically triggers an interrupt. An interrupt-service routine in the device then processes the received data and does whatever else the transaction requires. When a device receives an IN transaction containing its device address, if the device has data to send to the host, the hardware sends the data from the specified endpoint onto the bus and typically triggers an interrupt. An interrupt-service routine in the device then does whatever is required to get ready for the next IN transaction.

Pipes: Connecting Endpoints to the Host

Before a transfer can occur, the host and device must establish a pipe. A USB pipe isn't a physical object; it's just an association between a device's endpoint and the host controller's software.

The host establishes pipes shortly after system power-up or device attachment, on requesting configuration information from the device. If the device is removed from the bus, the host removes the no-longer-needed pipes. The host may also request new pipes or remove unneeded pipes at other times by requesting an alternate configuration for a device.

The configuration information received by the host includes a descriptor for each endpoint that the device has available. Each endpoint descriptor is a block of information that tells the host what it needs to know about the endpoint in order to communicate with it. This includes the endpoint address, the type of transfer to use, the maximum size of data packets, and, when appropriate, the desired interval for transfers.

In some cases, the host will establish a pipe only after ensuring that the bus has enough idle bandwidth to do the transfers within the requested time. This is true for pipes that will carry isochronous transfers, which have a guaranteed rate (transactions per second), and interrupt transfers, which have a guaranteed maximum latency (time between transactions).

In these cases, the host examines the available bandwidth before establishing the pipe. If the bandwidth is available, the host accepts the request and ensures that the transfers will have the time they need. If the bandwidth isn't available, the host denies the request to establish the pipe and the requesting software must try again, either waiting until the bandwidth is available or selecting a new configuration that reduces the requested bandwidth. For other pipes that carry requests without guaranteed timing, the host doesn't check available bandwidth; it just promises to fit the transfers into the available time.

Types of Transfers

The USB is designed to handle many types of peripherals with varying requirements for transfer rate, response time, and error correcting. The four types of data transfers each handle different needs, and a peripheral can support the transfer types that are best suited for its purpose. Table 3-1 summarizes the features and uses of each transfer type.

Control transfers are the only type with functions defined by the USB specification. These transfers enable the host to read and select configurations and other settings on the devices being enumerated. Control transfers may also send custom requests that send and receive blocks of data for any purpose. All USB devices must support control transfers.

Bulk transfers are intended for situations where the rate of transfer isn't critical, such as sending a file to a printer or receiving data from a scanner. In these cases, quick transfers are nice, but the data can wait if necessary. If the bus is very busy with other transfers that have guaranteed transfer rates, bulk transfers must wait, but if the bus is idle, bulk transfers are very fast. Only full-speed devices can do bulk transfers. Devices aren't required to support bulk transfers, but a specific device class might require it.

Interrupt transfers are for devices that must receive the host's or device's attention quickly. Other than control transfers, interrupt transfers are the only way that low-speed devices can transfer data. A keyboard or mouse can use interrupt transfers to send keypress or mouse-movement data. Both full- and low-speed devices can do interrupt transfers. Devices aren't required to support interrupt transfers, but a specific device class might require it.

Isochronous transfers are for devices that must transfer data at a constant rate, such as audio files to be played in real time, or other data that needs a guaranteed delivery rate or time. This is the only transfer type that doesn't support automatic re-transmitting of data received with errors, so occasional errors must be acceptable. Only full-speed devices can do isochronous trans-

Table 3-1: Each of the USB's four transfer types is suited for different application types.

Transfer Type	Control	Bulk	Interrupt	Isochronous
Typical Use	Configuration	Printer, scanner	Mouse, keyboard	Audio
Required?	yes	no	no	no
Allowed on low-speed devices?	yes	no	yes	no
Data bytes/millisecond per transfer, maximum possible per pipe (full speed)	832 (in thirteen 64-byte transactions)	1216 (in nineteen 64-byte transactions)	64	1023
Data bytes/millisecond per transfer, maximum possible per pipe (low speed)	24 (in three 8-byte transactions)	not allowed	0.8 (8 bytes per 10 milliseconds)	not allowed
Direction of data flow	bidirectional	one way	one way	one way
Reserved bandwidth for all transfers of the type (maximum %)	10	none	90 (isochronous & interrupt combined)	
Error correction?	yes	yes	yes	no
Message or Stream data?	message	stream	stream	stream
Guaranteed delivery rate?	no	no	no	yes
Guaranteed latency (maximum time between transfers)?	no	no	yes	yes

fers. Devices aren't required to support isochronous transfers, but a specific device class might require it.

Chapter 4 has more detailed descriptions of each transfer type, with the focus on what you need to know in order to use each. But before we get into that, there are additional things to understand about how the bus transfers data.

Stream and Message Pipes

In addition to classifying a pipe by the type of transfer it carries, the USB specification defines pipes as either stream or message type, according to whether or not information travels in one or both directions. Control transfers are the only transfers that use the bidirectional message pipes; all others use unidirectional stream pipes.

Control Transfers Use Message Pipes

In a message pipe, each transfer begins with a Setup transaction containing a request. To complete the transfer, the host and device may exchange data and status information, or the device may just send status information. There is always at least one transaction that sends information in each direction.

If the request is one that the device supports, it takes the requested action. A device may also respond with a code that indicates that it doesn't support the request.

All Other Transfers Use Stream Pipes

In a stream pipe, the data has no format defined by the USB specification. The receiving device just accepts whatever arrives. The device firmware or host software can then process the data in whatever way is appropriate for the application.

Of course, even with stream data, the sending and receiving devices will need to agree on some type of format. For example, a host application may define a code that requests a device to send a series of bytes indicating a temperature reading and the time of the reading. Although the host could use control transfers for this, it might prefer to use interrupt transfers to guarantee that the host will request a new reading at least once per millisecond. In an interrupt transfer, the data is in a stream pipe and doesn't have to conform to the format for control transfers.

Initiating a Transfer

When a device driver in the host wants to communicate with a device, it initiates a transfer. The specification defines a transfer as the process of making and carrying out a communication request. A transfer may be very short, sending as little as a byte of data, or very long, sending the contents of a large file.

An application identifies a device with a handle retrieved using standard API functions. To begin a transfer, an application may use the handle in calling an API function to request the transfer from the device's driver. Applications can request data from a device or provide data to send to the device. A request from an application might be "send the contents of the file *data.txt* on the host" or "get the contents of *Report 0* from the device." In some cases, the driver is configured to request periodic transfers automatically.

Other transfers, such as those done in the enumeration process, are initiated by the operating system on detecting the device.

The operating system passes requests to the appropriate device driver, which in turn passes the request to other system-level drivers and on to the host controller. The host controller then initiates the transfer on the bus.

Transactions: the Building Blocks of a Transfer

Figure 3-2 shows the elements of a typical transfer, and Table 3-2 lists the elements that make up each of the four transfer types. A lot of the terminology here begins to sound the same. There are transfers and transactions, stages and phases, data transactions and data packets, Status stages and handshake phases. Data stages have handshake packets and Status stages have data packets. It takes a while to absorb it all. I created Table 3-2 specifically to use as a memory-jogging reference when I found myself getting confused about the terminology. With that reminder to take it slowly, we can move on to the details.

Each transfer contains one or more transactions, and each transaction in turn contains one, two, or three packets.

The three transaction types are defined by their purpose and direction of data flow: Setup for sending control-transfer requests to a device, IN for receiving data from a device, and OUT for sending other data to the device. The specification defines a transaction as the delivery of service to an endpoint. *Service* in this case can mean either the host's sending a chunk of information to the device, or the host's requesting and receiving a chunk of information from the device.

Each transaction includes identifying, error-checking, status, and control information, as well as any data to be exchanged. While a complete transfer may take place over multiple frames, a transaction is a single communication that must complete uninterrupted. No other communication on the bus can break into the middle of a transaction. Devices must be able to respond quickly with requested data or status information. This means that although program code may prepare an endpoint to respond to a transaction request, hardware normally handles the actual responding.

A transfer with a small amount of data may require just one transaction. If the amount of data is large, a transfer may use multiple transactions, with a portion of the data in each.

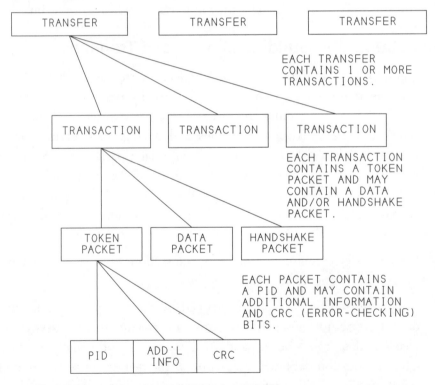

Figure 3-2: A USB transfer consists of transactions. The transactions in turn contain packets, and the packets contain a packet identifier (PID), error-checking bits, and sometimes additional information.

Table 3-2: Each of the four transfer types consists of one or more stages, with each stage made up of two or three phases.

Transfer Type	Stages (0 or more transactions)	Phases (packets). Each downstream, low-speed packet is also preceded by a PRE packet.
Control	Setup	Token
		Data
		Handshake
	Data (IN or OUT) (optional)	Token
		Data
		Handshake
	Status (IN or OUT)	Token
		Data
		Handshake
Bulk	Data (IN or OUT)	Token
		Data
		Handshake
Interrupt	Data (IN or OUT)	Token
		Data
		Handshake
Isochronous	Data (IN or OUT)	Token
		Data

Phases of a Transaction

Each transaction has up to three phases, or parts: token, data, and handshake. Each phase consists of one or two transmitted packets. Each packet is is a block of information with a defined format. All packets begin with a Packet ID (PID) that contains identifying information, as Table 3-3 shows. Depending on the transaction, the PID may be followed by an endpoint address, data, status information, or a frame number, along with error-checking bits.

The PRE PID is a special case. It contains a preamble code that tells hubs that the next packet is low speed and the hub should enable communica-

Table 3-3: The lower four bits of a PID (packet identifier) provides information about a transaction. The upper four bits are for error-checking.

Type	Name	Value (MSB first)	Description
Token	OUT	0001	Endpoint address for host-to-device transaction.
	IN	1001	Endpoint address for device-to-host transaction.
	SOF	0101	Start-of-Frame marker and frame number.
	SETUP	1101	Endpoint address for host-to-device Setup transaction.
Data	DATA0	0011	Data packet with even synchronization bit.
	DATA1	1011	Data packet with odd synchronization bit.
Handshake	ACK	0010	Receiver accepts error-free data packet.
	NAK	1010	Receiver can't accept data or sender can't send data or has no data to transmit.
	STALL	1110	A control request isn't supported or the endpoint is halted.
Special	PRE	1100	Preamble issued by host. Enables downstream traffic to low-speed device.

tions with any attached low-speed devices. The PRE PID precedes all token, data, and handshake packets directed to low-speed devices. Low-speed packets sent by a device don't require a PRE PID.

Packet Types

There are five packet types, summarized in Table 3-4. Three of these correspond to the phases of a transaction that transfers data. In the token phase, the host sends a communications request in a token packet. In the data phase, the host or device may transfer any kind of information in a data packet. In the handshake phase, the host or device sends status, or handshaking, information in a handshake packet. The specification sometimes uses the terms status phase and status packet to refer to the handshake phase and packet.

The token phase has one additional use. A token packet may carry a Start-of-Frame (SOF) marker, which is a timing reference that the host sends at 1-millisecond intervals. This packet also contains an 11-bit frame

Table 3-4: Three of the packet types correspond to the phases of a transaction. The fourth type is the Start-of-Frame marker.

Packet type	Transfer Type(s) that Use the Packet	Source	Contents (in addition to PID)
Token	All	Host	Endpoint Address
Data	All	Host or Device	Data or Handshake
Handshake	Control, Interrupt, Bulk	Host or Device	None (PID contains the handshake code)
Start of Frame (SOF)	None (sent alone)	Host	Start-of-Frame timing
Low-speed Preamble	All low-speed	Host	None

number, which rolls over on reaching the maximum. An endpoint may synchronize to the start-of-frame packet, or use the frame count as a timing reference. The Start-of-Frame marker also keeps devices from entering the low-power Suspend state when there is no other USB traffic.

Low-speed devices don't see the SOF packet. Instead, the device's hub translates the SOF to a simpler End-of-Packet (EOP) signal called the low-speed keep-alive signal. As the SOF does for full-speed devices, the low-speed keep-alive keeps low-speed devices from entering the Suspend state.

The fifth packet type contains the PRE PID and always precedes another packet.

Packet Sequences

Every transaction has a token packet. The host is always the source of the this packet, which sets up the transaction by identifying the packet type, the receiving device and endpoint, and the direction of any data that the transaction will transfer. If it's a low-speed transaction, a PRE packet precedes the token packet.

Depending on the transfer type and whether or not a device has information to send, a data packet may follow the token packet. The direction specified in the token packet determines whether the host or peripheral sends the data packet. Some transactions have no data packets. For example, in a control transfer sending a Set_Address request, the Setup transaction holds the address, so there's no need for a data packet.

In all transfer types except isochronous, the device that receives a data packet returns a handshake packet containing a code that indicates the success or failure of the transaction. (The absence of an expected handshake packet is an indication of a more drastic failure.)

Timing Constraints and Guarantees

The allowed delays between the token, data, and status packets of a transaction are very short, intended to allow only for cable delays and switching times, plus a brief time to allow the hardware to prepare a response, such as a status indication, in response to a received packet.

The maximum packet sizes for the transfer type and endpoint limit the amount of data a transaction can contain. A transfer with multiple transactions may take place over multiple frames, which don't have to be contiguous. For example, in a bulk transfer of 512 bytes, the maximum number of bytes in a single bulk transaction is 64, so transferring all of the data would require 8 transactions, assuming that the endpoint is configured for the maximum size.

Although each transaction must complete quickly, the bus can accommodate transfers with devices that need extra time to respond. The amount of time allowed varies with the transfer type, but can be as long as five seconds. If a request will take a long time to carry out, the request should be defined so that the request and response use separate transfers. This way, after receiving a request for data, the device can prepare its response for later retrieval by the host. The host uses this technique when it requests a hub to reset a port. The host requests the hub to reset a port, and the hub responds that it has received the request and has begun the reset signaling. Later, the host sends a second request to find out if the reset is complete.

Ensuring that Transfers Are Successful

To help ensure that every transfer succeeds, USB uses handshaking and error-checking.

Handshaking

Like other interfaces, the USB has status and control signals that help to manage the flow of data. Another name for these is handshaking signals. In hardware handshaking, dedicated lines carry the handshaking information. An example is the RTS and CTS lines in the RS-232 interface. In software handshaking, the same lines that carry the data also carry handshaking codes. An example is the XON and XOFF codes transmitted on the data lines in RS-232 links.

The USB uses software handshaking. A code indicates the success or failure of all transactions except in isochronous transfers. In addition, in control transfers, the Status stage enables a device to report the success or failure of the entire transfer.

Most handshaking signals transmit in the handshake packet, though some use the data packet. The three defined status codes are ACK, NAK, and STALL. A fourth status indicator is the absence of an expected handshake code, indicating a bus error. In all cases, the receiver of the handshake, or lack of one, uses the information to help it decide what to do next. Table 3-5 shows the status indicators and where they transmit in each transaction type.

ACK

ACK (acknowledge) indicates that a host or device has received data without error. Devices must return ACK in the handshake packets of Setup transactions. Devices may also return ACK in the handshake packet of OUT transactions. The host returns ACK in the handshake packets of IN transactions.

NAK

NAK (negative acknowledge) means the device is busy or has no data to return. If the host sends data at a time when the device is too busy to accept it, the device sends a NAK in the handshake packet. If the host requests data from the device when the device has nothing to send, the device sends a NAK in the data packet. In either case, NAK indicates a temporary condition, and the host retries later.

Table 3-5: The location, source, and contents of the handshake signal depend on the transaction type.

Transaction type	Data packet source	Data packet contents	Handshake packet source	Handshake packet contents
Setup	host	data	device	ACK
OUT	host	data	device	ACK, NAK, STALL
IN	device	data, NAK, STALL	host	ACK

Hosts never send NAKs. Isochronous endpoints don't support NAK because they have no handshake packet for returning the NAK. If a device or the host misses isochronous data, it's gone.

STALL

The STALL handshake can have any of three meanings: unsupported control request, control request failed, or endpoint failed.

When a device receives a control-transfer request that the endpoint doesn't support, the device returns a STALL to the host. The device also sends a STALL if it supports the request but for some reason can't take the requested action. For example, if the host sends a Set_Configuration request that requests the device to set its configuration to 2, and the device supports only configuration 1, the device returns a STALL. To clear this type of STALL, the host just needs to send another SETUP packet to begin a new control transfer. The specification calls this type of stall a protocol stall.

Another use of STALL is to respond to transfer requests when the endpoint's Halt feature is set, indicating that the endpoint is unable to send or receive data at all. The specification calls this type of stall a functional stall.

Bulk and interrupt endpoints must support the functional stall. Although control endpoints may also support this use of STALL, it's not recommended. A control endpoint in a functional stall must continue to respond normally to requests related to controlling and monitoring the STALL condition. And if the endpoint is capable of doing this, it's clearly capable of sending and receiving data and shouldn't be stalled! Isochronous endpoints don't support STALL because they have no handshake packet for returning the STALL.

On receiving a functional STALL, the host drops all pending requests to the device and doesn't resume communications until it has sent a successful request to clear the Halt feature on the device. Hosts never send STALL.

No Response

The final type of status indication occurs when the host or a device expects to receive a handshake, but receives nothing. This usually indicates that the receiver's error-checking calculation detected an error in the data, and informs the sender that it should try again, or take other action if multiple tries have failed.

Reporting the Status of Control Transfers

In addition to reporting the status of transactions, the same ACK, NAK, and STALL codes report the success or failure of complete control transfers. An additional status code is a zero-length data packet, which reports successful completion of a control transfer with a host-to-device Data stage. Table 3-6 shows the locations of the different status indicators for control transfers.

For control Write transfers. where the device receives data in the Data stage, the status is returned in the data packet of the Status stage. A zero-length data packet means that the transfer succeeded. Or the device may return a NAK or STALL, as appropriate. The host then returns an ACK in the handshake packet of the Status stage to indicate that it received the data packet.

For control Read transfers, where the host receives data in the Data stage, the device returns the status of the transfer in the handshake packet of the Status stage. The host usually waits to receive all of the data packets, then sends a zero-length data packet in the Status stage. The device responds with an ACK, NAK, or STALL. However, if the host begins the Status stage

Table 3-6: Depending on the direction of the Data stage, the status information for a control transfer may be in the data or handshake packet of the Status stage.

Data stage direction	Source of Data stages's data packet	Status stage's data packet	Status stage's handshake packet
OUT (Control Write transfer)	host	Device sends status: 0-length data packet (success), NAK (busy), STALL (failed)	Host returns ACK
IN (Control Read transfer)	device	Host sends 0-length data packet	Device sends status: ACK (success), NAK (busy), STALL (failed)

before all of the data packets have been sent, the device still must return an ACK.

Error checking

The specification for USB hardware, including the drivers, receivers, and cables, spells out design and performance requirements that ensure that errors due to line noise will be rare. Still, especially because the interface uses external cabling, there is a chance that a noise glitch or an unexpectedly disconnected cable could corrupt a transmission. For this reason, USB packets include error-checking bits that enable a receiver to identify virtually any received data that doesn't match what was sent. In addition, for transfers that require multiple transactions, a data-toggle value keeps the transmitter and receiver synchronized to ensure that no transactions are missed entirely.

Error-checking Bits

All token, data, and Start-of-Frame packets include bits for use in error-checking. The bit values are calculated using a mathematical algorithm, or procedure, called the cyclic redundancy check (CRC). The specification has details on how the CRC is calculated. It's not something you'll ever have to do in code, however, because the hardware handles it.

The CRC is applied to the data to be checked. The transmitting device performs the calculation and sends the result along with the data. The receiving device performs the identical calculation on the received data. If the results match, the data has arrived without error and the receiving device returns an ACK. If the results don't match, the receiving device sends no handshake. This tells the sender to retry.

Under Windows, the host will try to complete a transaction with no handshake response a total of three times. If there's still no handshake, the host will give up and inform the driver of the problem.

The PID field in token packets uses a simpler form of error checking. The lower four bits in the field are the PID, and the upper four bits are the complement. The receiver can check the integrity of the PID by complementing the upper four bits and ensuring that they match the PID. If not, the packet is corrupted and should be ignored.

The Data Toggle Bit

In transfers that require multiple transactions, the data-toggle bit can ensure that no transactions are missed by keeping the transmitting and receiving devices synchronized. The data-toggle bit is included in the PID field of the token packets for IN and OUT transactions. DATA0 is a code of 0011, and DATA1 is 1011. Bit 3 indicates the data-toggle state. In controller chips, a register bit often indicates the data-toggle state. Another name for this bit is DATA0/1, sometimes also called DATA1/0.

Both the sender and receiver keep track of the data toggle. On configuring the device, the bits on both are set to DATA0.

When the receiver detects an incoming data transaction, it compares the received data-toggle bit to the state of its own data toggle. If the bits match, the receiver toggles its bit and returns an ACK handshake packet to the sender. The ACK causes the sender to toggle its bit.

The next received packet in the transfer should contain a data-toggle of DATA1, and again the receiver toggles its bit and returns an ACK. The data toggle continues to alternate until the transfer completes.

If the receiver is busy, it returns a NAK. If it detects corrupted data, it returns no response. If the sender doesn't receive an ACK, it doesn't toggle its bit and instead tries again with the same data and data toggle.

If a receiver returns an ACK but for some reason the sender doesn't see it, the sender will think that the receiver didn't get the data and will try again, with the same data and data-toggle bit. In this case, the receiver of the repeated data doesn't toggle its bit and ignores the data, but it does return an ACK. This re-synchronizes the data toggles. The same thing happens if the sender mistakenly sends the same data toggle twice in a row.

The host handles the data toggles without requiring any user programming. Some peripheral controller chips also handle the data-toggles completely automatically, while others require some program control.

In some cases, if the device is interested only in the receiving the newest data and doesn't care about the sequence, it may not bother to compare the data toggles. Instead, it can just return ACKs without comparing or toggling the bit.

In isochronous transfers, the host always uses a data toggle of DATA0. Isochronous transfers can't use the data toggle because they have no handshake packet for returning an ACK or NAK and no time to resend missed data.

4

A Transfer Type for Every Purpose

Now that you know a little more about how transfers work, it's time to look in more detail at the transfer types: control, bulk, interrupt, and isochronous.

Control Transfers

Control transfers send requests and data relating to the device's abilities and configuration. They can also transfer blocks of information for any other purpose.

Availability

Every device must support control transfers over the default pipe at Endpoint 0. A device may also have additional pipes configured for control transfers, but in reality there's no need for more than one. Even if a device needs to send a lot of control requests, the host allocates bandwidth according to the number and size of requests, not by the number of control pipes, so there's no advantage to having multiple control endpoints.

Structure

As Chapter 3 explained, control transfers use a defined structure with two or three stages: Setup, Data (optional), and Status. A stage consists of one or more transactions. (Don't confuse these stages with the three transaction phases and packets: token, data, and handshake).

Every control transfer must have Setup and Status stages. The Data stage is optional, though a particular request may require it. Because every control transfer requires transferring some information in both directions, the control transfer's message pipe uses both the IN and OUT addresses of the endpoint.

In a control Write transfer, data travels from the host to the device. In a control Read transfer, data travels from the device to the host. Figure 4-1 and Figure 4-2 show the stages of each.

In the Setup stage, the host initiates a Setup transaction by sending information about the request. The token packet contains a PID that identifies the transfer as a control transfer. The data packet contains information about the request, including the request number, whether or not the transfer has a Data stage, and if so, in which direction the data will travel.

The USB specification defines 11 standard requests, though devices aren't required to support all of them. A device that belongs to a USB class must respond to the requests defined for the class, and any device may support vendor-specific or device-specific requests.

When a Data stage is present, it consists of one or more IN or OUT transactions, also called Data transactions. Depending on the request, the host or peripheral may be the source of these transactions, but all data packets in this (or any) stage must be in the same direction.

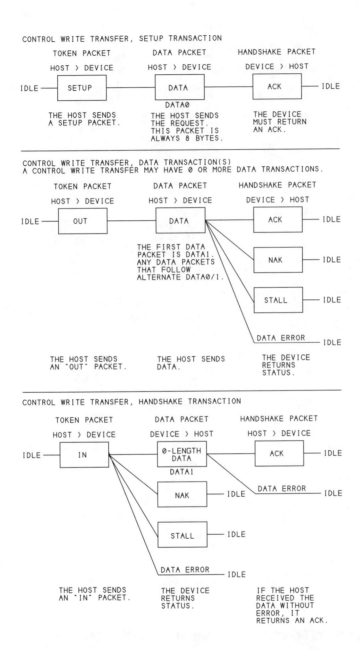

CONTROL WRITE TRANSFER, SETUP TRANSACTION

TOKEN PACKET	DATA PACKET	HANDSHAKE PACKET
HOST > DEVICE	HOST > DEVICE	DEVICE > HOST
IDLE — SETUP	DATA	ACK — IDLE
	DATA0	
THE HOST SENDS A SETUP PACKET.	THE HOST SENDS THE REQUEST. THIS PACKET IS ALWAYS 8 BYTES.	THE DEVICE MUST RETURN AN ACK.

CONTROL WRITE TRANSFER, DATA TRANSACTION(S)
A CONTROL WRITE TRANSFER MAY HAVE 0 OR MORE DATA TRANSACTIONS.

TOKEN PACKET	DATA PACKET	HANDSHAKE PACKET
HOST > DEVICE	HOST > DEVICE	DEVICE > HOST
IDLE — OUT	DATA	ACK — IDLE
	THE FIRST DATA PACKET IS DATA1. ANY DATA PACKETS THAT FOLLOW ALTERNATE DATA0/1.	NAK — IDLE
		STALL — IDLE
		DATA ERROR — IDLE
THE HOST SENDS AN "OUT" PACKET.	THE HOST SENDS DATA.	THE DEVICE RETURNS STATUS.

CONTROL WRITE TRANSFER, HANDSHAKE TRANSACTION

TOKEN PACKET	DATA PACKET	HANDSHAKE PACKET
HOST > DEVICE	DEVICE > HOST	HOST > DEVICE
IDLE — IN	0-LENGTH DATA	ACK — IDLE
	DATA1	DATA ERROR — IDLE
	NAK — IDLE	
	STALL — IDLE	
	DATA ERROR — IDLE	
THE HOST SENDS AN "IN" PACKET.	THE DEVICE RETURNS STATUS.	IF THE HOST RECEIVED THE DATA WITHOUT ERROR, IT RETURNS AN ACK.

Figure 4-1: A control Write transfer consists of a Setup transaction, zero or more Data transactions, and a Status transaction.

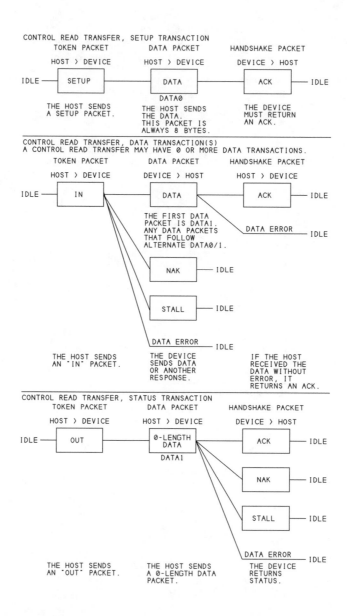

Figure 4-2: A control Read transfer consists of a SETUP transaction, zero or more data transactions, and a status transaction.

The Status stage consists of one IN or OUT transaction, also called the status transaction. The source of the Status stage's data is the receiver of the data in the previous transaction. When there is a Data stage, the receiver of the data sends the Status stage's data. When there is no Data stage, the device sends the Status stage's data.

Data Size

In full-speed devices, the maximum size for the data packet may be 8, 16, 32, or 64 bytes. On low-speed devices, the maximum is 8 bytes. These include only the information transferred in the data packet, excluding the PID and CRC bits. A transaction containing less than the maximum number of data bytes (including 0 bytes) identifies the last transaction in the transfer.

The host reads the maximum data size from the device. For the default control pipe, the host reads this value from the device descriptor retrieved on power-up or attachment. If a transfer requests more data than will fit in one transaction, the host controller divides the transfer into multiple transactions.

Speed

The host must make its best effort to ensure that all control transfers get through as quickly as possible. The host controller reserves 10 percent of the USB's bandwidth for control transfers. If the control transfers don't need this much time, bulk transfers may use the rest. Likewise, if the bus has unused bandwidth, control transfers may use more than 10 percent. The host attempts to parcel out the available time as fairly as possible to all requests. Within a transfer, one frame may carry multiple transactions, or each transaction may be in a different frame.

There are two opinions on whether control transfers are appropriate for transferring data other than configuration data. The specification recommends reserving control transfers for servicing the standard USB requests as much as possible. This helps to ensure that control transfers transmit quickly by keeping the bandwidth reserved for them as open as possible. But some believe there's no reason to limit to control transfers to a particular purpose, and that any device should be free to use control transfers for any purpose.

Control transfers aren't the most efficient way to transfer data. Each full-speed transfer with one data packet has an overhead of 45 bytes (46 for low-speed transfers) in addition to the data being transferred. Each data stage requires token and handshake packets, so stages with larger data packets are more efficient.

Low-speed transfers, which can transmit no more than 8 data bytes, are limited to three transactions per frame. A single low-speed control transfer with 8 data bytes uses 29% of a frame's bandwidth. (But the transfer's individual transactions may be spread among multiple frames).

If the bus is very busy, all control transfers may have to share the reserved 10 percent of the bandwidth. This allows just one 64-byte, full-speed transfer per frame (though again, any one transfer may be spread over multiple frames).

Devices don't have to respond immediately to control-transfer requests. In a transfer where the host requests data from the device, the device may delay as long as 500 milliseconds before it has the data ready for the host. To find out if data is available, the host sends a token packet requesting the data. If the data is ready, the device sends it immediately, in that transaction's data packet. If not, the device returns a NAK to advise the host to retry later. The host keeps trying at intervals, for up to 500 milliseconds.

In a transfer where the host sends data to the device, the device can delay as long as 5 seconds before accepting all of the data and completing the Status stage. The 5 seconds doesn't include any delays the host adds between packets.

In a transfer with no Data stage, the device must complete the request and the Status stage within 50 milliseconds.

A specific device class may require faster response to the standard requests as well as to class-specific requests.

Detecting and Handling Errors

If a device doesn't return an expected handshake packet during a control transfer, a PC's host controller will retry twice more. If the host receives no response after a total of three tries, it notifies the software that requested the transfer and stops communicating with the endpoint until the problem is corrected. The two retries include only those sent in response to no hand-shake at all. Retries in response to NAKs don't count.

If a new SETUP packet arrives before a previous transfer completes, the peripheral must abandon the previous transfer and start the new one.

Bulk Transfers

Bulk transfers are useful for transferring data where transfer time isn't criti-cal. A bulk transfer can send large amounts of data without clogging the bus, because the transfers defer to the other transfer types and will wait until time is available. Uses for bulk transfers include sending data from the host to a printer, sending data from a scanner to the host, and reading and writing to a disk. On an otherwise idle bus, bulk transfers are fast.

Availability

Only full-speed devices can do bulk transfers. Devices aren't required to sup-port bulk transfers, though a specific device class may require it.

Structure

A bulk transfer consists of one or more IN or OUT transactions. Figure 4-3 shows transactions in both directions. A bulk transfer is one-way; the trans-actions in a transfer must all be IN transactions, or all OUT transactions. Transferring data in both directions requires a separate pipe and transfer for each direction.

A bulk transfer ends in one of two ways: when the requested amount of data has transferred, or when the data-packet size is less than the maximum, including a 0-length packet.

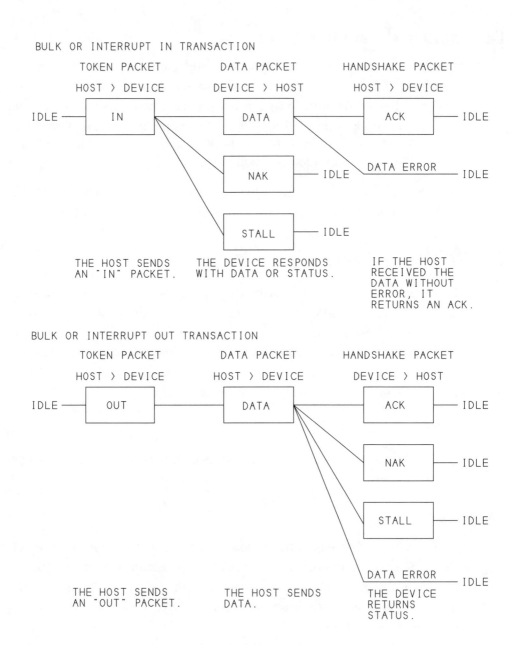

Figure 4-3: Bulk and interrupt transfers use IN and OUT transactions. Their structure is identical, but the host schedules them differently.

Data Size

A bulk transfer can have a maximum packet size of 8, 16, 32, or 64 bytes. During enumeration, the host reads the maximum packet size for each bulk pipe from the device. The amount of data in a transfer may be less than, equal to, or greater than the maximum size. If the amount of data won't fit in a single packet, the host controller divides the transfer into multiple transactions.

Speed

The host controller guarantees that bulk transfers will complete eventually, but doesn't reserve any bandwidth for the transfers. Control transfers are guaranteed to have 10 percent of the bandwidth, and interrupt and isochronous transfers may use up to 90 percent. So if a bus is very busy, a bulk transfer may take very long.

However, when the bus is otherwise idle, bulk transfers can use the most bandwidth of any type (up to 95%), and they have a low overhead, so they're the fastest of all. If the packet size is less than 64 bytes, the host may schedule only one packet per frame, even if more bandwidth is available.

On an otherwise idle bus, up to nineteen 64-byte bulk transfers can transfer up to 1216 data bytes per frame, for a data rate of 1.216 Megabytes per second. This leaves 18% of the bus bandwidth free for other uses. The protocol overhead for a bulk transfer with one data packet is 13 bytes.

Detecting and Handling Errors

Bulk transfers use error detecting. If a device doesn't return an expected handshake packet, host controllers in PCs will retry up to twice more. The host will also retry if it receives a NAK handshake. Bulk transfers also use data-toggle bits to ensure that no data is lost.

Interrupt Transfers

Interrupt transfers are useful when moderate amounts of data have to transfer within a specific amount of time. Typical applications include keyboards, mice and other pointing devices, joysticks, and hub status reports. Users don't want a noticeable delay between pressing a key or moving a mouse and seeing the result on screen. And a hub needs to report the attachment or removal of devices promptly. Low-speed devices, which support only control and interrupt transfers, are likely to use interrupt transfers for generic data. Interrupt transfers are also popular because Windows 98 includes drivers that enable applications to do interrupt transfers with HID-class devices.

The name *interrupt transfer* suggests that a device can cause a hardware interrupt that results in a fast response from the PC. But the truth is that interrupt transfers, like all other USB transfers, occur only when the host polls a device. The transfers are interrupt-like, however, because they guarantee that the host will request or send data with minimal delay.

Availability

Both low-speed and full-speed devices can do interrupt transfers. Devices aren't required to support interrupt transfers, but a device class may require it. For example, a device in the USB's HID class must support interrupt IN transfers for sending data to the host.

Structure

An interrupt transfer consists of one or more IN transactions or one or more OUT transactions. The structure of an interrupt transfer is identical to that of a bulk transfer (Figure 4-3). An interrupt transfer is one-way; the transactions must be all IN transactions, or all OUT transactions. Transferring data in both directions requires a separate transfer and pipe for each direction.

An interrupt transfer ends in one of two ways: when the requested amount of data has transferred, or when the data-packet size is less than the maximum, including a zero-length packet.

Data Size

A full-speed device can use a maximum packet size of 1 to 64 bytes. Low-speed devices have an 8-byte maximum. During enumeration, the host reads the maximum packet size for each interrupt pipe from the device. If the amount of data in a transfer won't fit in a single packet, the host controller divides the transfer into multiple transactions.

Speed

An interrupt transfer guarantees a maximum latency, or time between transaction attempts. In other words, there is no guaranteed transfer rate, just a guaranteed maximum time between transactions. The endpoint descriptor stored in the device specifies the latency, which may be any value between 1 and 255 milliseconds for full-speed devices, or between 10 and 255 milliseconds for low-speed devices. The host controller ensures that the transactions have no more than the specified time between them.

The host may begin each transaction at any time up to the specified maximum, compared to when the previous transaction began. So, for example, with a 10-millisecond maximum, 5 transfers could take as long as 50 milliseconds or as little as 5 milliseconds. However, under Windows, the host uses values that correspond to powers of 2. So, for example, if a device requests a maximum anywhere from 8 to 15 milliseconds, the host will begin a transaction every 8 milliseconds.

The host's freedom to transfer data more quickly than the requested rate means that the transactions don't guarantee a precise rate of delivery, with one exception. An interrupt pipe configured for 1 transfer per millisecond must do exactly one transfer per millisecond, because that's the fastest rate possible.

Before configuring a pipe for interrupt transfers, the host controller compares the requested buffer size with the available remaining, unreserved bandwidth on the bus to determine whether the required bandwidth is available. Because interrupt transfers use little bandwidth and because the host controller prevents any transfer from using all of the bandwidth, an interrupt-transfer request is likely to be accepted unless the bus is extremely busy. But if the bus doesn't have room for the transfer, the host controller will deny the request to configure the device. If the device supports an alternate configuration with smaller data packets, the driver can request this. Or the driver can try later, in the hope that the bandwidth will be available. When the device is configured, the transfers are guaranteed to have the time they need.

In order to use interrupt transfers effectively, both the sending and receiving devices have to be capable of getting the data in and out of the USB buffers at the required rate. The host controller guarantees that the USB bandwidth will be available, but it can't guarantee that the host application and device will be ready to transfer data at the requested times. If the sender doesn't write the data to send into the transmit buffer in time, the hardware can't send it on the bus. And if the receiver doesn't read the data from its buffer before the new data arrives, either the old data will be overwritten or the receiver will refuse the new data.

For devices such as keyboards and mice, the driver continually requests interrupt transfers. For other devices, the host may request no transfers until an application requests to send or receive data.

An otherwise idle bus can theoretically carry up to nineteen 64-byte, full-speed interrupt transfers in each frame. In reality, a host isn't likely to be able to schedule nineteen interrupt transactions in a single frame, so the actual maximum rate is less. An otherwise idle bus can theoretically carry up to eight low-speed, 8-byte transactions. The protocol overhead for both speeds is 13 bytes per transfer for transfers with one data packet.

Isochronous and interrupt transfers combined can use no more than 90 percent of the USB's bandwidth.

Detecting and Handling Errors

If a device doesn't return an expected handshake packet, host controllers in PCs will retry up to twice more. The host will also retry if it receives a NAK from a device. Interrupt transfers can use data-toggle values to ensure that all data is received without errors. As explained earlier, if the receiver is more interested in immediate data rather than keeping track of all data, it may ignore the data toggle.

Isochronous Transfers

Isochronous transfers are streaming, real-time transfers that are useful when data must arrive at a constant rate, or by a specific time. Isochronous transfers can transfer more data per frame than interrupt transfers. But there is no provision for retransmitting data received with errors, so occasional errors must be acceptable.

Examples of uses for isochronous transfers include encoded voice and music to be played in real time. But data that will eventually be used at a constant rate doesn't necessarily require an isochronous transfer. For example, a host may use a bulk transfer to send a music file to a device. After the device has received the entire file, it can play it at the appropriate rate.

Nor does the data in an isochronous transfer have to be used at a constant rate. An isochronous transfer is a way to ensure that a large block of data gets through quickly on a busy bus, even if the data doesn't need to transfer in real time. Unlike with bulk transfers, once an isochronous transfer begins, the sending of the data at a constant rate is guaranteed, so the completion time is predictable.

Availability

Only full-speed devices can do isochronous transfers. Devices aren't required to support isochronous transfers but a device class may require it.

Structure

Isochronous means that the data has a fixed transfer rate, with a defined number of bytes transferring in every frame. All of the other transfer types are asynchronous, which means that they don't guarantee to send a specific number of bytes in each frame (with the exception of 1-millisecond interrupt transfers).

An isochronous transfer consists of one IN or OUT transaction per frame in one or more contiguous frames. Figure 4-4 shows the packets in an isochronous IN and OUT transactions. An isochronous transfer is one-way; the transactions in a transfer must all be IN transactions, or all OUT transactions. Transferring data in both directions requires a separate transfer and pipe for each direction.

Before configuring a pipe for isochronous transfers, the host controller compares the requested buffer size with the available remaining, unreserved bandwidth on the bus to determine whether the requested bandwidth is available. A transfer of the maximum 1023 bytes per frame uses 69 percent of the USB's bandwidth. If two devices want to establish pipes for transferring 1023 bytes per frame, the host will refuse to configure the device requesting the second pipe because the data won't fit in the available time. If the device supports an alternate configuration with smaller data packets, the device driver can request this. Or the device can try again later in the hope

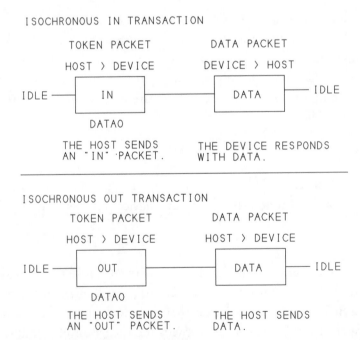

Figure 4-4: Isochronous transfers don't use status packets, so occasional errors must be acceptable.

that the bandwidth will be available. When the device is configured, the transfers are guaranteed to have the time they need.

Although isochronous transfers may send a fixed number of bytes per frame, the data doesn't transfer at a constant number of bits per second. Each transaction has overhead and must share the bus with other devices. So the data in each frame is actually a burst at 12 Megabits per second. If the receiving end wants to use the data at a constant rate, such as sending it to a speaker, the receiver must convert the received bits to signals that span the 1-millisecond frame time.

Isochronous transfers may also synchronize to another data source or recipient. For example, a microphone's input may synchronize to the output of speakers. The specification describes several methods of synchronizing to internal and external clocks.

Data Size

If the bandwidth is available, a transaction can carry up to 1023 data bytes. If the amount of data won't fit in a single packet, the host will divide the transfer into multiple transactions.

The amount of data in each frame doesn't have to be the same. For example, a transfer at 44,100 samples per second could use a sequence of 9 frames containing 44 samples each, followed by 1 frame containing 45 samples.

Speed

Isochronous and interrupt transfers combined can use up to 90 percent of the USB's bandwidth.

In order to use isochronous transfers effectively, both the sender and receiver have to be capable of getting the data into and out of the USB buffers at the required rate. If the sender doesn't write the data to the transmit buffer in time, the transmitting hardware can't send it on the bus. And if the receiver doesn't read the data from its buffer before the new data arrives, either the old data will be overwritten or the receiver will refuse the new data.

An isochronous transfer can transfer up to 1023 bytes per frame, or up to 1.023 Megabytes per second. This leaves 31% of the bus bandwidth free for other uses. The protocol overhead is 9 bytes per transfer for a transfer with one data packet, or less than 1% for a single 1023-byte transaction.

Detecting and Handling Errors

The price to pay for guaranteed on-time delivery of large blocks of data is a lack of error correction. Isochronous transfers are intended for uses where occasional, small errors are acceptable. For example, listeners may tolerate or not notice a short dropout in voice or music. In reality, under normal circumstances, a USB transfer should experience no more than a very occasional error due to line noise. Because isochronous transfers must keep to a schedule, the receiver can't request a retransmit of data if it's busy or detects an error. If the receiver suspects errors, it can ask the sender to resend the entire transfer, but this isn't very efficient.

5

Enumeration: How the Host Learns about Devices

Before applications can communicate with a device, the host needs to learn about what transfer types and endpoints the device supports. The host also must assign an address to the device. The host accomplishes these in an exchange of information called enumeration.

This chapter describes the enumeration process, including the structure of the descriptors that the host reads from the device during enumeration. You don't need to know every detail about enumeration in order to design a USB peripheral, but understanding a certain amount is essential in creating the descriptors that will reside in the device and writing the firmware that responds to enumeration requests.

The Process

One of the duties of a hub is to detect the attachment and removal of devices. Each hub has an interrupt IN pipe for reporting these events to the host. On system boot-up, the host polls its root hub to learn if any devices are attached, including additional hubs and devices attached to them. After boot-up, the host continues to poll periodically to learn of any newly attached or removed devices.

On learning of a new device, the host sends a series of requests to the device's hub, causing the hub to establish a communications path between the host and the device. The host then attempts to enumerate the device. Enumeration is the initial exchange of information that enables the host's device driver to communicate with the device. The process consists of assigning an address to the device, reading descriptive data from the device, assigning and loading a device driver, and selecting a configuration from the options presented in the retrieved data. The device is then configured and ready to transfer data using any of the endpoints in its configuration.

The host enumerates by sending control transfers containing standard USB requests to Endpoint 0. All USB devices must support control transfers, standard USB requests, and Endpoint 0. For a successful enumeration, the device must respond to each request by returning the requested information and taking other requested actions.

From the user's perspective, enumeration should be invisible and automatic, except for in some cases a window that announces the detection of a new device and whether or not the attempt to configure it succeeded. Sometimes on first use, the user will need to provide a disk containing the INF file and device driver.

When enumeration is complete, Windows adds the new device to the Device Manager display in the Control Panel. Figure 5-1 shows an example. To view the Device Manager, click the Start menu > Settings > Control Panel >System > Device Manager. When a user disconnects a peripheral, Windows automatically removes the device from the display.

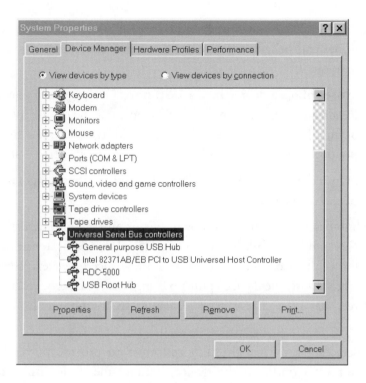

Figure 5-1: The Device Manager in Windows' Control Panel lists all detected USB devices. (Some devices will be listed by type, such as keyboard or modem, rather than under Universal Serial Bus controllers.)

In a typical peripheral, the peripheral's program code contains the information the host will request, and the program code must recognize and respond to requests for the information. Some application-specific chips (ASICs) manage the enumeration entirely in hardware and require no firmware support. On the host side, under Windows there's no need to write code for enumerating, because Windows handles it automatically. Windows will look for a special text file called an INF file that tells Windows what driver to use for the device.

Enumeration Steps

During the enumeration process, a device moves through four of the six possible device states: Powered, Default, Address, and Configured. (The other states are Attached and Suspended.) In each state, the device has defined capabilities and behavior. These are the events that cause and occur during enumeration:

1. The user plugs a device into a USB port. Or the system powers up with a device already plugged into a port. The port may be on the root hub at the host or on a hub that connects downstream of the host. The hub normally provides power to the port, and the device is in the Powered state.

2. The hub detects the device. The hub monitors the voltages on the signal lines of each of its ports.

The hub has a 15-kilohm pull-down resistor on each of the port's two signal lines (D+ and D-), while a device has a 1.5-kilohm pull-up resistor on either D+ (for a full-speed device) or D- (for a low-speed device). When a device plugs into a port, the device's pull-up brings that line high, enabling the hub to detect that a device is attached. Chapter 16 has more on how hubs detect devices.

On detecting a device, the hub continues to provide power but doesn't transmit USB traffic to the device, because the device isn't yet ready to receive it.

3. The host learns of the new device. Each hub uses its interrupt pipe to report events at the hub. The report indicates only whether the hub or a port (and if so, which port) has experienced an event. When the host learns of an event, it sends the hub a Get_Port_Status request to find out more. Get_Port_Status and the other requests described here are standard hub-class control requests that all hubs understand. The information returned tells the host when a device is newly attached.

4. The hub resets the device. When a host learns of a new device, the host controller sends the hub a Set_Port_Feature request that requests the hub to reset the port. The hub places the device's USB data lines in the Reset condition for at least 10 milliseconds. Reset is a special condition where both D+ and D- are a logic low. (Normally, the lines have opposite logic states.) The hub sends the reset only to the new device. Other hubs and devices on the bus don't see it.

5. The hub establishes a signal path between the device and the bus. The host verifies that the device has exited the reset state by sending a Get_Port_Status request. A bit in the data returned indicates whether the device is still in the reset state. When the hub has released the reset, the device is in the Default state. The device's USB registers are in their reset states and the device is ready to respond to control transfers over the default pipe at Endpoint 0. The device can now communicate with the host, using the default address of 0h. At this point, the device can draw no more than 100 milliamperes from the bus.

6. The hub detects the device's speed. Either just before or just after the Reset, the hub detects the device's speed by examining the voltages on the two signal lines. The hub detects the speed of a device by determining which line has the higher voltage when idle. The hub sends the information to the host in response to the next Get_Port_Status request.

7. The host sends a Get_Descriptor request to learn the maximum packet size of the default pipe. The host sends the request to device address 0, Endpoint 0. Because the host enumerates only one device at a time, only one device will respond to communications addressed to device address 0.

The maximum packet size is in the eighth byte of the descriptor, so the host needs to read only the first 8 bytes. A Windows host requests 64 bytes, but after receiving just one packet (whether or not it has 64 bytes), it begins the status stage. On completion of the status stage, the host requests the hub to reset the device (repeating steps 4 and 5). The specification doesn't require a reset here, because devices should be able to handle the host's abandoning a control transfer at any time by responding to the next Setup stage. Resetting is a precaution that ensures that the device will be in a known state when the reset ends.

8. The host assigns an address. The host controller assigns a unique address to the device by sending a Set_Address request. The device reads the request, returns an acknowledge, and stores the new address. The device is now in the Address state. All communications from this point on use the new address. The address is valid only until the device is detached or the system powers down. On the next enumeration, the device may be assigned a different address.

9. The host learns about the device's abilities. The host sends a Get_Descriptor request to the new address to read the device descriptor, this time reading the whole thing. The descriptor is a data structure containing the maximum packet size for Endpoint 0, the number of configurations the device supports, and other basic information about the device. The host uses this information in the communications that follow.

The host then continues to learn about the device by requesting the one or more configuration descriptors specified in the device descriptor. A Windows host begins by requesting just the configuration descriptor's nine bytes. Included in these bytes is the total length of the configuration descriptor and all of its subordinate descriptors.

Windows then requests the configuration descriptor again, this time using the retrieved total length, up to FFh bytes. This causes the device to send the configuration descriptor followed by the interface descriptor(s) for each configuration, followed by endpoint descriptor(s) for each interface. If the descriptors total more than FFh bytes, Windows obtains the full set of descriptors on a third request. Each descriptor begins with its length and type, to enable the host to parse (pick out the individual elements in) the data that follows. The Descriptors section in this chapter has more on what each descriptor contains.

10. The host assigns and loads a device driver (except for composite devices). After the host learns as much as it can about the device from its descriptors, it looks for the best match in a device driver to manage communications with the device. In selecting a driver, Windows tries to match the Vendor and Product IDs, Release Number, and/or class information retrieved from the device with the information stored in the system's INF files. After the driver is loaded, it often requests the device to resend descriptors or send class descriptors that apply to the device.

An exception to this sequence is composite devices, which have multiple interfaces, with each interface requiring a driver. The host can assign these drivers only after the interfaces are enabled, which requires the device to be configured (as described in the next step).

11. The host's device driver selects a configuration. After learning about the device from the descriptors, the device driver requests a configuration by sending a Set_Configuration request with the desired configuration number. Many devices support only one configuration. If a device supports multiple configurations, the driver can decide which to use based on whatever information it has about how the device will be used, or it may ask the user what to do, or it may just select the first configuration. The device reads the request and sets its configuration to match. The device is now in the Configured state and the device's interface(s) are enabled.

Drivers for the interfaces in compound devices may be assigned now. As with other devices, if Vendor and Product IDs are available, the host uses these to select the driver for an interface. Otherwise, the host uses whatever class, subclass, and protocol values are available.

The device is now ready for use.

The other two device states, Attached and Suspended, may exist at any time.

Attached state. If the hub isn't providing power (VBUS) to the port, the device is in the Attached state. This may occur if the hub detects an over-current condition, or if the host requests the hub to remove power from the port. With no power on VBUS, the host and device can't communicate, so from their perspective, the situation is the same as when the device isn't attached at all.

Suspended State. The Suspended, or Suspend, state means that the device has seen no activity on the bus for at least 3 milliseconds. In the suspended state, the device must consume minimal bus power. Both configured and unconfigured devices must support the Suspended state. Chapter 17 has more on this.

Enumerating a Hub

Hubs are also USB devices, and the host enumerates a newly attached hub in exactly the same way it enumerates a device. If the hub has devices attached, the host also enumerates each of these after the hub informs the host of their presence.

Device Removal

When a user removes a device from the bus, the hub disables the device's port. The host learns that the removal occurred after polling the hub, learning that an event has occurred, and sending a Get_Port_Status request to find out what the event was. Windows then removes the device from the Device Manager's display and the device's address becomes available to another newly attached device.

About Descriptors

Descriptors are data structures, or formatted blocks of information, that enable the host to learn about a device. Each descriptor contains information about either the device as a whole or an element within the device.

All USB peripherals must respond to requests for the standard USB descriptors. This means that the peripheral must do two things: store the information that the host may request, and respond to requests with the information in the expected format.

Types

As described above, during enumeration the host uses control transfers to request descriptors from the device. As enumeration progresses, the requested descriptors concern increasingly small elements of the device: first the entire device, then each configuration, each configuration's interface(s), and finally each interface's endpoint(s).

The higher-level descriptors inform the host of any additional, lower-level descriptors. Each device has one and only one device descriptor that contains information about the device as a whole and specifies the number of configurations the device supports. Each device also has one or more configuration descriptors that contain information about the device's use of power and the number of interfaces supported by the configuration. Each interface descriptor has zero or more endpoint descriptors that contain the information needed to communicate with an endpoint. (An interface with no endpoints can use only the control endpoint for communications.)

A fifth descriptor type, the string descriptor, can store text such as the vendor's or device's name. The other descriptors may store indexes that point to the string descriptors, and the host can read the string descriptors with the same Get_Descriptor requests it uses for the other descriptors.

In addition to the standard descriptors, a device may contain class- or vendor-specific descriptors. These offer a structured way for a device to provide more detailed information about itself. For example, an interface descriptor may specify that the device belongs to the HID class and supports a class descriptor.

Each descriptor contains a value that identifies the descriptor type. Table 5-1 lists values defined by the USB and HID specifications. Bit 7 is always zero. Bits 6 and 5 identify the descriptor type: 00h=standard, 01h=class, 02h=vendor, 03h=reserved. Bits 4 through 0 identify the descriptor.

Each descriptor consists of a series of fields. Most of the field names use prefixes to indicate something about the contents of the data in that field: b = byte (8 bits), w = word (16 bits), bm = bit map, bcd = binary-coded decimal, i = index, id = identifier.

Chapter 12 shows a set of descriptor tables stored in the firmware of an HID-class device.

Device Descriptor

The device descriptor has basic information about the device. It's the first descriptor that the host reads on device attachment. The descriptor includes the information the host needs in order to retrieve additional information from the device.

The descriptor has 14 fields. Table 5-2 lists the fields in the order they occur in the descriptor. The descriptor includes information about the descriptor itself, the device, its configurations, and its classes. The following descriptions group the information by function.

Table 5-1: Each descriptor has a value that specifies what kind of information the descriptor contains.

Type	Value (hexadecimal)	Descriptor
Standard	01	Device
	02	Configuration
	03	String
	04	Interface
	05	Endpoint
Class	21	HID
	29	Hub
Specific to the HID class	22	Report
	23	Physical

The Descriptor

bLength. The length in bytes of the descriptor.

bDescriptorType. The constant DEVICE (01h).

The Device

bcdUSB. The USB specification number that the device and its descriptors comply with. In BCD (binary-coded decimal) format. (For example, Spec. version 1.0 is 0100h; version 1.1 is 0110h.)

idVendor. Members of the USB Implementers Forum and others who pay an administrative fee receive a unique Vendor ID. The device descriptor for every commercial product must have a Vendor ID. The device's INF file on the host may also contain this value, and if so, Windows uses the value to help decide what driver to load for the device.

idProduct. The Product ID is assigned by the manufacturer to identify the device. Both the device descriptor and the device's INF file on the host may contain this value, and if so, Windows uses the value to help decide what driver to load for the device.

Table 5-2: The device descriptor has 14 fields in 17 bytes.

Offset (decimal)	Field	Size (bytes)	Description
0	bLength	1	Descriptor size in bytes
1	bDescriptorType	1	The constant DEVICE (01h)
2	bcdUSB	2	USB specification release number (BCD)
4	bDeviceClass	1	Class code
5	bDeviceSubclass	1	Subclass code
6	bDeviceProtocol	1	Protocol Code
7	bMaxPacketSize(0)	1	Maximum packet size for Endpoint 0
8	idVendor	2	Vendor ID
10	idProduct	2	Product ID
12	bcdDevice	2	Device release number (BCD)
14	iManufacturer	1	Index of string descriptor for the manufacturer
15	iProduct	1	Index of string descriptor for the product
16	iSerialNumber	1	Index of string descriptor containing the serial number
17	bNumConfigurations	1	Number of possible configurations

bcdDevice. The device's release number in BCD format. Assigned by the manufacturer. Optional. This value can also be used in deciding which driver to load.

iManufacturer. An index that points to a string describing the manufacturer. Optional. Zero if unused.

iProduct. An index that points to a string describing the product. Optional. Zero if unused.

iSerialNumber. An index that points to a string containing the device's serial number. Optional. Zero if unused. Serial numbers are useful if users may have more than one identical device on the bus and the host needs to keep track of which is which. They also enable the host to determine whether a peripheral is the same one used previously or a new installation of a peripheral with the same Vendor and Product ID. If a device has a serial number and a user plugs the device into a different port on a PC, Windows won't need to reload the device's driver.

The Configuration

bNumConfigurations. The number of configurations the device supports.

bMaxPacketSize0. The maximum packet size for Endpoint 0. The host uses this information in the requests that follow. Allowed values for full-speed devices are 8, 16, 32, and 64. Low-speed devices must use 8.

Classes

bDeviceClass. For devices in one of the USB's defined classes, this field may name the class. Values from 1 to FEh are reserved for the USB's defined classes. Examples of classes are hubs, printers, and communications devices. The value FFh means that the class is specific to the vendor and defined by the vendor. Some devices (such as HIDs) specify the class in the interface descriptor, so for these devices, this field in the device descriptor is 0. Not all devices belong to a class.

bDeviceSubclass. For devices in one of the USB's defined classes, this field may specify a subclass within the class. If DeviceClass is 0, the Subclass must be 0. If DeviceClass is between 1 and FEh, the Subclass must be a code defined in a USB specification. A value of FFh means that the subclass is specific to the vendor. A subclass may add support for additional features and abilities shared by a group of functions within a class.

bDeviceProtocol. May specify a protocol defined by the selected class or subclass. If DeviceClass is between 1 and FEh, the protocol must be a code defined by a USB specification.

Configuration Descriptor

After retrieving the Device Descriptor, the host is able to retrieve the device's Configuration, Interface, and Endpoint Descriptors.

Each device has at least one configuration that describes the device's features and abilities. Often a single configuration is enough, but a device with multiple uses or modes can have multiple configurations. Each configuration in turn has a configuration descriptor. The configuration descriptor contains information about the device's use of power and the number of interfaces supported.

The host selects a configuration with the Set_Configuration request, and reads the current configuration with a Get_Configuration request.

The descriptor has eight fields. Table 5-3 lists the fields in the order they occur in the descriptor. The fields in the descriptor contain information about the descriptor itself, the configuration, and the device's use of power in that configuration. For many configurations, some fields don't apply. The following descriptions group the information by function.

The Descriptor

bLength. The length (in bytes) of the descriptor.

bDescriptorType. The constant CONFIGURATION (02h).

wTotalLength. The number of data bytes that the device returns, including the bytes for all of the configuration's interfaces and endpoints.

The Configuration

bConfigurationValue. Identifies the configuration in Get_Configuration and Set_Configuration requests. A Set_Configuration request with a value of zero causes the device to enter the Not Configured state.

iConfiguration. Index to a string that describes the configuration. Optional.

bNumInterfaces. The number of interfaces the configuration supports. The minimum is 1.

Power Use

bmAttributes. Bit 6=1 if the device is self-powered. Bit 5=1 if the device supports remote wakeup, which enables a suspended USB device to tell its host that it wants to communicate. A USB device must enter the Suspend state if there has been no bus activity for 3 milliseconds. If an event at a suspended device requires action from the host, a device that supports remote

Table 5-3: The configuration descriptor has 8 fields.

Offset (decimal)	Field	Size (bytes)	Description
0	bLength	1	Descriptor size in bytes
1	bDescriptorType	1	The constant Configuration (02h)
2	wTotalLength	2	Size of all data returned for this configuration in bytes
4	bNumInterfaces	1	Number of interfaces the configuration supports
5	bConfigurationValue	1	Identifier for Set_Configuration and Get_Configuration requests
6	iConfiguration	1	Index of string descriptor for the configuration
7	bmAttributes	1	Self power/bus power and remote wakeup settings
8	MaxPower	1	Bus power required, expressed as (maximum milliamperes/2)

wakeup and has had this feature enabled can request the host to resume communications. The other bits are unused: bits 0 through 4 are 0, and bit 7 is 1.

MaxPower. Specifies how much bus current a device requires. MaxPower in milliamperes equals one half the number of milliamperes required. If the device requires 200 milliamperes, MaxPower=100. The maximum current allowed is 500 milliamperes. Storing half the number of milliamperes enables one byte to store values up to the maximum. If the host determines that the requested current isn't available, it will refuse to configure the device.

Interface Descriptor

The term interface may of course describe the USB as a whole, but in terms of a device and its descriptors, *interface* means a set of endpoints used by a device feature or function. A configuration's interface descriptor contains information about the endpoints.

Each configuration must support one interface, and for many devices, one is enough. When there are multiple ways to use a device, instead of using multiple configurations, a device may define multiple interfaces within a configuration. The interfaces may each use different endpoints, or each may specify alternate uses of the same endpoints. The host requests a new interface with a Set_Interface request, and reads the current interface with a Get_Interface request. Changing interfaces is simpler than changing configurations, which affects the entire device.

An Interface Descriptor has nine fields. Table 5-4 lists the fields in the order they occur in the descriptor. Many devices don't have a need for all of the fields, such as those that enable alternate settings and protocols. The following descriptions group the information by function.

The Descriptor

bLength. The number of bytes in the descriptor.

bDescriptorType. The constant INTERFACE (04h).

The Interface

iInterface. Index to a string that describes the interface.

bInterfaceNumber. The interface's number. Used in Get_Interface and Set_Interface requests. The default is 0.

bAlternateSetting. For interfaces with more than one setting, specifies the setting to use. The default is 0.

bNumEndpoints. The number of endpoints the interface supports in addition to Endpoint 0. For a device that supports only endpoint 0, NumEndpoints is 0.

bInterfaceClass. Similar to DeviceClass in the Device Descriptor, but for devices with a class defined by the interface. Values from 01h to FEh are reserved for USB-defined classes. HID is class 03h. FFh indicates a vendor-defined class. Zero is reserved.

bInterfaceSubClass. Similar to bDeviceSubClass in the Device Descriptor, but for devices with a class defined by the interface. For interfaces in one of the USB's defined classes, this field may specify a subclass within the class. If bInterfaceClass is 0, bInterfaceSubclass must be 0. If bInterfaceClass is between 1 and FEh, InterfaceSubclass must be a code defined by a USB

Table 5-4: The interface descriptor has 9 fields.

Offset (decimal)	Field	Size (bytes)	Description
0	bLength	1	Descriptor size in bytes
1	bDescriptorType	1	The constant Interface (04h)
2	bInterfaceNumber	1	Number identifying this interface
3	bAlternateSetting	1	Value used to select an alternate setting
4	bNumEndpoints	1	Number of endpoints supported, except Endpoint 0
5	bInterfaceClass	1	Class code
6	bInterfaceSubclass	1	Subclass code
7	bInterfaceProtocol	1	Protocol code
8	iInterface	1	Index of string descriptor for the interface

specification. A value of FFh means that the subclass is specific to the vendor.

bInterfaceProtocol. Similar to bDeviceProtocol in the Device Descriptor, used by devices whose class is defined by the interface. May specify a protocol defined by the selected bInterfaceClass or bInterfaceSubClass. If bInterfaceClass is between 1 and FEh, bInterfaceProtocol must be a code defined by a USB specification.

Endpoint Descriptor

Except for Endpoint 0, each endpoint specified in an interface descriptor has an endpoint descriptor. Endpoint 0 doesn't need a descriptor because the device descriptor contains its maximum packet size and everything else about the endpoint is defined by the specification. Table 5-5 lists the descriptor's six fields in the order they occur in the descriptor. The following descriptions group the information by function.

The Descriptor

bLength. The number of bytes in the descriptor.

bDescriptorType. The constant ENDPOINT (05h).

Table 5-5: The endpoint descriptor has 6 fields.

Offset (decimal)	Field	Size (bytes)	Description
0	bLength	1	Descriptor size in bytes
1	bDescriptorType	1	The constant Endpoint (05h)
2	bEndpointAddress	1	Endpoint number and direction
3	bmAttributes	1	Transfer type supported
4	wMaxPacketSize	1	Maximum packet size supported
5	bInterval	1	Polling interval, in milliseconds

The Endpoint

bEndpointAddress. Includes the endpoint number and direction. Bits 0 through 3 are the endpoint number. Low-speed devices can have a maximum of 3 endpoints (0 through 2), while full-speed devices can have 16 (0 through 15). Bit 7 is the direction: Out=0, In=1, Bidirectional (for control transfers)=ignored. Bits 4, 5, and 6 are zero and unused.

bmAttributes. Bits 1 and 0 specify the type of transfer the endpoint supports. 00=Control, 01=Isochronous, 10=Bulk, 11=Interrupt. Bits 2 through 7 are reserved. For Endpoint 0, Control is assumed.

wMaxPacketSize. The maximum number of data bytes the endpoint can transfer. For Endpoint 0, the device descriptor holds the maximum packet size. For low-speed devices, this must be 8. For full-speed devices, it can be 8, 16, 32, or 64.

bInterval. The frequency, in milliseconds, for polling interrupt and isochronous endpoints. For interrupt transfers, the value may range from 1 to 255 for full-speed devices and from 10 to 255 for low-speed devices. For isochronous transfers, the value is 1. For bulk and control transfers, the value is ignored.

String Descriptor

A string descriptor contains descriptive text. The USB specification defines string descriptors for the manufacturer, product, serial number, configura-

Table 5-6: A string descriptor has 3 or more fields.

Offset (decimal)	Field	Size (bytes)	Description
0	bLength	1	Descriptor size in bytes
1	bDescriptorType	1	The constant String (03h)
2	bSTRING or wLANGID	varies	Unicode string or an array of 1 or more Language Identifier codes

tion, and interface. A device may support additional string descriptors as well. String descriptors are optional. Table 5-6 shows the descriptor's fields and their purposes.

The Descriptor

bLength. The number of bytes in the descriptor.

bDescriptorType. The constant STRING (03h).

The String

Each string has an index. String 0 has the special function of providing language IDs, while the other strings may contain any information.

wLANGID[0...n]. String 0 is one or more 16-bit language ID codes that specify the languages that the strings are available in. The code for English is 0009h, and the subcode for U.S. English is 0004h. These seem to be the only codes that are valid in U.S. versions of Windows 98. This value must be valid in order for any of the other strings to be valid. For a list of codes, see the book *Developing International Software for Windows 95 and Windows NT* by Nadine Kano (Microsoft Press). The book is included in the Microsoft's MSDN library.

bString. For Strings 1 and up, the String field contains a Unicode string. Unicode uses 16 bits to represent each character. With a few exceptions, ANSI character codes 00h through 7Fh correspond to Unicodes 0000h through 007Fh. For example, a product string for a product called "Gizmo" would contain five 16-bit Unicodes representing the characters in the product name: 0047 0069 007A 006D 006F. The strings are not null-terminated.

6

Control Transfers: Structured Requests for Critical Data

Of the four transfer types, control transfers have the most complex structure. They're also the only transfer type with functions defined by the specification. This chapter takes a more detailed look at control transfers. The focus is on what you need to know to implement standard and custom requests in device firmware, along with some background about the structure of the requests.

Elements of a Control Transfer

As Chapter 3 explained, control transfers enable the host and a device to exchange information about the device's configuration. They also offer a way that any device can use to transfer any type of information. Each control transfer has a defined format consisting of a Setup stage, an optional Data stage, and a Status stage. Each stage consists of one or more transactions that contain a token phase, a data phase, and a handshake phase. Each phase transfers a token, data, or handshake packet. If the transfer is low speed, any phase that sends data to a device begins with a PRE packet. Each packet also contains error-checking bits. Chapter 4 included diagrams showing the packets that transfer in each stage.

The Setup Stage

The Setup stage consists of a Setup transaction, which has two purposes: to identify the transfer as a control transfer and to transmit the request and other information that the device will need in order to complete the request.

Devices must accept and acknowledge Setup transactions. If a device is in the middle of another control transfer, it must abandon that transfer and respond to the new Setup transaction. Here are more details about each of the packets in the Setup stage's transaction:

Token Packet

Purpose: identifies the receiver and identifies the transaction as a Setup transaction.

Sent by: the host.

PID: SETUP

Additional Contents: the device and endpoint addresses.

Data Packet

Purpose: transmits the request and related information.

Sent by: the host.

PID: DATA0

Additional Contents: eight bytes in five fields: bmRequestType, bRequest, wValue, wIndex, and wLength.

bmRequestType is a byte that specifies the direction of data flow, the type of request, and the recipient.

Bit 7 is a Direction bit that specifies the direction of data flow for requests that include a data packet. Zero indicates host-to-device; 1 indicates device-to-host.

Bits 6 and 5 are Request Type bits that specify whether the request is one of the USB's eleven standard requests (00), a request defined for a specific USB class (01), or a request defined by a vendor for use with a particular product or products (10).

Bits 4 through 0 are Recipient bits that define whether the request is directed to the device (0000) or to a specific interface (0001), endpoint (0010), or other element (0011) in the device.

bRequest is a byte that specifies the request. When the Request Type bits in bmRequestType are 00, bRequest contains the number of one of the USB's standard requests. When the Request Type bits are 01, bRequest names a request defined for the device's class. When the Request Type bits are 10, bRequest names a request defined by the device's vendor.

wValue is two bytes that the host may use to pass information to the device. Each request may define the meaning of these bytes in its own way. For example, in a Set_Address request, wValue contains the device address.

wIndex is two bytes that the host may use to pass information to the device. A typical use is to pass an index or offset such as an interface or endpoint number, but each request may define the meaning of these bytes in any way. When passing an endpoint index, bits 0-3 indicate the endpoint number, and bit 7 is 0 for a Control or OUT endpoint or 1 for an IN endpoint. When passing an interface index, bits 0-7 are the interface number. All unused bits are 0.

wLength is two bytes containing the number of data bytes in the Data stage that follows. For a host-to-device transfer, wLength is the exact number of bytes. For a device-to-host transfer, wLength is a maximum, and the device may return this number of bytes or fewer. If the wLength field is 0, there is no data packet.

Handshake Packet

Purpose: transmits the device's acknowledgement.

Sent by: the device.

PID: ACK.

Additional Contents: none. The handshake packet consists of the PID alone.

Comments: If the device detected an error in the received Setup or Data packet, it returns no handshake. The device's hardware typically handles the error checking and sending of the ACK, with no programming required.

The Data Stage

When a control transfer contains a Data stage, the stage consists of one or more IN or OUT transactions. The endpoint's descriptor specifies the number of data bytes that each transaction can carry. (The device descriptor specifies this value for Endpoint 0.)

When the Data stage uses IN transactions, the device sends data to the host. An example is Get_Descriptor, where the device sends a descriptor to the host. When the Data stage uses OUT transactions, the host sends data to the device. An example is Set_Report, where an HID-class device sends a report to the host. If the wLength field in the Setup transaction is 0, there is no Data stage at all. For example, in the Set_Configuration request, the host passes a configuration value to the peripheral in the wValue field of the Setup stage's data packet, so there's no need for the Data stage.

If all of the data can't fit in one packet, the stage uses multiple transactions. The number of transactions required to send all of the data for the transfer equals the value in the Setup transaction's wLength field divided by the wMaxPacketSize value in the endpoint's descriptor, rounded up. For example, in a Get_Descriptor request, if wLength is 18 and wMaxPacketSize is 8, the transfer requires 3 Data transactions. The transactions in the Data stage must all be in the same direction.

Each IN or OUT transaction in the Data stage contains token, data, and handshake packets. Here are more details about each of the packets in the Data stage's transaction(s):

Token Packet

Purpose: identifies the receiver and identifies the transaction as an IN or OUT transaction.

Sent by: the host.

PID: if the request requires the device to send data to the host, the PID is IN. If the request requires the host to send data to the device, the PID is OUT.

Additional Contents: the device and endpoint addresses.

Data Packet

Purpose: transfers all or a portion of the data specified in the wLength field of the Setup transaction's data packet.

Sent by: if the token packet's PID is IN, the device sends the data packet; if the token packet's PID is OUT, the host sends the data packet.

PID: The first packet is DATA1. Any additional packets in the Data stage alternate DATA0/DATA1.

Additional Contents: the data.

Handshake Packet

Purpose: transmits the status of the data packet's receiver.

Sent by: the receiver of the Data stage's data packet. If the token packet's PID is IN, the host sends the handshake packet. If the token packet's PID is OUT, the device sends the handshake packet.

PID: A device may return ACK (valid data was received), NAK (the endpoint is busy), or STALL (the request isn't supported or the endpoint is halted). The host can return only ACK.

Additional Contents: None. The handshake packet consists of the PID alone.

Comments: If the receiver detected an error in the token or data packet, it returns no handshake packet.

The Status Stage

The Status stage is where the device reports the success or failure of the entire transfer. Its purpose is similar to that of a transaction's handshake packet, and in fact the information sometimes travels in the handshake packet of the Status stage. But the Status stage reports the success or failure of the entire transfer, rather than of a single transaction.

In some cases (such as after receiving the first packet of a device descriptor during enumeration), the host begins the Status stage before the device has sent all of the transfer's data, and the device must detect this, stop sending data, and complete the Status stage.

Here are more details about each of the packets in the Status stage's transaction:

Token Packet

Purpose: identifies the receiver and indicates the direction of the Status stage's data packet.

Sent by: the host.

PID: the opposite of the direction of the previous transaction's data packet. If the Data stage's PID was OUT, or if there was no Data stage, the Status stage's PID is IN. If the Data stage's PID was IN, the Status stage's PID is OUT.

Additional Contents: the device and endpoint addresses.

Data Packet

Purpose: enables the receiver of the Data stage's data to indicate the status of the transfer.

Sent by: if the Status stage's token packet's PID is IN, the device sends the data packet; if the Status stage's token packet's PID is OUT, the host sends the data packet.

PID type: DATA1

Additional Contents: The host sends only the PID and error-checking bits, but no data bits. This is a called a zero-length data packet. A device may send a zero-length data packet (success), NAK (busy), or STALL (endpoint halted).

Comments: For most requests, the zero-length data packet indicates that the request has been carried out. An exception is Set_Address, which isn't carried out until the Status stage has completed.

Handshake Packet

Purpose: the sender of the Data stage's data indicates the status of the transfer.

Sent by: the receiver of the Status stage's data packet. If the Status stage's token packet's PID is IN, the host sends the handshake packet; if the token packet's PID is OUT, the device sends the data packet.

PID type: the device's response may be ACK (success), NAK (busy), or STALL (the request isn't supported or the endpoint is halted). The host's response to the received data packet must be ACK.

Additional Contents: none. The handshake packet consists of the PID alone.

Comments: The Status stage's handshake packet is the final transmission in the transfer. If the receiver detected an error in the token or data packet, it returns no handshake packet.

For any request that's expected to take many milliseconds to carry out, the protocol should define an alternate way to determine when the request has completed. This ensures that the host doesn't waste a lot of time looking for an acknowledgement that will take a long time to arrive. An example is the Set_Port_Feature(PORT_RESET) request sent to a hub. The reset signal lasts at least 10 milliseconds. Rather than forcing the host to wait this long for the device to complete the reset, the hub acknowledges receiving the request when it first places the port in the reset state. When the reset is complete, the hub sets a bit that the host can retrieve at its leisure, using a Get_Port_Status request.

Handling Errors

Control-transfer requests aren't always carried out. A request may be one that the device's firmware doesn't support. Or the device may be unable to respond because its firmware has crashed, the device is in the Halt condition, or the device is no longer attached to the bus. The host may also decide for any reason to end a transfer early, before all of the data has been sent.

An example of an unsupported request is one that uses a request code that the device's firmware doesn't know how to respond to. Or the device may support the request but other information in the Setup stage doesn't match what the device expects or supports. When this occurs, a Request Error condition exists and the device notifies the host by sending a STALL code in a handshake packet. Devices must respond to the Setup transaction with an ACK, so the STALL must transmit in the handshake packet of the next Data stage or the Status stage.

If the host fails to get an expected response, or if it detects an error in received data or a Halt condition at the device, it abandons the transfer. The host then tries to re-establish communications by sending the token packet for a new Setup transaction. If a device receives a token packet for a Setup transaction before it has completed a previous control transfer, it must abandon the previous transfer and begin the new one. If the transfer is using the default control pipe and the new token packet doesn't cause the device to recover, the host takes more drastic action, requesting the device's hub to reset the device's port.

The host may also end a transfer early by initiating the Status stage before completing all of the Data stage's transactions. In this case, the device must abandon the rest of the data and respond to the Status stage as if all of the data had transferred.

The 11 Standard Requests

Table 6-1 summarizes the USB's 11 standard requests, followed by a description of each request. All devices must respond to these requests (though the response may be just a STALL). The values range from 00 to 0Ch, with some values unused.

Most of the requests are in pairs, with each Set request having a corresponding Get or Clear request. The exceptions are Set_Address and Synch_Frame.

Table 6-1: The USB specification defines eleven standard requests for Control transfers.

Request #	Request	Data source	Recipient	Value	Index	Data Length (bytes)	Data
00h	Get_Status	device	device, interface, endpoint	0	device, interface, endpoint	2	status
01h	Clear_Feature	none	device, interface, endpoint	feature	device, interface, endpoint	0	none
03h	Set_Feature	none	device, interface, endpoint	feature	device, interface, endpoint	0	none
05h	Set_Address	none	device	device address	0	0	none
06h	Get_ Descriptor	device	device	descriptor type & index	device or language ID	descriptor length	descriptor
07h	Set_ Descriptor	host	device	descriptor type & index	device or language ID	descriptor length	descriptor
08h	Get_ Configuration	device	device	0	device	1	configura-tion
09h	Set_ Configuration	none	device	configura-tion	device	0	none
0Ah	Get_Interface	device	interface	0	interface	1	alternate setting
0Bh	Set_Interface	none	interface	interface	interface	0	none
0Ch	Synch_Frame	device	endpoint	0	endpoint	2	frame number

Set_Address

Purpose: The host specifies an address to use in future communications with the device.

Request Number: 05h

Source of Data: none

Data Length: 0

Contents of Value field: new device address. Allowed values are 1 through 127. Each device on the bus, including the root hub, has a unique address.

Contents of Index field: 0

Contents of Data field: none

Supported States: Default, Address.

Behavior on error: not specified.

Comments: When a hub enables a port after power-up or attachment, the port uses the default address of 0 until it receives a Set_Address request from the host.

This request is unlike most other requests because the device doesn't carry out the request until it has completed the Status phase of the request by sending a 0-length data packet. The host sends the Status phase's token packet to the default address, so the device must send the packet before changing its address.

After completion of this request, all communications use the new address.

A device using the default address of 0 is in the Default state. After completing Set_ Address request to set an address other than 0, the device enters the Address state.

A device must send the handshake packet within 50 milliseconds after receiving the request, and it must complete the request within 2 milliseconds after completing the Status phase.

Get_Descriptor

Purpose: The host requests a specific descriptor.

Request Number: 06h

Source of Data: device

Data Length: the number of bytes to return. If the descriptor is longer than Data Length, the device returns bytes up to Data Length. If the descriptor is shorter than Data Length, the device returns the descriptor, and the host detects the end of the descriptor when the device sends a data packet with less than the maximum packet size (including 0 bytes).

Contents of Value field: High byte: descriptor type. Low byte: descriptor value.

Contents of Index field: for String descriptors, Language ID. Otherwise 0.

Contents of Data field: the requested descriptor.

Supported states: Default, Address, Configured.

Behavior on error: If a device receives a request that it doesn't support, it should return a STALL.

Comments: There are five types of descriptors: Device, Configuration, Interface, Endpoint, and String. Chapter 5 described the purpose and contents of the descriptor types. Every USB device must support a device descriptor and at least one configuration descriptor.

A request for a configuration descriptor causes the device to return the configuration descriptor, plus all interface descriptors for that configuration and all endpoint descriptors for the interfaces.

Set_Descriptor

Purpose: The host adds a descriptor or updates an existing descriptor.

Request Number: 0Bh

Source of Data: host

Data Length: The number of bytes the host will transfer to the device.

Contents of Value field: high byte: descriptor type. (See Get_Descriptor) Low byte: descriptor index.

Contents of Index field: For string descriptors, Language ID. Otherwise 0.

Contents of Data field: descriptor length.

Supported states: Address and Configured.

Behavior on error: If a device receives a request that it doesn't support, it should return a STALL.

Comments: This request makes it possible for the host to add descriptors other than those stored in the device's firmware, or to change an existing descriptor. Many devices don't support this request because it allows errant software to place incorrect information in a descriptor.

Set_Configuration

Purpose: Instructs the device to use the selected configuration.

Request Number: 09h

Source of Data: none

Data Length: none

Contents of Value field: The lower byte specifies a configuration. If the value matches a configuration supported by the device, the device selects the requested configuration. A value of 0 indicates not configured. If the value is 0, the device enters the Address state and requires a new Set_Configuration request to be configured.

Contents of Index field: 0

Contents of Data field: 0

Supported states: Address, Configured.

Behavior on error: If Value isn't equal to 0 or a configuration supported by the device, the device returns a STALL.

Comments: After completing a Set_Configuration request specifying a supported configuration, the device enters the Configured state. Many of the standard requests require the device to be in the Configured state.

Get_Configuration

Purpose: The host requests the value of the current device configuration.

Request Number: 08h

Source of Data: device

Data Length: Configuration value

Contents of Value field: 0

Contents of Index field: 0

Contents of Data field: 1

Supported states: Address (returns 0), Configured

Behavior on error: not specified.

Comments: If the device isn't configured, it returns 0.

Set Interface

Purpose: For devices with configurations that support multiple interfaces, the host requests an interface setting.

Request Number: 0Bh

Source of Data: host

Data Length: 0

Contents of Value field: alternate setting

Contents of Index field: interface

Contents of Data field: none

Supported states: Configured

Behavior on error: If the device supports only a default interface, it may return a STALL. If the interface or setting doesn't exist, the device returns a STALL.

Comments: Many devices support only one interface.

Get_Interface

Purpose: For devices with configurations that include support multiple interfaces, the host requests the current interface number.

Request Number: 0Ah

Source of Data: device

Data Length: 1

Contents of Value field: 0

Contents of Index field: interface

Contents of Data field: the current interface number

Supported states: Configured

Behavior on error: If the interface doesn't exist, the device returns a STALL.

Comments: Many devices support only one interface.

Set_Feature

Purpose: The host requests to enable a feature on a device, interface, or endpoint.

Request Number: 03h

Source of Data: none

Data Length: none

Contents of Value field: the feature to enable

Contents of Index field: 0, interface number, or endpoint number

Contents of Data field: 0

Supported states: Default: undefined. Address: OK for address 0, Endpoint 0. Otherwise the device returns a STALL. Configured: OK.

Behavior on error: If the endpoint or interface specified doesn't exist, the device responds with a STALL.

Comments: The USB specification defines just two features.

DEVICE_REMOTE_WAKEUP, with a value of 1, applies to devices. When the host sets the DEVICE_REMOTE_WAKEUP feature, a suspended device can signal the host to resume communications.

ENDPOINT_HALT, with a value of 0, applies to endpoints. Bulk and interrupt endpoints must support the Halt condition. Two types of events may cause a Halt condition: a communications problem such as the device's not receiving a Status packet or receiving more data than expected, or the device's receiving a Set_Feature request to halt the endpoint. A Clear_Feature request to halt the endpoint removes a Halt condition caused by a Set_Feature request.

The Get_Status request tells the host what features, if any, are enabled.

Clear_Feature

Purpose: The host requests to disable a feature on a device, interface, or endpoint.

Request Number: 01h.

Source of Data: none

Data Length: none

Contents of Value field: the feature to disable

Contents of Index field: For a device feature, 0. For an interface feature, the interface number. For an endpoint feature, the endpoint number.

Contents of Data field: none

Supported states: Default: undefined. Address: OK for address 0, Endpoint 0. Otherwise the device returns a STALL. Configured: OK.

Behavior on error: If the feature, device, or endpoint specified doesn't exist, or if the feature can't be cleared, the device responds with a STALL. Behavior is undefined when Length is greater than 0.

Comments: The USB specification defines only two features. DEVICE_REMOTE_WAKEUP, with a value of 1, applies to devices. ENDPOINT_HALT, with a value of 0, applies to endpoints. See Set_Feature for more details.

Get_Status

Purpose: The host requests the status of the features of a device, interface, or endpoint.

Request Number: 00h

Source of Data: device

Data Length: 2

Contents of Value field: 0

Contents of Index field: For a device, 0. For an interface, the interface number. For an endpoint, the endpoint number.

Contents of Data field: the device, interface, or endpoint status

Supported states: Default: undefined. Address: OK for address 0, endpoint 0. Otherwise the device returns a STALL. Configured: OK.

Behavior on error: The device returns a STALL if the interface or endpoint doesn't exist.

Comments: For device requests, only two bits are defined. Bit 0 is the Self-Powered field: 0=bus-powered, 1=self-powered. The host can't change this value. Bit 1 is the Remote Wakeup field. The default on reset is 0 (disabled). All other bits are reserved. For interface requests, all bits are reserved. For endpoint requests, only bit 0 is defined. Bit 0=1 indicates a Halt condition. See Set_Feature for more details on Remote Wakeup and Halt.

Synch_Frame

Purpose: The device sets and reports an endpoint's synchronization frame.

Request Number: 0Ch

Source of Data: host

Data Length: 2

Contents of Value field: 0

Contents of Index field: endpoint number

Contents of Data field: frame number

Supported states: Default: undefined. Address: The device returns a STALL. Configured: OK.

Behavior on error: If the endpoint doesn't support the request, it should return a STALL.

Comments: In isochronous transfers, a device endpoint may request data packets that vary in size, following a sequence. For example, an endpoint may send a repeating sequence of 8, 8, 8, 64 bytes. The Synch_Frame request enables the host and endpoint to agree on which frame will begin the sequence.

When an endpoint receives a Synch_Frame request, it returns the number of the frame that will precede the beginning of a new sequence

This request is rarely used because there is rarely a need for the information it provides!

Other Control Requests

In addition to the eleven standard requests, USB allows classes and vendors to define their own requests.

Class-Specific Requests

When a group of devices has similar attributes, or when many devices provide or request similar services, it makes sense to define a series of requests that all can use. Classes make this possible. The USB Implementers Forum releases class specifications developed by teams whose members have expertise in the area of interest.

A special case is the hub class, which is defined in the main USB specification rather than in its own document. The operating system must support the hub class because the host requires a root hub to do any communications at all.

An advantage to classes is easier programming, because much of the work of developing the communications protocol has been done. In addition, the host's operating system may include a driver for the class, freeing device vendors from having to provide a device driver.

A class specification may include class-specific items to be included in the standard descriptors, as well as class-specific descriptors, interfaces, endpoint usages, and class-specific control requests. For example, the device descriptor for a hub includes a bDeviceClass value of 09h to indicate that the device belongs to the hub class. When the host sends a Get_Status request to a hub with a port number in the Index field, the hub responds with port-status information. Hubs also support one class-specific request (Get_Bus_State). (Chapter 16 has more on hubs.) A class may also require a device to support specific endpoints or comply with tighter timing requirements for standard requests.

In addition to the hub class, several other classes have completed specifications. However, just because a specification exists doesn't mean that Windows includes drivers for the class. The following descriptions note which drivers are present in the various editions of Windows:

Audio Device. Devices that transfer audio, voice, or sound and related controls. Windows 98 includes an audio driver.

Communications Device. Telephones, modems, and other telecommunications devices. Windows 98 SE includes a modem driver.

Mass Storage. CD-ROM, tape, floppy drives, etc. Windows 2000 includes a mass-storage driver.

Human Interface Device (HID). Keyboards, mice, joysticks, or any device that transfers blocks of information to or from the host at moderate rates, with or without guaranteed maximum latency. Windows 98 includes HID drivers.

Monitor Control. HIDs that provide user controls on display monitors (not the display interface itself).

Power Devices. HIDs that provide power-supply control, including control for power conservation and uninterruptible power supplies.

Printer. The printer interface (not the page-description protocols). Windows 2000 includes a printer driver.

More classes are under development, with the complete list available from the USB Implementers Forum website.

Device-Specific Requests

A vendor may also define custom requests for control transfers with specific devices. In order to use a custom request in a control transfer, you need all of the following:

- A protocol for the Setup, (optional) Data, and Status stages. Bits 6 and 5 in the Setup stage's data packet are set to 10 to indicate a vendor-defined request.

- Code in the device that detects the request number and knows how to respond. If you have code for the standard requests, you can use it as a model for custom requests.

- A custom device driver in the host that applications can access to initiate the request. Windows 98 has no built-in driver that enables applications to send custom control requests, so the only option is a custom driver with this ability.

7

Chip Choices

When it's time to select a USB controller for a project, the good news is that there are plenty of chips to choose from. The downside is that there are so many that deciding which chip to use in a project can be overwhelming at first.

As with any project involving embedded controllers, the decision depends on what functions the chip has to perform, cost, and ease of development. Ease of development depends on the availability and quality of development tools, device-driver software for the host, and sample code, as well as your familiarity with the device's architecture and instruction set or language compiler.

This chapter is a guide to selecting a USB controller. It includes a tutorial about what you need to consider and descriptions of a sampling of chips with a range of abilities. The chips covered include inexpensive ones with simple architectures and basic USB support as well as more full-featured, high-end chips.

Elements of a USB Controller

The complexity of the USB protocol means that USB peripherals must have intelligence. The controller chip has to know how to detect and respond to events at a USB port, and it has to provide a way for the device to store data to be sent and retrieve data that's been received.

Controller chips vary in how much support they require for USB communications. Some require little more than accessing a series of registers to store and retrieve USB data. Others require the device's program code to do more, including managing the retrieval of descriptors, setting data-toggle values, and ensuring that the appropriate handshake packets are sent.

Some controllers have a general-purpose CPU on chip, while others take a minimalist approach and interface to an external CPU that handles the non-USB tasks and communicates with the USB controller as needed. All USB controllers have one or more USB ports as well as buffers, registers, and other I/O. A controller chip with a general-purpose CPU also has program and data memory on-chip or an interface to these in external memory.

For high-volume applications that require fast performance, another option is to design and manufacture an application-specific integrated circuit (ASIC). VAutomation is one source for a USB controllers and other components that are available as synthesizable VHDL or Verilog Source code.

CPU

A controller chip's central-processing unit (CPU) controls the chip's actions by executing instructions in the firmware stored in the chip. Each CPU supports an instruction set that includes machine-language instructions for moving data, performing math and logic operations, and program branching. The CPU may be based on a general-purpose microcontroller such as the 8051, or it may be a design developed specifically for use in USB applications.

Chips that don't have a general-purpose CPU may support a command set for USB-related communications, or they may just use a series of registers for storing USB data and configuration information. These chips provide a way to add USB capabilities to any microcontroller with an external data bus.

Program Memory

The program memory holds the code that the CPU executes. The code configures the chip, accesses the USB port and other I/O pins, and does whatever else the chip is responsible for. This memory may be in the CPU chip or a separate chip.

The program storage may use any of a number of memory types: ROM, EPROM, EEPROM, Flash EPROM, or RAM. All except RAM (unless it's battery-backed) are nonvolatile; they retain the data stored in them after powering down. The amount of program memory may range from a couple of kilobytes on up. Chips that can access memory off-chip may support a Megabyte or more of program memory.

Another name for the code stored in program memory is firmware, which indicates that the memory is non-volatile and not as easily changed as program code that can be loaded into RAM, edited, and re-saved on disk. In this book, I use the term firmware to refer to a controller's program code, with the understanding that the code may be stored in a variety of memory types, some of them firmer than others.

ROM (read-only memory) must be mask-programmed at the factory and can't be erased. It's practical only for product runs of thousands.

EPROM (erasable programmable ROM) is user-programmable. Many chips have inexpensive programming hardware and software available. To erase an EPROM, you insert the chip into an EPROM eraser, which exposes the circuits beneath the chip's quartz window to ultraviolet light. Erasing typically takes 10 to 30 minutes. The chip is then ready to be reprogrammed. Data sheets rarely specify the number of erase/reprogram cycles that the chip can withstand, but it's typically at least 100.

OTP (one-time programmable) EPROMs are a cheaper, non-erasable alternative to erasable EPROMs. You program them exactly like EPROMs, but they lack the window for erasing. Erasable EPROMs are useful for product development. Then to save cost, you can switch to OTP EPROMs for the final product run. Many USB chips have both EPROM and OTP EPROM variants. OTP EPROM is sometimes called ROM, but it uses a different technology than mask-programmed ROM.

Flash EPROM is a more recent electrically-erasable memory technology that doesn't need a quartz window and often doesn't need the special programming voltage required by other EPROMs. Current Flash EPROM technology enables around 100,000 erase/reprogram cycles.

EEPROM (electrically erasable PROM) also doesn't need a window, nor does it need the special programming voltage required by other EPROMs. EEPROMs tend to have longer access times than Flash EPROMs. EEPROMs are available both with the parallel interface used by EPROM and Flash EPROM, and with a variety of synchronous serial interfaces: Microwire, I^2C, and SPI. The serial EEPROMs are useful for storing small amounts of data that changes only occasionally, such as configuration data. Current EEPROM technology enables around 10 million erase/reprogram cycles.

RAM (random-access memory) can be erased and rewritten endlessly, but the stored data disappears when the chip powers down. Still, it's possible to use RAM for program storage by loading the code from a PC or by using battery backup. Cypress Semiconductor's EZ-USB chip uses RAM for program storage, along with special hardware and driver code that loads a program into the chip on power-up or attachment to the bus. Any CPU with external program memory could use battery-backed RAM for program storage. A battery-backed or host-loadable RAM has no practical limit on the number of erase/rewrite cycles (except for battery life). Access times are fast.

Data Memory

Data memory provides temporary storage during program execution. The contents of data memory may include data received from the USB port, data to be sent to the USB port, values to be used in calculations, or anything else the chip needs to remember or keep track of. Data memory is usually RAM. Typical amounts of data memory are 128 to 1024 bytes.

Some chips may use EEPROM or other memory types for configuration data or other data that doesn't change often and needs to be preserved when the chip isn't powered.

Registers

Registers are another option for temporary storage. Registers are memory locations that are accessed using different instructions than those used for other data memory. Most have defined functions and can be accessed more quickly than other data memory.

USB controller chips typically have status and control registers that hold information about what endpoints are enabled, the number of bytes received or bytes to transmit, suspend-state status, error-checking information, and other information about how the chip will be used and the current status of transmitted or received data. For example, setting a bit in a configuration register may enable an endpoint. The number of registers and the specifics of their contents vary with the chip family.

USB Port

A USB peripheral controller must of course have a USB port and supporting circuits. The circuits that control the USB interface form the serial interface engine (SIE). Some chips have ports that support all of the USB's transfer types, while others may support only low-speed transfers or some transfer types. Few chips support the maximum number of endpoints (1 control + 30 others for full speed).

USB Buffers

A USB controller must have transmit and receive buffers for storing USB data. Some chips use registers for this, while others, such as Cypress' CY7C63000 and EZ-USB, reserve a portion of data memory for the buffers.

Registers that hold transmitted or received data are often structured as FIFOs (first in, first out buffers). Each read of a receive FIFO returns the byte that has been in the FIFO the longest. Each write to a transmit FIFO stores a byte that will transmit after all of the bytes already in the FIFO have transmitted. An internal pointer to the next location to be read or written to increments automatically as the firmware reads or writes to the FIFO.

In some chips, like Cypress' CY7C63000, the USB buffers are in ordinary data memory and the firmware explicitly selects each location to read and write to. There is no pointer that increments automatically. The bytes in the USB transmit buffer go out in order from the lowest address to the highest, and the bytes in a USB receive buffer are stored in the order they arrive, from lowest address to highest. These buffers technically aren't FIFOs, but are sometimes called that anyway.

For faster transfers, some chips have double buffers that can store two full sets of data in each direction. While one block is transmitting, the firmware can write the next block of data into the other buffer location so it will be ready to go as soon as the first block finishes transmitting. In the receive direction, the extra buffer enables a new transaction's data to arrive before the firmware has finished processing the previous transaction's data. The hardware automatically switches, or ping-pongs, between the two buffers.

Other I/O

Just about every controller will also have an interface to the world outside of itself, other than the USB Port. This often includes a series of general-purpose input and output (I/O) pins that will connect to other circuits. A chip may also have built-in support for other serial interfaces, such as an asynchronous interface for RS-232 or synchronous interfaces such as I²C, Microwire, and SPI.

Some chips have special-purpose interfaces. For example, Philips' USA1321 contains a digital-to-analog converter (DAC) for use in USB speakers and other audio devices. The chip converts received USB data to analog signals at sampling frequencies of up to 55 kilohertz.

Other Features

A chip may also have hardware timers, UARTs, and other features for general use. Just about any feature that you might find in a general-purpose microcontroller is likely to be available in a USB controller.

Simplifying the Development Process

Besides the features of the chip itself, ease of development can make a big difference in how long it takes to get a project up and running. The simplest and quickest USB project is one that uses a chip that has all of the following:

- A chip architecture and programming language that you're familiar with.

- Detailed, well-organized hardware documentation.

- Well-documented, bug-free sample firmware code for an application similar to yours.

- A development system that enables easy downloading and debugging of firmware.

- The ability to communicate using device drivers included with Windows or a vendor-provided, well-documented driver that you can use as-is or with minimal modifications.

These are not trivial considerations! The right choice will save you many hours and much aggravation.

Architecture Choices

In selecting a controller chip, you can use a chip designed from the ground up as a standalone USB controller, a chip that's compatible with an existing chip family, or a chip that requires an interface to a generic microcontroller. Which to use depends on your own background and experience as well as the project specifics.

Chips Designed for USB from the Ground Up

Some controllers are designed specifically for USB applications. Cypress Semiconductor has several chips of this type. Table 7-1 compares the features of a selection of these.

The CY7C63xxx family consists of inexpensive chips, each with a USB port, 12 to 32 lines of general-purpose I/O, and 35 instructions that cover the basics of moving data, performing mathematical operations, and program branching. The chips support low-speed transfers only. Other Cypress chips have more I/O and support full-speed transfers.

Because the instruction set is short, learning it isn't difficult. However, the short instruction set also means that you won't find fancy instructions that do a lot of the work for you. For example, there are no instructions for multiplying or dividing; all calculations must be done by adding, subtracting, and bit-shifting. (Cypress does offer a C compiler with extensive math functions and other features.)

Chips Based on Popular Families

Many USB controller chips are based on existing chip families. One way to get a quick start on a project is to use a controller based on a family you're familiar with. There are several controllers compatible with the popular 8051 family and its variants. Intel was the first to release a peripheral chip with a USB port. Intel/Cypress' 8x931 is based on the basic 8051, while the 8x930 is based on the high-speed, enhanced 80251. Cypress Semiconductor's EZ-USB is also based on an enhanced 8051. In 1999, Cypress Semiconductor gained control of both the 8x930/1 families and the EZ-USB by licensing Intel's technology and development tools for USB peripherals and acquiring Anchor Chips. Table 7-2 compares the chips.

The 8051-compatible chips have two advantages. One is that many developers are already familiar with the architecture and instruction set, and familiarity gives a big head start to any project. Certainly if you're designing a USB-capable version of an existing product that uses an 8051 variant, sticking with the 8051 makes sense. But even if you're not already familiar with the architecture, the family's popularity means that programming and

Table 7-1: Cypress Semiconductor has microcontrollers that are designed for USB from the ground up.

Feature	CY7C63000/1	CY7C63100/1	CY7C63513	CY7C64013
Speed	Low	Low	Low	Full
Number of End-points	2	2	3	4
USB buffer Size (bytes)	8	8	8	8/32
RAM (bytes)	128	128	256	256
Program Memory Type	EPROM	EPROM	EPROM	EPROM
Program Memory Size (bytes)	2K/4K	2K/4K	8K	8K
External Memory Bus	no	no	no	no
General Purpose I/O Pins	12	16	32	24
Other I/O	-	-	-	I^2C & hardware-assisted parallel interface
Number of Interrupts	15 + 2 Endpoint interrupts	15 + 2 Endpoint interrupts	34 + 3 Endpoint interrupts	19 + 2 Endpoint interrupts
Power Supply Voltage	5	5	5	5
Number of Pins	20	24	40/48	28

debugging tools are available, and sample code and other advice is likely to be available from other users on the Internet. Keil has C compilers for the Intel/Cypress chips, and both Keil and Tasking have a C compiler for the EZ-USB. If you're familiar with C, being able to program in C can save time even if you're not already familiar with the 8051.

The 8051 isn't the only microcontroller family with USB-capable chips. Other examples are Mitsubishi, which offers USB-capable chips in its 740, 7600, and M16C families, and Motorola, which has announced chips for its HC05 family.

Table 7-2: Comparison of three 8051-compatible USB chips.

Feature	8x930A	8x931A	EZ-USB
Manufacturer	Intel/Cypress	Intel/Cypress	Cypress Semiconductor
Full speed?	yes	yes	yes
Number of endpoints	4 or 6	3	32
USB buffer size	16-1024	8 or 16	64/2048
Compatibility	80251, 8051	8051	80C320, 8051
RAM (bytes)	1024	256	8192 combined data and program memory
Program memory type	ROM, external	ROM, external	RAM
Program memory size (bytes)	0-16k	0-8k	8k combined data and program memory
External memory bus (bytes)	16M	256k	64k
General-purpose I/O pins	32	32	24
Other I/O	async. serial	async. serial, keyboard	async. serial, I^2C
Number of interrupts		2external, 10 total	5 external, 10 total
Number of timers	3	3	3
C Compiler Available?	yes	yes	yes
Power Supply Voltage	5	5	3.3
Number of Pins	68	68	44, 80
Comments	-H version has embedded hub	-H version has embedded hub	firmware loads from PC or EEPROM on powerup or attachment

Chips that Interface to a Generic Microcontroller

Some USB controllers handle only the USB communications and must be controlled by an external microcontroller. These enable you to add a USB port to just about any microcontroller. The downside is that the circuits require two chips, while other USB controllers have both the CPU and the USB controller on a single chip. Also, the chip vendor may not have example circuits and code for the CPU you want to use. Table 7-3 compares a selection of these chips.

The chips have external data buses that may use a serial or parallel interface to connect to the CPU. An interrupt pin can signal the CPU when the controller has received USB data or needs new data to send. The external interface may be slower than the USB's maximum speed, making the chip suitable only for transferring intermittent data.

Netchip's NET2888 uses a parallel data bus with 8 data lines and 5 address lines. It can read and write data at 10 Megabytes per second, or faster in DMA mode. The external data bus on National Semiconductor's USBN9602 is more flexible, and requires fewer lines. It has a parallel data bus that you can configure to transfer multiplexed or non-multiplexed parallel data or Microwire serial data. The Microwire interface requires just four lines, and can interface to any microcontroller with four spare I/O pins. Philips Semiconductors also has chips with serial and parallel interfaces.

Chip Documentation

The ultimate authority on a chip's abilities is its data sheet and (for chips with CPUs) the documentation for the instruction set. The data sheet documents the hardware, including the functions of the registers and voltages and timing for all pins.

The documentation for the chip's instruction set defines the assembly-code syntax for each of the instructions that the CPU understands. If you're programming in assembly code, these are the instructions you must use in writing the firmware. If you're using a higher-level language such as C, you may not need to use the assembly-code instructions at all (though compilers typically allow in-line assembly code.)

To supplement the basic documentation, many vendors provide a user manual with more detailed information about how to use the chip. The manuals for some of the more complex chips are large! The 8x930's user manual is over 600 pages, though this also includes the documentation for the instruction set. A thick manual is good if it provides a lot of detail, but it's also an indication of complexity.

Table 7-3: A Selection of USB Controllers that Interface to a Generic Microcontroller.

Chip	USS820/825	USBN9602	NET2888	PDIUSBD11	PDIUSBD12
Manufacturer	Lucent	National Semiconductor	NetChip	Philips	Philips
Speed	Full	Full	Full	Full	Full
Number of Endpoints	1 control + 14 others	1 control + 6 others	1 control + 5 others	1 control + 6 others	1 control + 6 others
Maximum Packet Size (bytes)	16/64/256/512 /1024	8/32/64	64	8	16, 64, 128
Double Buffered?	yes	no	no	no	yes
Microprocessor Interface	Non-multiplexed parallel	Multiplexed or non-multiplexed parallel, Microwire	Non-multiplexed parallel	I^2C	Multiplexed or non-multiplexed parallel
Power Supply Voltage	3.3	5	3.3	3.3	3.3
Number of Pins	44/48	28	48	16	28
Comments	Programmable FIFO size	Has programmable clock output	Occupies 32 bytes of address space	Has programmable clock output	Has programmable-clock and status-LED outputs

Sample Firmware

The best way to get a head start on writing firmware is to begin with sample code that's similar to what you want to achieve. Having an example to refer to is much, much easier than trying to put something together from scratch. Chip and tool vendors vary widely in the amount and quality of sample code provided.

Cypress provides code for a keyboard, mouse, joystick, uninterruptable power supply, and thermometer application for its low-speed chips. The code is generally well-commented and thoroughly debugged, as documented by the included revision histories.

Other vendors provide code for a simple loopback test and leave the rest to you. Of course, in some cases you may be able to find code samples from other sources, especially via the Internet, from other users who are willing to share what they've done.

Driver Choices

The other side of programming a USB device is the driver and application software on the host. Here again, samples are useful.

If your device fits into the HID class, you can use Windows' HID drivers and you don't have to worry about writing or finding a driver. Applications can use standard API functions to access the device, and the code in this book will get you started. A chip vendor may offer a sample as well, as National Semiconductor does in its sample HID application for its '9602.

Some vendors provide a generic driver that you can use to exchange data with the device. Cypress' EZ-USB is an example. The chip has a unique architecture that enables the PC to load the chip's firmware on attachment. To use this feature, the chip requires a special driver, and Cypress provides it. As an application example, Cypress provides the source code for the development system's monitor program.

For bulk and isochronous transfers, many chips can use the *bulkusb.sys* and *isousb.sys* drivers included in the Windows 98 DDK. Although the drivers were written for the 82930, they have no chip-specific functions and other chips can also use the driver.

Debugging Tools

Ease of debugging also makes a big difference in how easy it is to get a project up and running. Most controller-chip manufacturers offer a development board and basic debugging software to make it easier for developers to use their chips. The development board enables you to load a program from a PC to the program memory of the chip itself, or to circuits that emulate the chip's hardware.

Typical debugging software uses a monitor program, which enables you to control program execution and watch the results. Standard features include the ability to step through a program line by line, set breakpoints, and view the contents of the chip's registers and memory. You can run the monitor program and a test application at the same time. You can look inside the emulated chip and see exactly what happens when your application communicates with it.

Another useful debugging tool is a USB protocol analyzer. Because the data on the bus is encoded, the conventional troubleshooting tools of oscilloscopes and logic analyzers used alone aren't much use in viewing the data on the bus. A protocol analyzer captures USB data and displays it in meaningful formats. Protocol analyzers aren't specific to a particular chip. Chapter 9 and Chapter 15 have more on debugging tools.

Project Needs

In addition to looking for a chip that will be easy to work with, you can further narrow the choice of controllers by specifying your project's needs and looking for chips that meet the needs. These are some of the areas to consider:

How fast does the data need to transfer? The rate of data transfer depends on several things: whether the device is low- or full-speed, the transfer type being used, and how busy the bus is. As a peripheral designer, you don't control how busy the users' buses will be, but you can design your product to work in the worst case expected.

If a product requires no more than low-speed interrupt and control transfers, a low-speed chip may save money not only in chip cost, but also in the circuit-board design and cables. However, you may find a full-speed chip that can do the job at the same or even a lower price.

If you do consider low speed, remember that low-speed devices can transfer only 8 data bytes per transaction. Because low-speed devices can't use isochronous transfers, they can't transfer data at a guaranteed rate, although interrupt transfers do have a guaranteed maximum latency. HID-class devices can use low-speed chips.

How many and what type of endpoints do you need? Each endpoint is configured to support a transfer type and direction. A simple device that does only control transfers needs just the default endpoint. If you want to do interrupt transfers, you'll need only one or two additional endpoints. If you want to be able to do different types of transfers, additional endpoints are useful, even though the host can request a new configuration or interface to use a different transfer type on an endpoint.

Do you want the device to be software upgradable? For program memory, many USB devices use EPROM or other memory that isn't easily erased and re-written. To change the program, you need to insert a new chip or remove, erase, re-program, and replace a chip. Cypress' EZ-USB supports an easier way, using a re-enumeration process that loads the program code into the chip from the host on each power-up. Another option is to store the program code in a microcontroller with electrically reprogrammable memory. In this case, you'll also need to provide the hardware and software to update the code. If you take this approach, see the *Device Class Specification for Device Firmware Upgrade* (available from the Implementers Forum's website), which describes a mechanism for loading new firmware from a host to a device.

Do you need a flexible cable? One reason why mice are almost certain to be low-speed devices is that the less stringent requirements for a low-speed cable mean that the cable can be thinner and more flexible.

Do you need a long cable? Low-speed cables are limited to three meters, while full-speed cables can be five meters.

What other hardware features and abilities do you need? These include everything from general-purpose or specialized I/O, the size of program and data memory, on-chip timers, and so on. As with any embedded computer project, the requirements depend on the application.

A Look at Some Chips

The following descriptions of popular USB controller chips will give an idea of what's available. They include only a sampling, and new chips are being released all the time, so any new project warrants checking the latest offerings. (See Lakeview Research's website at *www.lvr.com* for links to chips.)

Intel/Cypress 8x931 and 8x930

The 8x931 and 8x930 are full-featured chips that are compatible with the 8051 microcontroller family. The 8x931 is an 8051 with an embedded USB controller. The 8x930 is compatible with Intel's enhanced, fast 8051, the 80251. Intel was the first to release peripheral chips with USB controllers, but is now focusing on the PC side of USB and has granted Cypress the license to their USB chips.

Both chips have full USB capabilities in a microcontroller that's powerful enough to control complex tasks. Some versions have an embedded hub that can connect to additional USB devices.

These chips have two advantages: many system designers and programmers are already familiar with the 8051 family, and language compilers and other development tools are available. The architecture and programming are compatible with other 8051s and 80251s, except for the USB-specific registers and instructions.

If you're not familiar with the chips, you will have a learning curve, as the architecture is complex. The 8x930 has over 300 machine-code instructions.

CPU Architecture

The 8x931 is based on the 8xC51FX, which in turn is based on Intel's 8051, the original member of an early but still popular microcontroller family. The chip can access up to 64 kilobytes each of external data and program memory and has 32 general-purpose I/O bits, three timers, an asynchronous serial port, and a keyboard interface.

The 8x930 is based on Intel's 80251, which has the same general architecture as the 8x931. But the 8x930 is much faster and has more RAM, the ability to access more external memory, and more USB endpoints.

The 8x930 is faster than the 8051 for two reasons. It has a redesigned core that takes from two to ten clock cycles per instruction, compared to the

8051's twelve. Also, the 80251 has added hardware and 62 new machine-code instructions that speed program execution. For example, a second general-purpose register enables faster data transfers, and page mode enables fast data access within a 256-byte block. Also, code fetches are 16-bit instead of 8, and some internal data transfers are 16- or 32-bit rather than 8-bit.

To remain as compatible as possible with the 8051, the 80251 supports two modes: source and binary. A configuration bit determines which mode the chip uses. Binary mode is compatible with the 8051, while source mode is faster on devices that make liberal use of the new 80251 features. In binary mode, each of the new instructions has a prefix of A5, which is the 8051's single unused machine code. In source mode, the new instructions don't use the prefix, but 159 of the original instructions do require it.

The USB Controller

Both the 8x930A and 8x931A contain a peripheral-side USB port. The 8x930H and 8x931H add hub circuits that enable attaching downstream devices.

The chips have special-function registers (SFRs) that store received data and data to transmit as well as status and control information. The transmit and receive buffers can each hold two sets of data. The chips can also be configured to automatically reread or retransmit data after an error has been detected.

Of the 8x931's three endpoints, Endpoint 0 supports control transfers only, Endpoint 1 supports all four transfer types, and Endpoint 2 supports all but isochronous transfers. On the 8x930, Endpoint 0 supports control transfers, endpoints 1 through 4 support all types, and endpoint 5 supports all but isochronous transfers.

To transmit data, the firmware writes the data to a transmit buffer and stores the number of bytes written in the TXCNTL register. This tells the USB controller how many bytes are available to transmit when the host polls the device. In a similar way, the USB controller stores received data in a receive buffer and generates an interrupt to let the firmware know that the data is available.

Intel provides source and object code for a host driver that handles enumeration and bulk transfers with the chips, as well as sample firmware.

Cypress Semiconductor EZ-USB

Cypress' EZ-USB is another 8051-compatible family of chips with USB capability. These chips uses a different approach to storing firmware. Rather than storing the firmware on-chip, an EZ-USB can store its firmware on the host, which loads it into the chip on each power-up or attachment. The EZ-USB was originally a product of Anchor Chips, which began as an independent company but in 1999 became a business unit of Cypress Semiconductor.

Having the firmware stored on the host has pluses and minuses. The obvious advantage—and it's a big one—is easy updates to firmware. To update the firmware, just store it on the host and the driver will send the firmware to the device on the next power-up or attachment. There's no need to replace the chip or use a special programmer.

The downsides are increased driver complexity, the need to have the firmware available on the host, and longer enumeration time. Cypress helps with the driver by providing complete source and executable code for a driver that handles the downloading of the firmware, enumeration of the device with the new firmware, and other data transfers of all types. You can use the supplied driver as-is, or use it as the base for a custom driver.

If you don't want to download from the host, the chip also supports storing its firmware in an external serial EEPROM. On power-up, the code loads into the EZ-USB's RAM.

CPU Architecture

The EZ-USB's architecture is similar to Dallas Semiconductor's DS80C320, which is another 8051 with a redesigned core. The chip uses four clock cycles per instruction cycle, compared to the 8051's twelve. Each instruction takes between one and five instruction cycles. The CPU is clocked at 24

Megahertz. On average, the EZ-USB is 2.5 times as fast as an 8051 with the same clock speed.

The instruction set is compatible with the 8051's. All of the chip's 8-kilo-bytes of combined code and data memory is RAM; there is no non-volatile memory. However, the chip does support non-volatile storage in its I²C serial interface that can read and write to serial EEPROM.

There are 32 general-purpose I/O pins.

USB Controller

The chip supports the maximum number of endpoints: one control end-point, plus 30 additional endpoints and all four transfer types.

The enumeration process for this chip is unique. As with any USB device, when the host detects the EZ-USB, it will attempt to enumerate it. But how can it enumerate the device when it has no stored firmware? The answer is that the chip's core includes circuits that know how to respond to the host's enumeration requests. The circuits also respond to the vendor-specific request AnchorLoad, which receives and stores the downloaded firmware. These circuits are independent from the 8051 core. They communicate with the host while holding the normal 8051 circuits in the reset state.

On power-up, before enumeration, the core circuits attempt to read a byte from a serial EEPROM on the I²C interface. The results tell the core what to do next: use the default mode, identify the device from EEPROM bytes, or load firmware from EEPROM.

Default Mode for Basic Testing. If the core detects no EEPROM, or if the first byte read is not B0h or B2h, the core reads no data from the EEPROM. This is the most basic mode of operation.

When the host enumerates the device, the chip's core circuits respond to requests. During this time, the 8051 is held in the reset state. This reset state is controlled by a register bit in the chip. The host can write directly to this bit to place the chip in and out of reset. This reset affects the 8051 circuits; it's unrelated to the reset state of the USB interface.

The descriptors retrieved by the host identify the device as a Default Anchor Device. This instructs the host to use Cypress' General Purpose Driver to communicate with the chip. The driver uses the AnchorLoad request to download firmware (provided by Cypress) to the device. The firmware contains a new set of descriptors and code that enables transferring data using all four transfer types. On completing the download, the 8051 exits the reset state and is configured so that the firmware, rather than the core circuits, responds to requests.

On exiting reset, the firmware causes the chip to electrically simulate a disconnect and reattachment to the bus. When the host detects the simulated re-attachment, it enumerates the device again, retrieving the new descriptors. Cypress has trademarked the term ReNumeration to describe this process.

This mode of operation is intended for use in debugging. You can use it to get the chip up and running and to transfer data without having to write any drivers or firmware.

Identify the Device from EEPROM Bytes. The core can also read identifying bytes from the EEPROM on power-up, and provide this information to the host during enumeration. If the first value read from the EEPROM is B0h, the core reads EEPROM bytes containing the chip's product, version, and device IDs. When the host enumerates the device the first time, it uses these bytes to find a matching INF file that identifies the driver that specifies which firmware to download on re-enumerating.

Load Firmware from EEPROM. A third mode of operation provides a way for the chip to store its own firmware. If the first byte read from the EEPROM is B2H, the core loads the EEPROM's entire contents into RAM. This must include the Vendor and Product ID bytes as well as all descriptors required for enumeration and whatever other code and data the device requires for USB communications. When the chip exits the reset state, it has everything it needs for USB communications. When the host enumerates the device, it reads the stored descriptors and loads the appropriate driver. There is no re-enumeration.

Additional Tools

For a quick start to EZ-USB designs, J. Gordon Electronic Design (*http://www.jged.com*) has an inexpensive business-card-sized SimmStick with an EZ-USB and related circuits. John Hyde's excellent book *USB Design by Example* includes assembly code and circuits for many projects with this chip. John's website at *http://www.usb-by-example.com* has more information and code examples.

Cypress Semiconductor CY7C63X00

The chips in Cypress Semiconductor's CY7C63000 and '63100 series are inexpensive and simple in design. They're intended for use in applications that transfer small blocks of information at moderate speed. Examples of uses include standard peripherals such as mice and joysticks, as well as specialized devices such as data-acquisition units and controllers. Microsoft's original IntelliMouse uses a CY7C63001A microcontroller. The Microsoft IntelliMouse Explorer uses the CY7C63613.

CPU Architecture

Unlike other USB chips, the CY7C63000 series isn't based on an existing chip family. Using one of these chips means having to learn a new instruction set. However, the instruction set is small and the instructions are similar to those used by other microcontrollers, Learning the syntax is fairly painless if you have experience with assembly-code programming. A C compiler is also available.

The chips in the series share a common architecture, but they vary in the amount of program memory, number of I/O pins, and packaging. All have 128 bytes of RAM. The options include 2 or 4 kilobytes of EPROM for program memory, 12 or 16 I/O pins, and surface-mount or through-hole packaging. The through-hole packages are useful for prototyping on hand-assembled boards because they don't require soldering a tiny surface-mount chip.

The chips themselves are inexpensive, and they can use inexpensive ceramic resonators rather than crystals as timing references.

USB Controller

The simplicity of the design is a benefit but also a limitation. Although the chips comply fully with the USB specification, they don't support the full range of USB capabilities. They're limited to low-speed transfers, which means that they can't use bulk or isochronous transfers. The chip has just two endpoints, the required Endpoint 0 for control transfers, plus Endpoint 1. Endpoint 1 can be configured for Interrupt IN transfers, but doesn't support Interrupt OUT transfers. (The chip was designed to be compatible with version 1.0 of the HID specification, and Version 1.1 added the option to use Interrupt OUT transfers.) Each endpoint has an 8-byte buffer in RAM.

For project development, Cypress offers a Developer's Kit with a monitor program as well as a Starter Kit that contains a programmer for the chips' EPROMs and a circuit board and code for an example thermometer application. The thermometer includes a custom host driver. Early versions of the kit didn't include source code, though it is available as one of the examples in BlueWater Systems' WinDK driver toolkit. Cypress plans to make driver source code available on its website.

If you like the Cypress chips but need more I/O or full-speed transfers, see Cypress' CY7C634xx and CY7C640xx families.

NetChip NET2888

NetChip's NET2888 doesn't contain a general-purpose CPU or memory. It has only a USB controller and an interface to a generic data bus, which you can connect to any CPU with a complimentary bus.

Architecture

The NET2888 has no program or data memory other than its USB buffers. The external bus has five address bits (A0 - A4) and eight data bits (D0-D7) to enable reading and writing bytes to 32 addresses.

Transferring data over the external bus uses a *ChipSelect line to select the chip and separate *IOR and *IOW signals to control reads and writes. Most microcontrollers that support external data buses can use this interface with little or no added logic.

The chip also supports direct memory access (DMA) transfers, for the fastest possible transfer of blocks of data. In a DMA transfer, the chip takes control of the external bus. Once the DMA transfer is requested, the transfer of data to or from memory is automatic.

The chip reserves a block of memory to hold the data that will transfer. A DMA address counter holds the address of the block, and a DMA byte counter holds the number of bytes left to transfer. In a host-to-device transfer, on receiving USB data, the device copies the data into the reserved memory. In a device-to-host transfer, the device copies data into the transmit buffer whenever space is available.

The chip responds to the standard control requests without requiring any firmware support other than storing the appropriate information (such as Vendor and Product IDs) in registers.

USB Controller

The NET2888 supports five endpoints and all four transfer types. Endpoint 0 supports control transfers. Endpoint 1 supports bulk transfers from the host. Endpoint 2 supports interrupt transfers to the host. Endpoint 3 supports bulk or isochronous transfers from the host. Endpoint 4 supports bulk or isochronous transfers to the host.

The 32 bytes that the CPU can access using the address and data buses correspond to registers in the chip. For transfers of small blocks of data, Endpoints 1 and 2 enable the peripheral's CPU to send and read USB data using two 8-byte mailbox registers. Each mailbox's data uses a single address on the external bus, with a second address containing an index that indicates the byte in the mailbox to be read or written to. For transferring larger blocks of data, Endpoints 3 and 4 enable the peripheral's CPU to send and receive USB data using two 64-byte buffers. Each buffer uses a single address, with a count register that indicates the number of data bytes in the buffer.

The NET2888 automatically stores data received from the host. To detect data received from the host at Endpoint 1, the peripheral's CPU can poll the chip's receive-mailbox-valid bit or respond to an interrupt that occurs when the bit is set.

To send data from Endpoint 2 to the host, the peripheral's CPU writes the data to the transmit mailbox and sets the chip's transmit-mailbox-valid bit. The NET2888 then handles the details of sending the data on the USB.

Other registers hold various status and handshaking values and configuration information.

The peripheral's CPU is responsible for writing some configuration information to the NET2888's registers. But because the endpoints are configured in hardware, there's less to do than for other chips.

NetChip provides a device driver for bulk transfers. The driver is based on the *bulkusb* example included in the Windows 98 DDK. The only change to the source code is the device name, from I82930 to NCUSB.

National Semiconductor USBN9602

National Semiconductor's USBN9602 is another chip that requires an interface to a microcontroller. It can interface to any microcontroller with a parallel data bus, a Microwire interface, or even just four spare I/O pins controlled entirely in firmware

Architecture

The '9602 has a serial interface engine for handling USB transmissions, a set of USB Endpoint buffers, and a series of status and control registers. A CPU can access the endpoint buffers and status and control registers at addresses 00h through 3Fh via the external bus.

The chip offers three options for accessing the external data bus: non-multiplexed and multiplexed parallel, and Microwire synchronous serial.

Multiplexed parallel transfers read or write a byte of data in one bus cycle. The address is latched with *ALE, and the data with *RD or *WR. Most microcontrollers with external data buses can use these signals with little or no glue logic.

For non-multiplexed parallel transfers, the '9602 transfers both data and addresses on D0-D7, but in separate bus cycles. One bus cycle sends the address to the '9602, and another transfers data to or from the chip. To save on bus accesses, the chip supports a burst mode, where the CPU writes a starting address to the controller chip, and then transmits or receives multiple bytes that go to consecutive addresses. The CPU must also support this mode. The parallel interface also supports DMA transfers.

Not all microcontrollers have an external parallel data bus, and for those that don't, the '9602 offers a solution in its Microwire interface. Microwire is a synchronous serial interface that uses four lines: the two data lines SIN (serial in) and SOUT (serial out), *CS (chip select), and SYNC (the clock line). Command/address and data bytes shift in and out, bit by bit, using transitions on the SYNC line as a timing reference. The external CPU controls SYNC. There is no minimum SYNC frequency, and the signal doesn't have to have a specific frequency at all; the CPU can toggle line as needed. The interface just has to be fast enough to keep up with the USB traffic. If the USB port transfers only small, occasional blocks of data, you can program a Microwire interface in firmware without having to worry about critical timing. Some microcontrollers, such as National Semiconductor's COP888, have Microwire interfaces built in.

USB Controller

The '9602 supports seven endpoint addresses: Endpoint 0 for control transfers, three IN endpoints, and three OUT endpoints. The buffers for Endpoints 5 and 6 are 64 bytes each. An endpoint may also send or receive packets larger than the buffer size, if the firmware reads data from the buffer as it arrives to prevent the buffer from overflowing, or writes data to the buffer as it transmits to prevent the buffer from emptying before all of the data has transmitted.

Philips Semiconductors PDIUSBD11/12

Philips Semiconductors offers additional choices for minimalist USB controllers in its PDIUSBD11 and PDIUSBD12.

Architecture

The chips are similar except for their external data buses. The '12 has a parallel data bus, while the '11 has an I²C bus. Like Microwire, I²C is a synchronous serial bus. It requires just two signal wires: serial clock (SCK) and a bidirectional serial-data line (SDA). In a typical transfer, the CPU sends a command that specifies the function of the data to follow, followed by transmitted or received data. The bus can transfer data at up to 1 Megabit per second (but some of the bits are commands). There is no minimum speed for SCK. Some microcontrollers have built-in I²C interfaces.

Like the USBN9602, the '12 supports multiplexed, non-multiplexed, and DMA parallel transfers. The interface can transfer data at up to 2 Megabytes per second.

Instead of using status and control registers, the chips respond to commands for performing functions such as selecting an endpoint or reading or writing to a buffer.

USB Controller

Both chips are full speed. The '12 supports three USB endpoints. One endpoint holds up to 128 bytes, with double buffering for a total of 256 bytes. The '11 supports four endpoints of 8 bytes each.

On both chips, the connection to the USB is under firmware control. The chip appears detached from the host until the peripheral's CPU sends a command to simulate attachment to the bus. This can ensure that the chip has time to initialize on power-up before being enumerated by the host. A status output on the '12 can connect to an LED that lights when a USB connection has been established and blinks on data transfers.

8

Inside a USB Controller: the Cypress CY7C63001

Now that you know something about the USB protocols and the controller chips available for USB peripherals, it's time to take a closer look at a controller chip and how to use it. The chip I've chosen for the examples in the book is Cypress Semiconductor's CY7C63001.

This chapter explains how I chose the chip to use for my examples, then describes the chip and its abilities in detail. The focus as always is on what you'll need to know to put the chip to use. No matter which chip your project uses, this chapter will give you an idea of how USB controllers carry out their responsibilities.

I've also included code fragments that show how to perform various functions. If you're not familiar with assembly-language coding, you'll find it helpful to read the first part of Chapter 8 before beginning this chapter.

Selecting a Chip

If you're going to design a USB peripheral, you eventually need to decide which controller chip the peripheral will contain. The same principle holds true for the examples in this book. In order to show application examples, I need to choose a chip to base the examples on. So the first order of business is selecting the chip.

Requirements

The purpose of this chapter and the next are to show how to design and program a USB peripheral. I wanted a chip that would be suitable for simple monitoring and control projects. The focus is on getting a basic design up and running quickly, rather than on supporting a complex design and every capability of USB. With this in mind, the requirements for the chip are:

- Easy to learn. A simple design is good.

- Supports interrupt transfers. One of the easiest ways to communicate with a USB device is using Windows 98's HID driver. The driver uses interrupt and control transfers for transferring data in both directions.

- Low speed. A low-speed device has less critical requirements for printed-circuit-board design of the USB interface, so it's good for experimenting.

- Inexpensive.

- Available.

- Has an inexpensive, easy-to-use development system. The development system should enable transferring of code from a PC to the controller, viewing the code and chip registers, and debugging functions such as single-stepping and breakpoints.

- Reprogrammable. A chip whose program memory is easily reprogrammed makes development simpler and cheaper.

- Available sample code.

The Choice

There are several fine chips that meet all or most of these requirements. In the end, I chose Cypress' CY7C63001, mainly because it's one of the most basic USB controllers. The chip can do USB communications and a little bit of generic I/O. There are no external buses; the chip stands alone as a complete controller for managing USB communications and other processing. The main downside is that the USB communications require a fair amount of firmware support. You have to do some things in firmware that other chips handle automatically.

If you're using a different chip, following my Cypress examples will give you a head start on figuring out what you'll need to do. Even if you need a full-speed interface or a custom driver, the examples will introduce many topics that are relevant to all USB devices.

Inside the Chip

Chapter 7 introduced Cypress Semiconductor's CYC763000 series. The chips are inexpensive and simple in design. They're intended for use in applications that transfer small blocks of information at moderate speeds. Uses include standard peripherals such as mice and other pointing devices, as well as specialized devices such as data-acquisition units and controllers.

For example, a data acquisition unit might send periodic sensor readings to a PC. The controller chip's I/O pins might connect to analog-to-digital converters that convert sensor readings to digital signals. Periodically, a host PC might use the USB link to request the latest readings. Or the PC might send signals to control relays, motors, or any machine controlled by the chip's I/O pins.

The following paragraphs summarize the features of the CY7C63001 chip (with some unavoidable repetition from Chapter 7's summary). Of course, the ultimate source for chip documentation is Cypress' data sheet. Instead of just repeating what's in the data sheet, I'll focus on what's important to know before you start working with the chip. I'll also explain in detail anything that I found difficult or confusing to understand from the data sheet alone. You can check the data sheet for details when it's time to use the chip.

One thing that's missing from the data sheet is a compact reference that lists the addresses of the I/O registers and the functions of the bits in the registers that contain status and control signals, so I've provided this in Appendix B.

Features and Limits

One compelling reason for choosing the '63001 for a project is inexpensive chips and development tools. Typical prices for the chip are a few dollars each in small quantities. Because the chip is low speed, it has a wider tolerance on the timing reference (1.5%, versus 0.25% for full speed) and can use an inexpensive ceramic resonator instead of a quartz crystal. Low-speed cables are cheaper as well.

The chip is available in both through-hole (DIP) and surface-mount (SOIC) packages. The DIP is handy for prototyping because you don't have to solder a tiny surface-mount chip to a printed-circuit board. The fact that the chip is low speed also makes printed-circuit board design less critical. The CerDIP package's windowed EPROM is useful for program development because you can erase and reprogram it. When the code is debugged, the final product can use chips with the cheaper OTP (one-time programmable) EPROMs.

If you're comfortable with assembly-language programming (or willing to learn), the 35 assembly-code instructions aren't too hard to master.

The chip has 4 kilobytes of program memory. With optimization, the code required to support USB communications can fit in 1 kilobyte, leaving 3 kilobytes for other functions.

The essential tool for developing is the $499 Developer's Kit, which contains a development board, assembler, and monitor program. You'll probably also want the $99 Starter Kit, which includes a device programmer and a USB thermometer demo board. It's possible to develop a project using only the Starter Kit, but you'll need to erase and reprogram an EPROM with

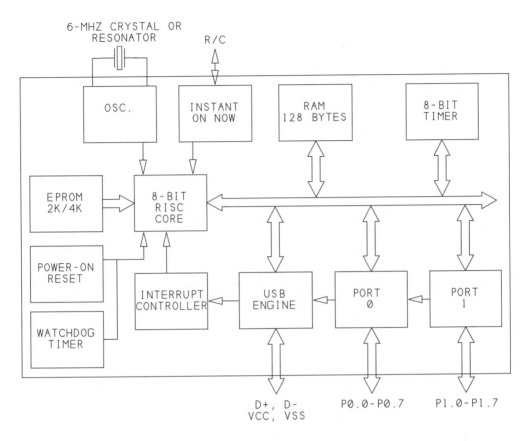

Figure 8-1: The chips in Cypress' CY7C63xxx series have the essentials for USB communications and general port I/O.

each code change, and you won't have the troubleshooting abilities available from the development board and monitor program.

The '63001 isn't suitable for every project. The hardware and code requirements must be simple. Peripherals with complex responsibilities will need more program memory. There are just twelve I/O pins. The chip is low speed, which means that you can't specify a transfer rate, though you can specify a maximum latency of up to 8 bytes every 10 milliseconds for device-to-host transfers. The chip doesn't support Interrupt OUT transfers,

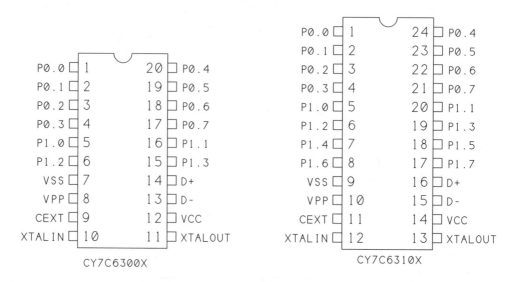

Figure 8-2: The CY7C63xxx series includes chips with 12 and 16 I/O pins.

so data sent from the host to the chip must use control transfers, which have no guaranteed delivery time.

If the '63001 doesn't have all you need, Cypress offers a number of other chips, including ones with more memory, endpoints, and I/O, plus full-speed communications.

Architecture

Figure 8-1 shows an overview of the chip's architecture. The CPU is an 8-bit RISC (reduced instruction set computer). It can access program memory, RAM, general-purpose I/O ports, and of course, a USB port. A variety of interrupt and reset sources can interrupt the CPU. A timing reference drives an oscillator that clocks the CPU. Figure 8-2 shows the pinout of the '6300X and the '6310X, which has four additional I/O pins.

Memory

The on-chip memory of the '63001 consists of 4 kilobytes (0000h to 0FFFh) of EPROM memory for program storage and 128 bytes of RAM

(00h to 7Fh) for temporary data storage. There are also 32 byte-wide registers, each with a defined purpose.

The organization of the program memory is similar to that of other microcontrollers. The first 16 bytes are interrupt vectors that hold the addresses to jump to when one of the chip's seven interrupts occurs. (One vector is reserved.) Here is an example interrupt-vector table in firmware:

```
org   00h                    ; Reset vector
jmp   Reset                  ; Begin here after a reset.
org   02h                    ; 128-microsecond interrupt
jmp   128_microSec_ISR
org   04h                    ; 1.024-millisecond interrupt
jmp   One_mSec_ISR
org   06h                    ; Endpoint 0 interrupt
jmp   USB_EP0_ISR
org   08h                    ; Endpoint 1 interrupt
jmp   USB_EP1_ISR
org   0Ah                    ; Reserved interrupt
jmp   Reset
org   0Ch                    ; general purp. I/O interrupt
jmp   GPIO_ISR
org   0Eh                    ; Wakeup or Resume interrupt
jmp   Wakeup_ISR
```

Each interrupt vector jumps to the location specified by a label. Unused interrupts should jump to a do-nothing interrupt-service routine that returns the firmware to the calling location with registers unchanged (in case the interrupt accidentally triggers).

For clarity, the example code has an *org* directive preceding each jump. However, since each jump uses two bytes, the only required directive is the first (*org 00h*), and the rest fall into place.

Program execution begins at address 0000h, which should contain the address that begins the main program's execution. The interrupt vectors are stored in order of priority, with the highest priority at 0002h. The area from 0010h to 0FFFh is available for storing the rest of the code.

The 128 bytes of RAM store two data stacks and a total of 16 bytes of buffer data for Endpoints 0 and 1, as well as any other temporary data. The stacks are last in, first out (LIFO) structures for short-term storage of addresses and register contents. The RAM has two pointers for accessing the two stacks. The Program Stack Pointer (PSP) begins at 00h on reset and grows up, while the Data Stack Pointer (DSP) may be set to 70h or lower and grows down. The firmware needs to be sure that the stacks don't grow so large that they bump into each other in the middle. If you need to reserve general-purpose RAM for another use, you can set the DSP to an address lower than 70h. This reserves the locations from that address through 6Fh for another use.

The Program Stack Pointer

The PSP holds the address the code will jump to on returning from a call to a subroutine or interrupt-service routine. The firmware doesn't have to do anything to manage the PSP. It's all done automatically as the firmware calls and returns from routines.

On reset, the PSP points to 00h. The PSP can handle multiple, nested subroutines and interrupts. Each will return to the instruction after the last instruction that executed before the call.

As an example, if the PSP is pointing to 00h when an instruction at 100h in program memory calls a subroutine, the CALL instruction will cause the PSP to save the value 100h in addresses 00h and 01h. The CALL also increments the PSP by two bytes (to 02h in the example) so it's ready to store another location if needed. When the subroutine returns, the RET instruction decrements the PSP by two bytes, causing the PSP to point to the value placed on the stack when the subroutine was called (100h at 00h and 01h). The RET instruction places the 2-byte value pointed to by the PSP (100h) in the program counter, and program execution continues where it left off before the interrupt.

The Data Stack Pointer

The DSP holds data stored by PUSH instructions. For example, PUSH A stores the contents of the accumulator on the data stack. The DSP decrements one byte before storing a byte. A POP instruction removes the most recently stored byte and increments the DSP.

The default value of DSP on reset is *not* where it should remain; the firmware *must* set it to a new value before doing any PUSH instructions. On reset, the DSP is 00h. From here, the first PUSH instruction would cause the DSP to decrement to the top of RAM (7Fh), which is byte 7 in Endpoint 1's buffer. For this reason, before pushing any bytes, the firmware should set the DSP to 70h or lower. Here is the code to do it:

```
;Store the DSP's beginning address in the accumulator.
    mov A, 70h
;Swap the contents of the accumulator with the DSP.
    swap A, dsp
```

Use a lower value if you want to reserve some bytes for a use besides the program and data stacks.

I/O

For interfacing to circuits besides the USB port, the chip has twelve versatile I/O pins. Each can function as an input or output. Each can trigger an interrupt. The sink current of Port 1's pins is capable of driving phototransistors and other components directly, in contrast to the outputs of many microcontrollers, which require external drivers for high-current loads.

Several registers control various qualities of each pin: whether a pin is an input or output, the interrupt polarity, maximum sink current of an output, and whether or not an input has a pull-up resistor.

The Circuits Inside

Figure 8-3 shows the circuits inside each port pin, and the combinations of settings available with the Data and Port Pull-up registers. The sink current available at an output is controlled by a digital-to-analog controller (DAC) that provides the output sink current (Isink).

To configure a bit as an output, the firmware writes 0 to the bit's Port Pull-up bit. This enables the bit's Data register to control the gate of the output transistor. Writing 0 to the pin's Data register bit enables the Isink DAC and results in a logic-low output. When the pin connects to a load, which may be a logic input or another circuit, the Isink register and DAC control

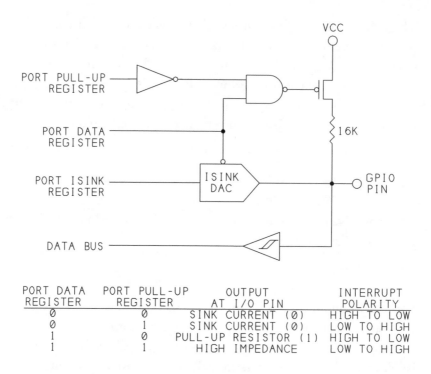

Figure 8-3: Two register bits for each pin determine whether the pin is an input or output and whether interrupts trigger on the rising or falling edge.

the amount of current the output sinks to ground. Writing 1 to the pin's Data register disables the Isink DAC. The logic low at the MOS transistor's gate then switches the transistor on and allows current to flow from the power supply, through the transistor and pull-up resistor, to the load. The result is a logic-high output at the pin. The 16-kilohm pull-up limits the pin's source current.

To configure a bit as an input, the firmware writes 1 to the bit's Data register. The Isink DAC is then disabled. You can configure each input bit to have an internal pull-up or not. With the internal pull-up enabled, the input is a logic high when no external signal is connected. Without the internal pull-up, the input is high impedance (with no guaranteed logic state) when no external signal is connected.

To disable the internal pull-up, write 1 to the Port Pull-up bit and the Data bit:

```
;Disable pull-ups on all Port 1 bits.
mov A, 0FFh
iowr Port1_Pullup
mov A, 0FFh
iowr Port1_Data
```

A logic high at the MOS transistor's gate switches the transistor off, so no current flows through the pull-up resistor. An external signal, which may be a logic output or other signal, drives the input of the Schmitt trigger buffer. The firmware can read the buffer's output state in the bit's Data register.

To enable the internal pull-up, write 0 to the Port Pull-up bit and 1 to the Data bit:

```
;Enable pull-ups on all Port 0 bits.
mov A, 0h
iowr Port0_Pullup
mov A, 0FFh
iowr Port0_Data
```

A logic low at the gate of the MOS transistor switches the transistor on, and the pull-up is enabled.

Output Features

The maximum sink current of pins configured as outputs is programmable. Each port has a dedicated Isink register with four bits that set the sink current. (The other four bits are unused.)

```
;Set maximum ISink current on port bits:
    mov A, 0ffh
    iowr Port1_Isink0
    iowr Port1_Isink1

;Set minimum ISink current on port bits.:
    mov A, 0h
    iowr Port0_Isink0
    iowr Port0_Isink1
```

Port 1 has higher current drive than Port 0. The maximum sink current available from all Port-1 outputs combined is 60 milliamperes.

The programmed value doesn't set the current precisely. For example, at the maximum value (1111), Port 1's pins may sink a maximum of anywhere from 8 to 24 milliamperes at an output of 2V. To save power and protect components that connect to the pins, you can program the pins for lower maximum currents.

Input Features

As described above, port pins configured as inputs can have internal pull-ups or not. To reduce noise susceptibility, the pins have a Schmitt-trigger circuit at each input. The Schmitt trigger adds hysteresis, which prevents the inputs from triggering on small noise glitches.

When a port pin is configured as an input, a transition on the pin can cause an interrupt. The polarity of the transition that triggers the interrupt is set by the Port-pull-up bit, which is the same bit that determines whether or not the pin uses a pull-up resistor. If the internal pull-up is enabled, interrupts are triggered by a high-to-low transition. This makes sense because logic high is the default state for the pulled-up pin with no external signal connected. If the internal pull-up is disabled, interrupts are triggered by a low-to-high transition. If the interrupt signal is a short pulse, it doesn't matter which edge triggers the interrupt unless timing is extremely critical.

Interrupt Processing

A Global Interrupt Enable register allows the firmware to control which interrupts are enabled. The register has bits for these interrupts: Endpoint 0, Endpoint 1, Wake-up, General-purpose I/O, 1.024-millisecond timer, and 128-microsecond timer. Writing 1 to an interrupt's bit enables the interrupt, while writing 0 masks, or disables, the interrupt.

When an interrupt occurs, the chip's hardware disables all interrupts, clears that interrupt's bit in the Global Interrupt Enable register, and jumps to the address stored in the interrupt's assigned interrupt-vector location in program memory. The interrupt-service routine is responsible for carrying out whatever needs to be done to service the interrupt and ensure that all registers are in the expected states on exiting the routine.

On a 1-millisecond timer interrupt, the code might check for bus activity to decide if the chip should enter the Suspend state. On an Endpoint 0 or Endpoint 1 interrupt, the code should determine what kind of USB activity occurred at the endpoint, then handle it.

Every interrupt-service routine for the '63001 must do two things: save the contents of the accumulator and re-enable interrupts. Here is an example do-nothing interrupt-service routine that does only these:

```
DoNothing_ISR:
push A
;Enable interrupts and return
mov A,[interrupt_mask]
ipret Global_Interrupt
```

On entering the interrupt-service routine, the code pushes the contents of the accumulator onto the data stack. This is required, because the IPRET instruction that exits the interrupt-service routine automatically pops a value from the data stack into the accumulator. Even if the code doesn't need to preserve the value in the accumulator, you need to push a value onto the stack to cause the DSP to decrement. Otherwise, when IPRET increments the DSP, the DSP could end up pointing to a reserved location, such as Endpoint 1's buffer.

An interrupt-service routine must also re-enable interrupts, because interrupts are automatically disabled on entering the routine. At different times, different combinations of interrupts will be enabled. A way to ensure that the correct interrupts are re-enabled is to keep a copy of the contents of the Global Interrupt Enable register in RAM. Every time you enable or disable an interrupt, copy the new register value to this location. This value is the *interrupt mask*.

On exiting an interrupt-service routine, the IPRET instruction can ensure that the correct interrupts are enabled. The instruction copies the contents of the accumulator into the address specified in the instruction's operand. So just before exiting an interrupt-service routine, the firmware should copy the interrupt mask to the accumulator. The IPRET instruction should specify the address of the Global Interrupt Enable register (Global_Interrupt in the example). IPRET then copies the contents of interrupt_mask into the address specified by Global_Interrupt.

An interrupt-service routine, or any subroutine, should also preserve the contents of other registers whose contents the routine changes, if there is any chance that the calling code will need the original contents. You can PUSH and POP the accumulator (A) and index (X) registers directly. You'll need to copy other values into the accumulator or index register before pushing and popping. Values should be popped in the reverse order they're pushed:

```
       push A
       push X
;do something that uses these registers
       pop X
       pop A
```

For the general-purpose I/O (GPIO) interrupts, a Port Interrupt Enable register for each port allows the firmware to enable or disable the interrupt for each I/O pin. A transition on a port pin will result in an interrupt only if several things are true:

- The GPIO bit in the Global Interrupt Enable register must be set to 1.
- The pin's bit in the Port Interrupt Enable register must be 1.
- The polarity of the transition on the port pin must match the polarity determined by the pin's bit in the Port Pull-up register.
- If any previous GPIO interrupt has occurred, that pin's state must have returned to the inactive, or non-trigger state, or the pin's bit in the Port Interrupt Enable register must have toggled to 0, then back to 1. (For a low-to-high interrupt trigger, the non-trigger state is low; for a high-to-low trigger, the non-trigger state is high.)

The USB endpoint interrupts trigger on sending or receiving USB data. An Endpoint 0 interrupt occurs on receiving data from the host, or after receiving an ACK from the host in response to a sent packet. Endpoint 1 is transmit-only, so an Endpoint-1 interrupt occurs only after receiving an ACK from the host in response to a sent data packet.

The timer interrupts occur at intervals of 1.024 milliseconds and 128 microseconds. The firmware can use these interrupts for any purpose. One use for the 1-millisecond interrupt is to measure the amount of time with no USB activity to determine whether or not to enter the Suspend state.

Deciding whether to enter the Suspend state requires firmware support. The code must maintain a count of the number of milliseconds that the bus has been idle and cause the chip to enter the Suspend state when the count equals or exceeds 3. The count can be stored in any spare location in RAM.

You find out if the bus has been idle by checking the bus-activity bit in the USB Status and Control register. If the bit is 0, there has been no bus activity and the firmware should increment the suspend counter. If the bit is 1, there has been activity, and the firmware should clear the suspend counter and the bus activity bit by writing 0 to each:

```
;Check for bus activity.
      iord USB_Status_Control
      and A, 01h
      cmp A,0h
;If no bus activity, increment the suspend counter.
      jz Inc_counter
;If bus activity detected, clear the bus-activity bit,
      iord USB_Status_Control
      and A, 0FEh
      iowr USB_Status_Control
;and clear the suspend counter.
      mov A, 0h
      mov [suspend_counter], A
      jmp Suspend_end


Inc_counter:
;Keep track of the amount of time
;with no bus activity.
      inc [suspend_counter]
```

If the counter reaches 3, the firmware must place the chip in the Suspend state by setting the Suspend bit in the Status and Control register:

```
;Get the number of milliseconds the bus has been idle.
      mov A, [suspend_counter]
;Has it been 3 milliseconds?
      cmp A, 03h
;If no, there's nothing else to do.
      jnz Suspend_end
```

```
;If yes, put the chip in the Suspend state.
;Clear the Suspend counter.
     mov A, 0h
     mov [suspend_counter], A
;Set the Suspend bit.
     iord Status_Control
     or A, 08h
     iowr Status_Control
;The chip is now in the Suspend state.
;No instructions will execute until the chip
;exits the Suspend state on detecting
;non-idle USB activity
;or a GPIO or Cext interrupt.
     nop
Suspend_end:
```

The Wake-up interrupt is triggered by non-idle activity at the USB port or a transition on the Cext or a GPIO pin whose interrupt is enabled. Any of these brings the chip out of the Suspend state and enables the firmware to check for activity on the I/O pins.

The Timer

An on-chip timer counts at 1/6 the 6-Mhz oscillator frequency, or once per microsecond. A Timer register holds the count, which rolls over at a count of FFh. This timer is the reference for the 1-millisecond and 128-microsecond interrupts. The count is also directly readable by firmware.

Resets

On reset, the chip is placed in a known state: the PSP and DSP are set to 0, the USB address is set to 0, interrupts are disabled, and registers return to their default states. After reset, the firmware is responsible for setting all of these values to their desired states. The USB address must be set to 0 until the host specifies a new address in a Set_Address request. After a reset, the chip has to wait to be enumerated by the host before it can do other USB communications.

The chip supports three types of resets: Power On, Watch Dog, and USB. Bits in the chip's Status and Control register record the type of reset that has occurred and whether the chip is in the Suspend state.

The Power On reset occurs when the chip powers up. After this reset, the chip enters the Suspend state until it detects a non-idle condition at the USB port, indicating that the host is ready to communicate.

A watchdog reset occurs if the firmware crashes or if for any reason the watchdog timer overflows. This ensures that the firmware will restart if something drastic happens. The watchdog timer counts in increments of 1.024 milliseconds from 0 to 8.192 milliseconds. Firmware must reset the timer by writing any value to the Watchdog Reset register before it overflows:

```
iowr Watchdog
```

The code to reset the watchdog should be in the firmware's main program loop, and in any other routine that might otherwise enable the count to exceed 8 milliseconds. Although the 1-millisecond interrupt-service routine might seem like a good place to reset the watchdog, this will prevent the watchdog from triggering if the main program loop hangs but the 1-millisecond interrupt is triggering. The Watchdog reset also disables the USB transmitter until the firmware has cleared the Watchdog Reset bit in the Status and Control register.

When using the Cypress development board, you can set a switch that causes the circuits to ignore the Watchdog, so your firmware will run even if it doesn't reset the Watchdog. This enables you to single-step through the code without having the Watchdog time out. But the firmware won't run on a stand-alone chip unless the Watchdog is reset. Don't forget to add the Watchdog code!

A USB Bus reset occurs when the host sends a reset by bringing both USB signal lines low for at least 10 milliseconds.

Power Management

The chip requires a power supply of 4 to 5.25V DC.

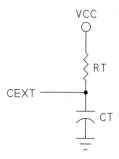

Figure 8-4: The resistor and capacitor values at Cext determine the period between wake-ups. The period is approximately equal to RT (ohms) * CT (Farads).

To save power, the chip can enter a Suspend state that powers down everything except what's needed to detect USB activity and external interrupts. The on-chip oscillator stops, so there is no clock to cause program instructions to execute. The chip just waits for an event that will end the Suspend state.

The events that will end the Suspend state are non-idle activity at the USB receiver, the triggering of an enabled interrupt on an I/O pin, or a Cext interrupt (if enabled). On detecting one of these events, the chip exits the suspended state within 256 microseconds. Cypress calls this the Instant-on Feature.

The Cext interrupt uses a resistor/capacitor timing circuit connected to the Cext pin, as Figure 8-4 shows. The Cext pin connects to the open drain of an output transistor and a Schmitt-trigger input. Writing 1 to the Cext register disables the driver and allows capacitor CT to charge through resistor RT. When the input rises above the Schmitt trigger's threshold, the Cext interrupt triggers. Writing 0 to the Cext register switches the driver on and provides a path to discharge CT. Writing 1 to the register allows CT to recharge.

Because the timing depends on resistor and capacitor values, the intervals are difficult to set precisely. For example, assuming 20% component tolerance, if you want an interrupt to occur once per second, typical component values may result in interrupts every 0.8 or 1.2 seconds. However, this interrupt does provide an inexpensive way to wake up the chip periodically, and you can easily choose values small enough to ensure a minimum triggering frequency.

The Serial Interface Engine (SIE)

In addition to all of the above, the '63001 of course has a serial interface engine (SIE) to control USB communications. The SIE and the USB transceivers, which provide the hardware interface to the USB cable, together comprise the USB engine.

Many of the firmware's responsibilities involve accessing registers that relate to USB communications. First we'll take a look at each of the USB-related registers, then we'll put it all together with a look at what the hardware and firmware must do when the host communicates. Again, Appendix B shows all of the registers.

The USB Registers

There are five registers whose functions relate directly to USB communications: an address register, three configuration registers, and a status and control register.

The **USB Device Address register** holds the address assigned by the host during enumeration. The firmware must detect the Set_Address request, send a handshake in response to the request, and store the received address in the register.

The **USB Endpoint 0 RX Configuration register** contains information about the last received data packet at Endpoint 0.

Three bits indicate whether the transaction's token packet indicated a Setup, In, or Out transaction. On receiving a Setup packet, the SIE sets the Setup bit to 1. Firmware can't change this bit until all of the transaction's data bytes have been received. To prevent incoming data from being overwritten, the chip doesn't allow firmware to write to any USB buffer while the Setup bit is 1.

On receiving a data packet, the SIE sets either the IN or OUT bit to 1, as appropriate. The Data Toggle bit contains the data-toggle state for received data. The Count bits contain the number of data bytes received, plus the two CRC bytes.

After receiving a data packet, the SIE updates the contents of this register and generates an Endpoint 0 interrupt. Any write to this register clears all of the bits except the Data-Toggle bit.

There's one additional receive-status bit that doesn't fit in this register. This bit is in the transmit configuration register, discussed next.

The complement to Endpoint 0's RX register is the **USB Endpoint 0 TX Configuration register**. This register contains information about the data packet that is next to transmit, is being transmitted, or has just transmitted, along with one receive-status bit. Similar to the RX register, the TX register has four bits that indicate the number of bytes to transmit (not including the CRC bytes) and a Data-Toggle bit to indicate the Data-Toggle state for the bytes. The firmware must set the Data-Toggle bit to the appropriate value for the transaction.

Setting the Stall bit causes the SIE to respond to all IN and OUT packets with a Stall.

The Enable-Respond-to-IN-Packets bit tells the SIE to respond to a received IN packet by transmitting the number of data bytes indicated in the register's Count bits. The firmware must set this bit to 1 when the chip is ready to send data. After the data transmits and the chip received an ACK from the host, the hardware clears the Enable-Respond-to-IN-Packets bit and generates an Endpoint 0 interrupt. The interrupt-service routine then prepares for the next transmission, if any.

The receive bit in this register is the Receive Invalid bit, which the SIE sets to 1 if it detects an error in received data.

Endpoint 1 is transmit-only, so it has no RX register. Its **USB Endpoint 1 TX Configuration register** is identical to Endpoint 0's corresponding register, except that instead of the receive Data-Invalid bit, it has an Endpoint-1-Enable bit. Endpoint 0 must always be enabled, so it has no need for this bit. Enabling Endpoint 1 is under firmware control. If the bit is 0, the chip ignores any transmissions to Endpoint 1.

The **USB Status and Control register** has five bits that relate to the overall status of the chip's USB communications.

The SIE sets the Bus Activity bit to 1 on detecting any USB activity except an idle bus. The firmware can use this bit along with the 1-millisecond interrupt-service routine to determine if the chip should enter the Suspend state. After clearing the Bus-Activity bit, if the bit remains 0 for three milliseconds, the chip must enter the Suspend state.

If the host has previously enabled a device's Remote-Wakeup ability with a Set_Feature request, the firmware can use the Force-Resume and Forced-J bits to send a Resume signal to tell the host that the device wants to communicate. Chapter 17 has more on resume signaling.

The StatusOuts bit automates the sending of the final packet in a control Read transfer. The firmware should set this bit before the device sends data in response to control Read requests such as Get_Descriptor, which require the device to send data to the host. In a control Read transfer, the host sends a request in the Setup phase, the device sends data in the Data phase, and the host sends status in the Status phase. When the StatusOuts bit is set, in the Status phase the SIE automatically sends the handshake packet in response to the token and data packets sent by the host. The SIE sends either an ACK in response to a valid Status-stage OUT packet, or a STALL in response to any other OUT packet. The next Setup transaction received at Endpoint 0 clears this bit, so there's no need for the firmware to do so.

The EnableOuts bit is set to 1 to enable Endpoint 0 to receive OUT packets. The firmware must set this bit to 1 on receiving a Setup packet for a transaction with a control Write request, such as Set_Report, where the host will send data to the device in the Data stage. If the bit is 0, the SIE won't write the received data to the USB buffer and the device will return a NAK. The next Setup or OUT transaction clears this bit, so there's no need for the firmware to do it.

Hardware and Firmware Responsibilities

In a USB transfer, the CY7C63001's SIE handles many of the tasks, but the firmware that you write still has plenty to do. Here is a look at the responsibilities of each.

What the Hardware Does

These are the tasks the hardware does on its own:

- Detects new incoming transactions.
- Translates received information from the encoded format used on the USB's data lines.
- Determines whether a transaction is directed to the chip's USB address and if not, ignores the transaction.
- Determines the transaction type (Setup, IN, or OUT) and sets a bit in the endpoint's receive (RX) register to indicate which type it is.

For received data, the hardware also does the following:

- Stores valid received data in the endpoint's buffer or toggles a register bit to indicate an error in received data.
- Stores the data-toggle state of valid received data.
- Calculates CRC values, compares them to the received CRC values, and takes appropriate action on detecting an error.
- Sends the appropriate handshake to the host.

For data to be transmitted, the hardware also does the following:

- Translates data to be transmitted from the bytes in the USB buffer to the format used on the USB's data lines.
- Sends the number of bytes specified in the TX register onto the USB lines in response to the host's request.
- Calculates and sends CRC bits with the data.
- Sends a data-toggle code with the data.
- On receiving a handshake from the host, triggers an interrupt.

What the Firmware Does

But the hardware doesn't do everything. These are the tasks that the firmware must do for received data:

On receiving an Endpoint 0 interrupt:

- PUSH the accumulator and check the RX register to find out if a Setup, IN, or OUT token packet was received. In the following example, the firmware checks for a Setup or OUT packet. An IN packet occurs only after receiving a Setup transaction with a request that requires sending data to the host, so the code checks for an IN packet in a different location.

```
USB_EP0_ISR:
     push A
     iord USB_EP0_RX_Status
;Has a Setup packet been received?
     and A, 01h
;If no, ignore.
     jz check_for_out_packet
;If yes, handle it.
; (code to handle the packet here)
check_for_out_packet:
     iord USB_EP0_RX_Status
;Is it an OUT packet?
     and A, 02h
;If no, ignore it.
     jz done_with_packet
;If yes, process the received data.
; (code to do so here)
```

If it's a Setup transaction:

- Re-enable all interrupts except Endpoint 0.

```
     mov A, [interrupt_mask]
     and A, 0F7h
     mov [interrupt_mask], A
     iowr Global_Interrupt
```

- Clear the Setup bit in the RX register.

```
     mov A, 00h
     iowr USB_EP0_RX_Status
```

- Read the received request from Endpoint 0's buffer and do whatever needs to be done to handle it.

```
;bmRequestType contains the request.
      mov A, [bmRequestType]
;jump to the routine for the request number
```

- If the Setup transaction contains a request that will be followed by an OUT data transaction where the host sends data to the device (Set_Report is an example), do the following:

  From the USB buffer, read and store the number of data bytes that will follow in the data (OUT) transaction.

```
;Find out how many bytes to read.
;This value is in wLength.
;Save the length in data_count.
      mov A, [wLength]
      mov [data_count], A
```

  In the USB Status and Control register, Set the EnableOuts bit to 1 and set the StatusOuts bit to 0 to enable receiving data in an OUT transaction at Endpoint 0.

```
;Enable receiving data at Endpoint 0
;by setting the EnableOuts bit
;The bit is cleared following any
;Setup or Out transaction.
      iord USB_Status_Control
      or A, 10h
;Clear the StatusOuts bit to disable auto-Ack
;after receiving a valid status packet in response
;to a control Read (IN) transfer.
;Otherwise, the SIE will respond to a
;data OUT packet with a stall.
      and A, F7h
      iowr USB_Status_Control
```

- If the Setup transaction contains a request that will be followed by an IN data transaction where the device sends data to the host (Get_Descriptor is an example), do the following:

  In the USB Status and Control register, set the StatusOuts bit to 1 to cause the chip to send an automatic handshake packet after receiving a 0-byte data packet in the Status stage.

```
;Set StatusOuts bit to enable auto-handshake
;of IN data packets
     mov A, 08h
     iowr USB_Status_Control
```

Write the bytes to send to the USB buffer.

```
;Copy the data to send into Endpoint 0's buffer.
;The X register indexes the address in the buffer.
dma_load_loop:
;Get the data's starting address.
     mov A, [data_start]
     index control_read_table
;Place the byte in the Endpoint's buffer.
     mov [X + Endpoint_0], A
;Increment the data address, buffer address, & counter
     inc [data_start]
     inc X
     inc [loop_counter]
;Decrement the count.
     dec [data_count]
;If the count = 0, there's no more data to send.
     jz dma_load_done
;If 8 bytes have been sent, it's the maximum.
     mov A, [loop_counter]
     cmp A, 08h
     jnz dma_load_loop
```

Set the data-toggle bit to the appropriate value.

```
;Toggle the Data 0/1 bit.
     mov A, [endp0_data_toggle]
     xor A, 40h
     mov [endp0_data_toggle], A
```

In the USB Endpoint 0 TX Configuration register, set the
Enable-Respond-to-IN-Packets bit to 1 to cause the hardware to
respond to an IN token packet. Set the lower four bits to the number
of bytes to send.

```
;Enable responding to IN packets.
     or A, 80h
;The low 4 bits hold the number of bytes to send.
     or A, [loop_counter]
```

```
    iowr USB_EP0_TX_Config
```

Re-enable interrupts.

```
    mov A, [interrupt_mask]
    iowr Global_Interrupt
```

Wait for the Enable-Respond-to-IN-Packets bit to clear, indicating that all of the data has transferred.

```
wait_control_read:
;Wait for the data to transfer,
;indicated by Bit 7 = 0.
    iord USB_EP0_TX_Config
    and A, 80h
```

Wait for the host to send a 0-byte data packet in the Status phase to acknowledge receiving the data. The StatusOuts bit will cause the handshake packet to transmit automatically.

```
;Wait for the host to send an OUT packet
;to acknowledge.
    and A, 02h
    jz wait_control_read
```

If the transfer requires sending more data, the firmware should prepare to send it in additional IN transactions.

- Return from the interrupt-service routine.

If the received token packet specifies an OUT data packet, the previous Setup phase contained a request requiring the host to send data to the device, as described above. The firmware must do the following:

- Enable all interrupts except Endpoint 0.

```
    mov A,[interrupt_mask]
    and A, 0F7h
    mov [interrupt_mask], A
    iowr Global_Interrupt
```

- Read the received data in the buffer and do whatever needs to be done with it.

```
    push X
;data_count holds the number of bytes left to read.
;X holds the index of the address to read and the
```

```
;index of the address to store the received data.
;Initialize the X register.
      mov X, 0

      Get_Received_Data:
;Find out if there are any bytes to read.
      mov A, 0
      cmp A, [data_count]
;Jump if nothing to read.
      jz DoneWithReceivedData

;Get a byte.
      mov A, [X + Endpoint_0]
      inc A
;Save it.
      mov [X + Data_Byte0], A
;Decrement the number of bytes to read.
      dec [data_count]
;Increment the address to read.
      inc X
;Do another
      jmp Get_Received_Data
;(Do anything else that needs to be done
;with the data.)
      DoneWithReceivedData:
      pop X
```

- In the Status phase, the host sends an IN token packet. The device responds with a 0-byte data packet.

```
Send0ByteDataPacket:
;Send a data packet with 0 bytes.
;Use this handshake after receiving an IN data packet
;in the Status phase.
;Enable responding to IN packets.
;Set Data 0/1 to Data 1.
      mov A, C0h
      iowr USB_EP0_TX_Config
;Enable interrupts.
      mov A, [interrupt_mask]
      iowr Global_Interrupt
      WaitForDataToTransfer:
;Wait for the data to transfer.
;Bit 7 of USB_EP0_TX_Config is cleared
```

```
        ;when the host acknowledges receiving the data.
            iord USB_EP0_TX_Config
            and A, 80h
            jnz WaitForDataToTransfer
            ret
```

- Re-enable Endpoint 0 interrupts and return from the interrupt-service routine.

```
        ;Re-enable Endpoint 0 interrupts.
            mov A,[interrupt_mask]
            or A, 08h
            mov [interrupt_mask], A
            ipret Global_Interrupt
```

Endpoint 1 supports only IN transactions in interrupt transfers. On receiving an Endpoint-1 interrupt the firmware must do the following:

- PUSH the accumulator.

```
            push A
```

- Toggle the Data-Toggle bit so it will be correct for the next transaction.

```
            iord USB_EP1_TX_Config
            xor A,40h
            iowr USB_EP1_TX_Config
```

- Re-enable interrupts and return from the interrupt-service routine.

```
            mov A, [interrupt_mask]
            ipret Global_Interrupt
```

That's the essence of USB communications with the CY7C63001. There are other details, of course. For example, during Control transfers the firmware must check periodically to find out if another Setup token has arrived, and if so, abandon the current transfer and start the new one. The firmware must also remember to clear the watchdog timer in any loop that might otherwise allow its count to exceed 8 milliseconds. I also haven't covered the specifics of how to respond to each control request. This book's CD-ROM has a complete firmware example for USB communications.

9

Writing Firmware: the Cypress CY7C63001

Whatever controller chip you select for a project, it won't be much use until you write the code that enables it to communicate with the host and the other circuits in your peripheral. In this chapter, I again use the Cypress CY7C63001 as an example, this time to show what's involved in writing and debugging USB firmware. Included are an overview of the assembly codes supported by the chip, an introduction to using Cypress' assembler and Developer's Kit, and a look at a C compiler for the chip. Even if you're using a different chip, this chapter will give you an idea of what the process involves.

The Assembler

The '63001's CPU supports 35 instructions. Everything that the firmware has to do must use these instructions. Cypress provides a free assembler for converting the assembly code you write into object files for programming into the chip's EPROM. If you prefer to program in C, Cypress also offers a C compiler.

If you have experience with microcontroller assembly-language programming, programming for the '63001 will be familiar. If you're used to programming in Basic, C, or another high-level language, the limited operations available in assembly code may come as a shock. There are no FOR or WHILE loops, no fancy variable types, and no object-oriented anything. But for a chip like the '63001, which is intended for fairly uncomplicated control and monitoring tasks, using assembly code is feasible. For short programs, the code is manageable and executes quickly. And there are no compilers to buy.

This book isn't a tutorial on assembly-language programming, but I will present some basic information for beginners, as well as specific details about the '63001 for those who have programming experience and want to see how the Cypress chip compares.

Assembly Programming Basics

An assembly-language program contains a series of instructions, each corresponding to a machine code that the chip supports. For example, the instruction IORD, which reads an I/O location, corresponds to the code 29h. Instead of having to remember 29h, you can write IORD, and the assembler will translate for you. The IORD instruction also requires an operand that specifies the location to read. For example, IORD 00h reads the port at address 00h.

An assembly-language program may also contain directives and comments. A directive is an instruction for the assembler, rather than for the CPU. Directives enable you to assign locations in program memory, define variables, and in general instruct the assembler to perform operations besides specifying what machine-code instructions to execute. A semicolon (;) or double slash (//) introduces a comment, which the assembler ignores.

The assembler provided by Cypress, *cyasm.exe*, is a command-line program that you can run in a DOS window. Cypress provides a User's Guide that documents the instructions, directives, and how to use the assembler.

The assembler supports two similar instruction sets, for the A- and B-series CPUs. The CY7C63001 is A-series. Cypress' newer chips are B-series and support the same instructions, plus a few additional and enhanced ones.

Assembler Codes

The User's Guide has complete documentation for the assembly codes and directives, and I won't repeat the details here. Table 9-1 is a summary of the codes, and Table 9-2 is a summary of the directives. The chip's 71 machine codes translate to 35 instructions, with some supporting multiple sources or destinations.

The instructions do basic arithmetic and logic functions, program branching and control, and copying of data to and from registers, ports, and RAM. Two flag bits, the carry flag and zero flag, provide additional information, such as whether an ADD instruction resulted in an overflow or whether the result of an instruction is zero.

The chip supports three addressing modes that determine how an instruction uses its operand.

In immediate addressing, the instruction uses the operand's value directly. This instruction uses immediate addressing to add 60h to the value in the accumulator.

```
Add A, 60h
```

In direct addressing, the instruction treats the operand as an address and uses the value stored at that address. This instruction uses direct addressing to add the value stored at address 60h in RAM to the contents of the accumulator:

```
Add A, [60h]
```

In indexed addressing, the instruction uses the data stored at an address obtained by adding a value to the contents of the X register. Indexed addressing is useful for copying blocks of data. The X register can hold the starting address of data to be copied. The code can then add an index value to the contents of the X register to obtain the address of any byte in the data

Table 9-1: The Cyasm assembler supports 35 assembly-language instructions. (Sheet 1 of 2)

Instruction Type	Instruction	Description
Arithmetic and logic functions	ADD	Add without carry
	ADC	Add with carry
	AND	Bitwise AND
	ASL	Arithmetic shift left
	ASR	Arithmetic shift right
	CMP	Non-destructive compare
	CPL	Complement accumulator
	DEC	Decrement
	INC	Increment
	OR	Bitwise OR
	RLC	Rotate left through carry
	RRC	Rotate right through carry
	SUB	subtract without borrow
	SBB	Subtract with borrow
	XOR	Bitwise XOR
Program branching and control	CALL	Call function
	HALT	Halt execution
	IPRET	Return from interrupt
	JACC	Jump accumulator
	JC	Jump if carry
	JMP	Jump
	JNC	Jump if no carry
	JNZ	Jump if not zero
	JZ	Jump if zero
	RET	Return
	XPAGE	Memory page

Table 9-1: The Cyasm assembler supports 35 assembly-language instructions. (Sheet 2 of 2)

Instruction Type	Instruction	Description
Moving data	INDEX	Table read
	IORD	Read I/O
	IOWR	Write I/O
	IOWX	Indexed I/O write
	MOV	Move
	POP	POP data stack into register
	PUSH	PUSH register into data stack
	SWAP	Swap
Other	NOP	No operation

to be copied. By incrementing the index value after each copy, the code can step through the block of data.

Chapter 8 had an example of using indexed addressing to copy data to an endpoint's buffer for transmitting.

Not all instructions support all three addressing modes.

Using the Assembler

The assembler uses a command-line interface that you can run from a DOS window. This command:

```
cyasm test.asm
```

assembles the file *test.asm*.

The assembler creates three files:

test.rom is the assembled code in a format for use with the Developer's Kit. Use this file to load the code from a PC to the development board's RAM.

Here is a portion of a *.rom* file as it appears when loaded into a text editor:

```
80 99 80 10 80 15 81 24
80 8C 80 99 80 85 80 10
2D 1A 20 1E 20 2D 2A 21
1A 37 16 00 A0 20 27 37
```

Table 9-2: The Cyasm assembler supports 13 directives.

Directive	Description
CPU	Product specification
DB	Define byte
DS	Define ASCII string
DSU	Define UNICODE string
DW	Define word (2 bytes)
DWL	Define word with little endian ordering
EQU	Equate label to variable value
FILLROM	Define value for unused program memory
INCLUDE	Include source file
MACRO	Macro definition
ORG	Origin
XPAGEON	XPAGE enable
XPAGEOFF	XPAGE disable

The file contains sets of eight ASCII hex bytes, with a space between each and a carriage return/line feed at the end. In ASCII hex format, each byte is represented by two ASCII codes, with each code representing a hexadecimal character. For example, the byte 80h is represented by the ASCII codes 38h for *8*, and 30h for *0*. Using ASCII hex format enables you to easily view the byte values (*80* in the example) in a text editor. When the code is stored in the development board's RAM, the RAM contains the binary bytes represented by the ASCII Hex bytes. For example, 80h translates to 10000000 in binary.

test.hex is the assembled code in Intel Hex format. Many EPROM programmers, including the one included with Cypress' Starter Kit, support this format. Intel Hex format uses ASCII hex characters and adds checksums for error-checking and addressing information to enable the file to specify where each line of bytes should be stored.

Here is the same data in one line of a **.hex* file (the line wraps on the page):

```
:20000000809980108015812480 8C8099808580102D1A201E202D
2A211A371600A0202737A1
```

cyasm.lst is the listing file generated by the assembler. It shows each line of the assembly code and comments, along with the program code generated from it and the address where each byte will be stored. The listing file is useful when you're using the monitor program. For example, if you want to stop program execution at a breakpoint, you can use the listing file to find the address that corresponds to the line of code where you want to break.

Here is an excerpt from a *.lst* file, showing an interrupt-service routine for Endpoint 1:

```
008C                 USB_EP1_ISR:
008C 2D     [05] push A
008D                 ;Toggle the data 0/1 bit.
008D 29 11 [05] iord USB_EP1_TX_Config
008F 13 40 [04] xor A,40h
0091                 ;The interrupt clears TXConfig, bit 7.
0091                 ;Set this bit to 1.
0091 0D 92 [04] or A, 92h
0093 2A 11 [05] iowr USB_EP1_TX_Config
0095                 ;Enable interrupts and return.
0095 1A 20 [06]     mov A, [interrupt_mask]
0097 1E 20 [13]     ipret Global_Interrupt
```

The leftmost column is the addresses in program memory. The address doesn't change when a line contains only a comment or label. The next two columns are the bytes stored at each address. For example, at location 008D, 29h is the code for *iord*, and 11h identifies the register to read. The next column is the number of clock cycles the instruction uses (5). The rightmost columns contain your assembly code and comments.

If You Prefer C...

Another option for developing code for these Cypress chips is to use Byte Craft's C compiler and development environment.

Advantages to C

Compared to assembly-language programming, C has several advantages:

- Standardization. If you're an experienced C programmer, you know the syntax and can get a quick start. You may be able to use C code written for another chip with minimal changes.

- More structures. Instead of being confined to simple jumps, your code can use structures like *if...else* and *case* statements and *for* and *do...while* loops.

- More operators. The compiler supports many more math and relational operators than the assembler. You can add, subtract, multiply, divide, and do a variety of comparisons.

- Libraries and examples. The included libraries will save you much time in performing common functions. There are libraries for a firmware UART, I²C and Microwire interfaces, delay timing, LCD and keypad interfacing, and more math functions. The examples include complete code for a keyboard and mouse/trackball.

- Optimization. The compiler optimizes the code for compactness and speed.

The downside is that you have to buy the compiler, while the assembler is free. But it's likely that the time saved with even a single project will justify the expense.

Using the Compiler

You can run the compiler from DOS or use the included Windows-based BCLIDE development environment (Figure 9-1). BCLIDE enables you to create a project, add files, define file paths, and set compiler and editor options. You can edit source-code files and compile and link the file or files to create executable code. The compiler can create a file in Intel hex format for use with EPROM programmers, and in the **.rom* format used by the Cypress development board, so you can load your code into the board's RAM.

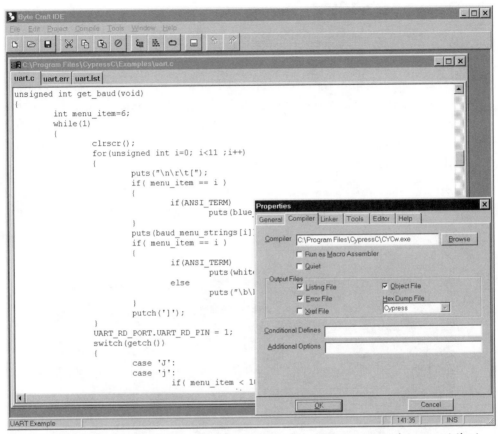

Figure 9-1: Byte Craft's C compiler includes a development environment that enables you to set project options and edit and compile code.

Hardware Development Tools

For project development for the '63001, Cypress offers a Starter Kit and a Developer's Kit. Although it's possible to develop code with the Starter Kit alone, you'll probably want the Developer's Kit for debugging. The Starter Kit is useful for its EPROM programmer, even if you don't need the rest of the kit.

The Developer's Kit

The CY3650 Developer's Kit enables you to test your code and circuits and find problems quickly.

The system includes a circuit board (Figure 9-2) and a monitor program that together enable you to load your assembled code from a PC to the board, then run and debug the code while using your PC to monitor and control program execution. Manufacturers of other USB chips have similar development systems for their chips.

To use the Developer's Kit, you need a PC running Windows 98 or later with available USB and RS-232 ports. A logic analyzer and prototyping

Figure 9-2: Cypress' development board has a USB port as well as an RS-232 port for loading program files and exchanging information with the monitor program.

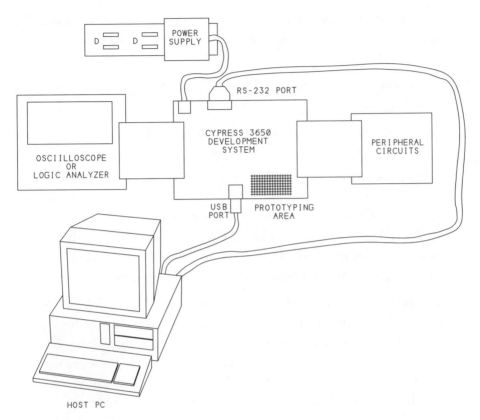

Figure 9-3: The development board connects to a USB port for USB communications with the host and to an RS-232 port for exchanging data with the monitor program.

board can connect to the board with 60-pin ribbon cables, but these are optional.

The PC Board

The Developer's Kit's printed-circuit board doesn't contain a '63001 chip. Instead it has circuits that emulate the functions of the chip while allowing you to control and monitor program execution.

Figure 9-3 shows a typical setup. The circuit board connects to a PC via both USB and RS-232 interfaces. The USB interface of course carries the USB communications between the PC and the device's USB port. The monitor program uses the RS-232 interface to send object code and to send and receive debugging information such as breakpoints and register contents.

The board uses an external 6V DC, 800-milliampere power supply, which is included.

Two connectors enable testing and monitoring of the emulated chip and connecting external circuits. The board has a small prototyping area as well.

One of the connectors has pins that are tied to the Port 0, Port 1, and Cext pins. You can run a cable from the connector to a prototyping board that holds whatever circuits you want to connect to the port pins. You might want to add a header for attaching probes for monitoring the signals on the prototyping board as well. The connector also has pins for the USB data signals, +5V, and ground. Only 22 of the 60 pins are used.

The other connector enables you to monitor what's going on inside the emulated chip. It has connections for addresses and data for both program memory and RAM, control signals for accessing program memory, RAM, and I/O ports, +5V and ground, a 12-Mhz clock, and a master reset. With an oscilloscope or logic analyzer and the monitor program, you can watch exactly what goes on inside the emulated chip when instructions execute.

You can use the monitor program to download code into RAM that emulates the EPROM. Downloading to RAM makes it easy to modify the code. You can also store program code in a socketed EPROM, if you have a programmer that supports the CY7C261 EPROM. The EPROM comes programmed with sample mouse firmware.

There are a few functions that the development board doesn't emulate. On the I/O pins, there are no programmable pull-up resistors or programmable output currents. And the board can't be bus powered; it always requires its own supply. In the Suspend state, the oscillator on the development board continues to run, while on the chip, the oscillator stops and everything remains in a static condition.

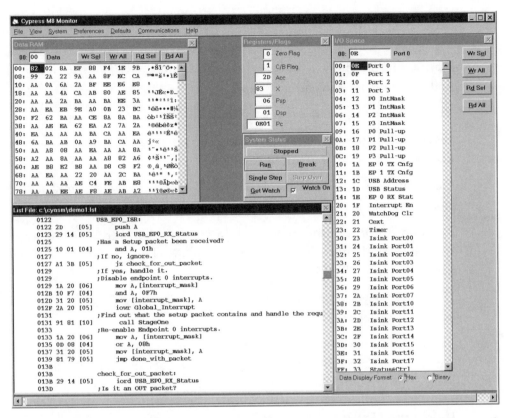

Figure 9-4: Cypress' M8 Monitor enables you to control program execution and view the status of memory and registers.

The Monitor Program

The companion to the development board is the monitor program. In addition to enabling you to load and run your firmware, the monitor program has debugging features that can help enormously in tracking down bugs.

Figure 9-4 shows one setup for the user screen, which you can customize to show the information you want. The View window allows you to select which windows display. These are the windows and what they enable you to do and see:

Download Object File: send an assembled object file to the board's program RAM.

Status: run the program in program RAM, stop, break, single-step, and update the values being monitored.

Breakpoints: add and delete breakpoints. Turn breakpoints on or off.

List File: view the *.lst* file for the object code downloaded to the board's program RAM.

Data Ram: view the contents of the board's data RAM, which emulates the chip's RAM, in hexadecimal and ASCII and write to data RAM.

Program RAM: view the contents of the board's program RAM in hexadecimal and ASCII and write to the program RAM. The program RAM emulates the chip's EPROM program memory.

I/O Space: view and modify the contents of 38 registers, including the I/O ports and the registers that control them.

Registers/Flags: view and modify the contents of the zero flag, carry flag, accumulator, X register, program stack pointer, data stack pointer, and program counter.

Using the Monitor Program

The Developer's Kit comes with a manual that guides you through setting up the system and getting started with the monitor program.

Switch settings enable you to do a few things that you wouldn't be able to do with the chip itself. You can ignore USB bus resets and Watchdog resets. You can skip going into the Suspend state on detecting a Power On reset. Other switches enable you to disable the Cext interrupt and configure the I/O ports as input only. You can select whether to use RAM or EPROM program memory, and whether to run the program or halt after a reset.

Here's an example of how to use the Developer's Kit to run your firmware:

1. Write your source file in assembly code and use the Cyasm assembler to create an object file. The object file has the extension *.rom*, and contains your firmware's machine-code instructions in ASCII Hex format. In order

for your device to enumerate, it will also need an INF file on the host, as described in Chapter 11. If your firmware identifies the device as HID class, you can use Windows' *hiddev.inf* file.

2. On the development board, set switch S3-2 open to cause the board to run the downloaded code on reset. Set switch S3-1 open to cause the board to use program RAM. Set switch S1-2 closed to disable the watchdog reset.

3. Plug in the board's power supply and connect the RS-232 and USB cables to the host PC.

4. Run the monitor program.

5. From the View window, select DnldObject, or from the File menu, select Download Object File. Select your file and click Download. A progress bar shows the code loading into RAM.

6. When the code has finishing loading, press the Reset switch on the development board. This will cause the code to begin executing. However, your code is probably written to wait for a bus reset and enumeration by the host, which is the normal chain of events when you attach a device. So to get things started, unplug and plug in the USB cable to cause a bus reset. There may be a short delay as Windows searches for the correct driver. Or Windows may ask for your help in finding the driver. To find out if Windows enumerated the device successfully, look for it in Windows' Device Manager (Start Menu > Settings > Control Panel > System > Device Manager).

7. From this point, you have several options. You can use the monitor program by itself, close the monitor program and do your debugging on your own application, or use both together.

Debugging Tips

In combination with the development board and your application's development environment, the monitor program enables you to precisely monitor and what the device's firmware is doing.

You can execute a portion of your application, then examine the states of all of the device's registers and RAM, or even change their contents on the fly. You can set a breakpoint to find out when and if a section of code executes.

You can single-step through the code to find out exactly what the code does and where it branches.

For example, if you suspect that a routine in your firmware never executes, you can use the monitor program to set a breakpoint in the routine. If the monitor stops program execution at the breakpoint, you know that the routine is executing. If you suspect the routine isn't doing what you intended, you can single-step through it and watch the contents of any registers and memory locations of interest in each step. The Registers/Flags window show the current state of the program counter (PC) and the listing file's display shows your code. Clicking Read All in the I/O Space window updates the display of the contents of the registers.

You can use your own application along with the development tools to test the firmware in its intended use. For example, you can run an application that enables users to click buttons to send and receive HID reports. You can keep the monitor program open at the same time as you run your own application. This way, you can watch what's going on inside the emulated chip as your application runs.

Tips for Use

Here are a few tips that might save you some time and trouble when using the monitor program and assembler:

To save some typing, copy the *cyasm.exe* file to the folder where you store your assembly code. Then you won't have to enter a path with the filename each time you assemble the code.

When you want to load code into the development board's RAM, the monitor program defaults to the folder containing the monitor program's executable file. This is probably not where you want to store your project's object code, but to minimize clicking, you might want to store it in a location that's easily accessible from this folder, such as *C:\cyasm* (one level down from the root directory).

The monitor program is 16-bit, so it truncates long file and folder names. To avoid this, stick with filenames that have 8 characters + 3-character extensions.

If you leave the development board attached and your PC doesn't boot the next time you power up, remove the development board's USB cable. After boot-up, you can run the monitor program, reload your firmware, and re-attach the device.

Inside the Development Board

If you're curious about how the development board emulates the '63001, the chips on the board offer some clues. Not surprisingly, the board uses Cypress chips for all of the logic and memory functions

Two large surface-mount chips are programmable-logic devices that emulate the logic of the '63001. The CY7C386A and CY7C387 are Macrocell Flash CPLD (complex programmable logic devices).

Six memory chips emulate the '63001's memory and provide additional program and data storage. There are two RAM chips: the 2-kilobyte CY7C128 and the 8-kilobyte CY7C185. The CY7C261 is an 8-kilobyte windowed EPROM that contains the sample mouse firmware for the emulated chip (but you can reprogram it with any code you want). There are three 2-kilobyte OTP EPROMs, all CY7C291s, which contain the program code for the emulated controller.

Several other chips provide additional functions. A Philips PDIUSBP11 provides the electrical interface to the USB port. There are two low-dropout voltage regulators, a National Semiconductor LM2940 with 1-ampere output and a Linear Technology LT1121 with 150-milliampere output. A Maxim MAX232 translates between the board's 5V signals and RS-232 voltages. A Maxim MAX 708 supervisory circuit has a power-supply watchdog circuit and an output to indicate a low or failed supply. The board's timing reference is a 12-Megahertz crystal.

The Starter Kit

The Starter Kit for the CY7C63001 is useful for demonstrating a USB application, and also includes a device programmer. The kit has a circuit board with a thermometer project, microcontroller source code for the thermometer, a custom Windows driver for the thermometer, a thermometer

Figure 9-5: The USB Starter Kit includes this circuit board with a thermometer circuit that uses Dallas Semiconductor's DS1623 temperature sensor.

application, an EPROM programmer, and three sample chips, two of them erasable.

The thermometer board and application are of some use in getting familiar with USB, but the options for experimenting are limited. The EPROM programmer is useful, however, if you plan to do any small-scale EPROM programming, and it alone is worth the price of the kit.

The Thermometer

Figure 9-5 shows the thermometer's circuit board. The application displays either the current temperature as a thermometer or a graph of temperature over time.

A thermometer is a natural application for the human-interface device class. As Chapter 13 shows, the HID report format even includes Unit codes for converting values into Fahrenheit and Celsius degrees. However, because the Starter Kit was an early USB product (predating Windows 98), it instead uses a custom driver.

The driver was written using BlueWater Systems' WinDK Developer's Kit (described in Chapter 10). WinDK includes source code for the thermometer driver as one of the examples. You need WinDK to compile the driver.

Applications communicate with the thermometer using a series of vendor-specific control requests. There are requests to read the thermometer, set the brightness of the on-board LEDs, read and write to ports and RAM, and read the chip's EPROM.

The kit includes some documentation of the vendor-specific requests, including a Visual-Basic declaration for the DeviceIOControl API function and a chart of the request codes and the values they pass and return. Using these, you could write your own Visual-Basic application to access the thermometer. The source code for the application isn't included.

You do get to see the chip's source code, and studying this can teach you a lot about USB. You can also add your own code to the firmware, within the limits of the host software that communicates with the device. Or you could modify the code so that it enumerates as an HID, and write your own application to communicate with it.

When you attach the board and install the drivers, the Device Manager lists the device under Thermometers.

The temperature sensor is Dallas Semiconductor's DS1623 chip, which uses a synchronous serial interface to communicate with the controller chip. Its two signal pins and one clock pin connect to port pins on the CY7C63001.

The sensor's 8-pin socket is mounted on the circuit board, so you can't subject it to different environments without bringing the entire circuit board along. You could, however, remove the chip and make a cable that attaches to the chip, possibly even encasing the chip so you can immerse it in liquids.

The sensor chip's I/O interface isn't designed for use over long-distances, however, so it's best to keep the cable to six feet or less.

The board has a considerable breadboarding area and a header and a series of holes that enable accessing the device's pins via a cable or direct wiring. A switch enables selecting Fahrenheit or Celsius, and an LED indicates when the device is enumerated, but you can easily rewire both of these for other purposes. There's also a power-on LED and a jumper to disable it.

EPROM Programming

The EPROM programmer included with the Starter Kit enables you to program the windowed CY7C6300X-series chips. With adapters available from Cypress it will also program CY7C63400- and CY7C63500-series chips. Figure 9-6 shows the programmer, and Figure 9-7 shows the programmer application's display. You'll need to have your own EPROM eraser.

The programmer connects to the PC via an RS-232 serial port. (The unit was probably adapted from an existing design that predates USB.) As with other EPROM programmers, you place the chip to be programmed in a zero-insertion-force (ZIF) socket and flip the lever to lock in the chip.

These are the steps to program a chip:

1. Insert an erased chip into the programmer.

2. In the Setup window, select a COM port and bit rate. A message will inform you when the software has located the programmer.

3. From the Device menu, select the device to be programmed.

4. From the File menu, select Load File to Buffer. Select a .hex file created by the cyasm assembler. The software is 16-bit, so long file and folder names will be truncated. In the window that appears, select file format = Intel Hex, File Start = 0000, File End = 1FFF, Buffer Start = 0000, and Unused Bytes = Don't Care.

4. Click Auto, then OK. This will cause the programmer to do four things in sequence. The programmer will verify that the chip is erased (contains all

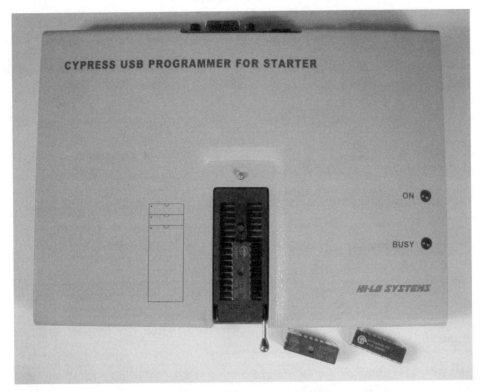

Figure 9-6: Cypress' Starter Kit includes an EPROM programmer.

FFs). It will program the buffer's file into the EPROM, beginning at 0000h. It will verify that the chip's contents match the buffer.

The Security button blows the chip's security fuse to prevent anyone from reading the code stored in the chip. Anyone who tries to read the code in the device will see only FFs. Once the security fuse is blown, the device can no longer be programmed.

You can also do an individual blank check, program, verify, and security protection of the code. An edit menu enables you to edit individual bytes in buffer, search, move blocks of bytes, and fill areas with a value.

I found the programming software to be a little quirky. At higher bit rates, the programmer sometimes failed to read or program the device. After

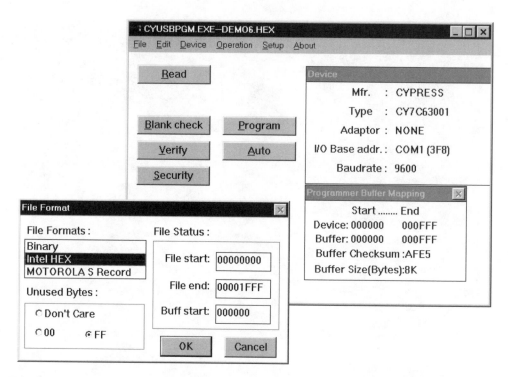

Figure 9-7: The software for Cypress Semiconductor's EPROM programmer enables you to program a file in any of several formats into Cypress chips, verify, and protect the code from copying by blowing the security fuse.

switching to 9600 bps, a device that failed at the higher bit rate passed the blank test but refused to be programmed until I re-erased. At slower rates, I had no problems. Because the amount to be programmed is small, the programming completes quickly enough even at a slower bit rate.

To erase a programmed EPROM, you'll need an EPROM eraser that exposes the chip's quartz window to ultraviolet light. Place the chip in the eraser and erase for 5 to 30 minutes. (Use the recommended time for your eraser.)

10

How the Host Communicates

A USB peripheral is of no use if its host PC doesn't know how to communicate with it. Under Windows, any communication with a USB peripheral must pass through a device driver that knows how to communicate with the system's USB drivers and the applications that access the device.

This chapter explains how Windows applications communicate with USB devices and explores the options for device drivers.

Device Driver Basics

A device driver is a software component that enables applications to access a hardware device. The hardware device may be a printer, modem, keyboard, video display, or just about any collection of electrical circuits connected to the computer. The device may be inside the computer's enclosure (an internal disk drive, for example) or it may use a cable to connect to the computer (as with the keyboard and mouse). The device can be a standard peripheral type or not, including one-of-a-kind, custom devices.

Insulating Applications from the Details

A device driver insulates applications from having to know details about the physical connections, signals, and protocols required to communicate with a device. Applications are the programs the users run, including special-purpose applications to support custom hardware. A device driver can enable application code to access a peripheral using only the peripheral's name (such as HP LaserJet) or a port designation (such as COM1 or LPT2). The application doesn't have to know the physical address of the port the peripheral attaches to (such as 378h), and it doesn't have to explicitly monitor and control the handshaking signals that the peripheral requires (Busy, Strobe, etc.).

A device driver accomplishes its mission by translating between application-level and hardware-specific code. The application-level code typically uses a set of functions supported by the operating system. The hardware-specific code handles the protocols necessary to access the peripheral's circuits, including detecting the states of status signals and toggling control signals at appropriate times.

Windows includes application programmer's interface (API) functions that enable device drivers and applications to communicate with each other. These functions are part of a set of thousands of functions that enable applications to control the display, handle messages, access memory, read and write to disks and other devices, and more. API functions used to read and write to USB devices are ReadFile, WriteFile, and DeviceIOControl. Applications written in Visual Basic, C/C++, and Delphi can call API functions.

Although API functions simplify the process of communicating with hardware, some programming tasks remain challenging. API functions tend to have specific and rigid requirements for the values they pass and return, and it's not unusual for a mistake to result in an application or system crash.

To make programming simpler and safer, Visual Basic has its own controls for common tasks. For example, applications can use the Printer Object to send data to printers and the MSComm control to communicate with serial ports. The controls provide a simpler and more bulletproof programming interface for setting parameters and exchanging data. The underlying code within the control will likely use API functions to communicate with device drivers, but using the control insulates application programmers from dealing with the sometimes arcane details of the API calls. However, Visual Basic doesn't include a control for generic access to generic USB devices.

Third-party vendors offer controls for specialized tasks such as communicating with bar-code scanners and other data-acquisition devices. A vendor may offer a control for communicating with a specific USB peripheral, and controls for generic USB communications may appear eventually as well.

On the hardware side of the communication, some device drivers are monolithic drivers that handle everything, from communicating with applications to reading and writing to the ports or memory addresses that connect to the device's hardware. Other drivers, including the Windows drivers for USB devices, use a layered driver model, where each driver in a series performs a portion of the communication. The top layer communicates with applications, the bottom layer communicates with the hardware, and in between there may be one or more additional layers. The layered driver model is more complicated as a whole, but it actually simplifies the job of writing drivers because devices can share code for tasks they have in common. The drivers that handle communications with the system's USB hardware are built into Windows 98, so peripheral vendors don't have to provide these.

Options for USB Devices

There are several approaches to writing or obtaining a driver for a device. Often there is more than one way that will work, and the choice depends on a combination of what's easier, cheaper, and offers better performance.

Standard Device Types

Many peripherals fit into standard classes such as disk drives, printers, modems, keyboards, and mice. For these, Windows includes universal drivers that any device in the class can use. If a device has unique features, a vendor can provide a supplemental driver called a mini-driver that adds capabilities to the universal driver.

Some peripheral types are available with a choice of interfaces, which may include USB. A keyboard may use the original legacy keyboard interface or USB. A disk drive may use an IDE, SCSI, printer-port, or USB interface. In cases like these, a mini-driver can communicate between the universal driver and the interface that the device uses. Windows provides a USB mini-driver for HID-class devices, which include keyboards, mice, and joysticks. For other devices, Windows may not have built-in support for a USB interface, so the product vendor must supply either a mini-driver or a complete, custom driver for the device.

Custom Devices

Some peripherals are custom devices intended for use only with specific applications. One example is the development boards for USB chips, which are designed for use with a vendor's monitor application. Other examples are data-acquisition units, motor controllers, and test instruments. Windows has no knowledge of these specialized devices, so it has no built-in drivers for them.

However, just because Windows doesn't know about a device doesn't mean that applications can't access it. There are several options for communicating with custom devices, not all requiring a custom driver.

These are the options for drivers for any device under Windows 98:

- A generic driver suitable for communicating with a variety of devices. Example device: a test instrument whose host uses the *bulkusb.sys* driver included in the Windows 98 DDK to receive data in bulk transfers.

- A class driver and a mini-driver that supports the device's USB interface. Example device: an HID-class mouse, which uses Windows' HID-class driver along with the HID mini-driver that enables the class driver to communicate with the system's USB drivers.

- A custom driver written specifically for the device. Example device: a data-acquisition unit with a driver that defines a series of control requests that applications can use to configure the unit and read data from it. The custom driver may be adapted from a generic driver.

How Applications Communicate with Devices

To understand what the device driver has to do, you need to understand where the driver fits in the communications path of a data transfer. Even if you don't need to write a driver for your device, understanding the driver's role will help in understanding the application-level code that you do write.

What Is a Device Driver?

In the most general sense, a device driver is any code that handles communication details for a hardware device that interfaces to a CPU. Even a short subroutine in an application can be considered a device driver. But under Windows, the code for most drivers, including USB drivers, differs from application code because the operating system allows the driver code a greater level of privilege than applications.

User and Kernel Modes

Code that runs under Windows 98 runs in one of two modes: user or kernel. Each allows a different level of privilege in accessing memory and other system resources. Applications must run in user mode. Most drivers run in kernel mode.

In user mode, Windows limits access to memory and other system resources. Windows won't allow an application to access an area of memory that the operating system has designated as protected. This enables a PC to run multiple applications at the same time, with none of the applications interfering with each other. In theory, even if an application crashes, other applications are unaffected. (Of course in reality it doesn't always work that way, but that's the theory.) Under Windows 98, applications can access I/O ports directly, unless a low-level driver has reserved the port, preventing access. On Pentiums and other x86 processors, user mode corresponds to the CPU's Ring 3 mode.

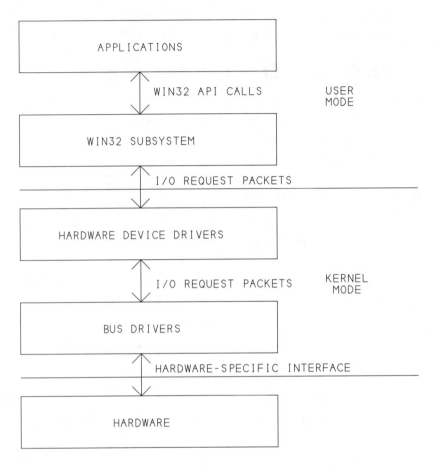

Figure 10-1: Windows 98 uses a layered driver model, with separate drivers for devices and the buses they connect to.

In kernel mode, the code has unrestricted access to system resources, including the ability to execute memory-management instructions and control access to I/O ports. On Pentiums and other x86 processors, kernel mode corresponds to the CPU's Ring 0 mode. Figure 10-1 shows the major components of user and kernel modes in a USB communication.

Applications and drivers each use their own language to communicate with the operating system. Applications use Win32 API functions. Drivers communicate with each other using structures called I/O request packets (IRPs).

Windows defines a set of IRPs that drivers can use. Each IRP requests or carries out a single input or output action. A device driver for a USB device uses IRPs to pass communications to and from the bus drivers that handle USB communications. The bus drivers in turn use IRPs to pass communications to and from drivers that manage aspects of communications closer to the bus. The final bus driver in the series communicates directly with the hardware. The bus drivers are included with Windows and require no programming by applications programmers or device-driver writers.

The Win32 Driver Model

USB device drivers for Windows must conform to the Win32 Driver Model defined by Microsoft for use under Windows 98 and later. These drivers are known as WDM drivers and have the extension *.sys*. (Other file types may also use the *.sys* extension.)

Like other low-level drivers, a WDM driver has abilities not available to applications because it communicates with the operating system at a more privileged level. A WDM driver can permit or deny an application access to a device. For example, a joystick driver can allow any application to use a joystick, or it can allow one application to reserve the joystick for its exclusive use. Other abilities that Windows reserves for WDM and other low-level drivers include DMA transfers and responding to hardware interrupts.

Driver Models for Different Windows Flavors

The Win32 Driver Model was designed to provide a common driver model for use by any device under Windows 98 and later, including Windows 2000 (the successor to Windows NT 4).

Earlier versions of Windows used different models for device drivers. Windows 95 used VxDs (virtual device drivers). NT 4 used a type of driver called kernel-mode drivers. Developers who wanted to support both Windows 95 and Windows NT had to develop a driver for each. But one WDM driver will work under both Windows 98 and Windows 2000.

The USB bus drivers included with Windows 98 are WDM drivers. Although Windows 98 continues to support VxDs (as well as drivers contained in DLLs), USB devices must use WDM device drivers because their drivers must communicate with the system's bus drivers.

The Win32 Driver Model isn't completely new; it's mostly a combination of what was available in Windows 95 and NT. A WDM driver is an NT kernel-mode driver with the addition of Windows 95's Plug-and-Play and power-management features. The final editions of Windows 95 (versions OSR 2.1 and higher) had some support for WDM drivers as well. These editions weren't available to retail customers, but were available only to vendors who installed the software on the computers they sold. In Windows 98, the WDM support was much expanded and improved.

How can two different operating systems, which previously required very different drivers, now use the same drivers? Windows 98 includes the driver *ntkern.vxd*, which tricks WDM drivers into thinking they're communicating with an NT-like operating system. All WDM drivers running on Windows 98 require this driver, which is included with Windows 98.

Programming Languages

Application programmers have a choice in programming languages, including Visual Basic, Delphi, and Visual C++. To write a USB device driver, however, you need a tool that is capable of compiling a WDM driver, and this means using Visual C++.

Layered Drivers

USB communications use a layered driver model, where each layer handles a piece of the communication process. Dividing communications into layers is efficient because it enables different devices that have some tasks in common to use the same driver for those tasks. For example, all kinds of devices may connect to the USB, so it makes sense to have one set of drivers, accessible to all and included in the operating system, to handle the USB-specific communications. The alternative would be to have each device driver communicate directly with the USB hardware, with much duplication of effort.

USB Driver Layers

The portion of Windows that manages communications with devices is the I/O subsystem. The subsystem has several layers, with each layer containing one or more drivers that handle a set of related tasks. Requests pass in sequence from one layer to the next. Within the I/O subsystem, the I/O manager is in charge of communications. One element within the I/O subsystem is the USB subsystem, which includes the drivers that handle USB-specific communications for all devices.

The set of protocols used by the drivers is called a stack. (This is different from the CPU stack introduced in Chapter 8.) You can think of the layers as being stacked one above the next, with communications passing in sequence up and down the stack.

Device and Bus Drivers

Under Windows, USB communications use two types of drivers: device drivers and bus drivers. A device driver handles communications that are specific to a single device or to a class of devices. A single USB device may use one or more device drivers. Below the device driver are three drivers that handle aspects of bus communications: the hub driver, the bus-class driver, and the host-controller driver. Figure 10-2 shows how these work together in USB communications.

The Device Driver

A device driver enables applications to talk to USB devices using API functions. The API functions are part of Windows' Win32 subsystem, which is also in charge of user functions such as running applications, managing user input via the keyboard and mouse input, and displaying output on the screen. To communicate with a USB device, an application doesn't have to know anything about the USB protocol, or even if the device uses USB at all.

A device may use a class driver or a custom driver. A class driver handles functions that are common to a set of similar devices. Windows includes

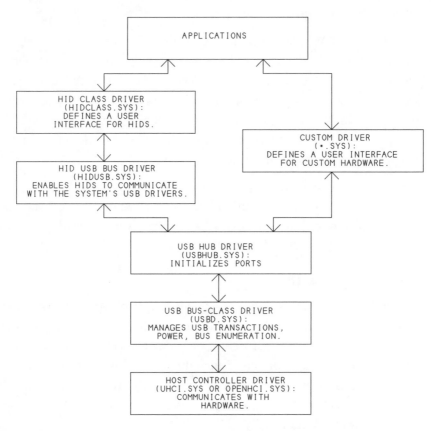

Figure 10-2: USB communications use a host controller driver, class driver, hub driver, and a device driver that may consist of one or more files.

class drivers for HIDs and other common peripherals. (These driver classes are distinct from the USB's device classes, although HIDs are considered a class in both.) The class driver handles functions that are common to all peripherals in the class.

When a device or subclass has requirements beyond what the class driver handles, a mini-driver can add the needed capabilities. For example, not all HIDs have a USB interface, so Windows provides a separate mini-driver that enables the HID driver to communicate with the USB subsystem when needed.

The Bus Drivers

The USB's bus drivers consist of the root-hub driver, the bus-class driver, and the host-controller driver. The root-hub driver manages the initializing of ports and in general manages communications between device drivers and the bus-class driver. The bus-class driver in turn manages bus power, enumeration, USB transactions, and communications between the root-hub driver and the host-controller driver. The host-controller driver knows how to talk to the host controller's hardware, which connects to the bus. The host-controller driver is separate from the bus-class driver because Windows 98 supports two types of host controllers, each with its own driver. The bus-class driver can communicate with either controller type.

The bus drivers are part of Windows, and application and device-driver writers don't have to know the details about how they work. Perhaps because of this, Microsoft provides very little in the way of documentation for them.

The Communications Flow

One way to better understand what happens during a USB transfer is to look at an example. The following are the steps in a USB transfer with a data-acquisition device that uses a custom driver.

Preliminary Requirements

Before an application can communicate with a device, several things must happen. The device must be attached to the bus. Windows must enumerate the device and identify the driver for the device. And the application that will access the device must obtain a handle that identifies the device and enables communications with it.

Plugging in the cable attaches the device. Windows handles enumeration automatically when it's notified of the device's attachment, as described in Chapter 5. To identify which driver to use, Windows compares the retrieved descriptors with the information in its INF files, as described in Chapter 11.

The handle is a unique identifier that Windows assigns to the device. An application gets the handle by calling the CreateFile API function with a symbolic link that identifies the device.

Some drivers explicitly define a symbolic link for each device they control. For example, Cypress' *ezusb.sys* driver identifies the first EZ-USB chip as ezusb-0. If there are additional EZ-USBs, the driver identifies them as ezusb-1, ezusb-2, and so on up.

Other drivers use a newer method supported by Windows, where the symbolic link contains a globally unique identifier (GUID). The GUID is a 128-bit number that uniquely identifies an object, which may be any system class, interface, or other entity that the software treats as an object.

Windows defines GUIDs for standard objects such as the HID class. For unique devices, developers can obtain a GUID using the *guidgen.exe* program included with Visual C++. The GUID is then included in the driver code.

The *guidgen* program uses a complex algorithm that takes into account a machine identifier, the date and time, and other factors that make it extremely unlikely that another device will end up with an identical GUID. The algorithm was originally defined by the Open Software Foundation.

The standard format for expressing GUIDs divides the GUID into five sets of hex characters, separated by hyphens. This is the GUID for the HID class:

745a17a0-74d3-11d0-b6fe-00a0c90f57da

Applications can use API calls to retrieve class and device GUIDs from the operating system.

The User's Role

When a device is attached and ready to transfer data, the host initiates a transfer by requesting it. To read data from a data-acquisition unit, the user might click a button in a data-acquisition application to cause the application to request data from the device. Or the user might select an option that causes the application to request a reading once per minute. Or periodic data acquisitions might start automatically when the user runs the application.

The Application's Role

After the user requests a transfer, the application begins communications with the device. The Windows API offers two ways of accessing devices: using the ReadFile/WriteFile pair or DeviceIOControl. A driver may use either or both. Each call includes the request, other required information such as the data to write or amount of data to read, and the device's handle. The Platform SDK section in the MSDN library documents the calls.

Although the names suggest that they're used only with files, ReadFile and WriteFile are actually general-purpose functions that can transfer data to and from any driver that supports them. The data read or to be written is stored in a buffer specified by the call. Chapter 14 has more on how to use ReadFile and WriteFile.

DeviceIOControl is another way to transfer data to and from buffers. Included in each DeviceIOControl request is a code that identifies a specific request. Unlike ReadFile and WriteFile, a single DeviceIOControl call can transfer data in both directions. The driver specifies what data, if any, to pass in each direction for each code. Some codes are commands that don't need to pass additional data.

Windows defines control codes used by disk drives and other common devices. These are examples:

> IOCTL_STORAGE_CHECK_VERIFY determines if media is present and readable on removable media.
>
> IOCTL_STORAGE_LOAD_MEDIA loads media on a device.
>
> IOCTL_STORAGE_GET_MEDIA_TYPES returns the types of media supported by a drive.

A driver may also define its own control codes. Because the codes are sent only to a specific driver, it doesn't matter if other drivers use the same codes. The driver for Cypress' thermometer application for the CY7C63001 defines codes to get the temperature and button state, set LED brightness, and read and write to the controller's RAM and ports. This is a Visual-Basic declaration for DeviceIOControl:

```
Declare Function DeviceIoControl Lib "kernel32" _
    (ByVal hDevice As Long, _
```

```
        ByVal dwIoControlCode As Long, _
        lpInBuffer As Any, _
        ByVal nInBufferSize As Long, _
        lpOutBuffer As Any, _
        ByVal nOutBufferSize As Long, _
        lpBytesReturned As Long, _
        lpOverlapped As OVERLAPPED) _
    As Long
```

This is a call that uses the control code 04h, which requests the thermometer to send the temperature:

```
ltemp = DeviceIoControl _
    (hgDrvrHnd, _
    4&, _
    lIn, _
    lInSize, _
    lOut, _
    lOutSize,_
    lSize, _
    gOverlapped)
```

The Device Driver's Role

When an application makes an API call, Windows passes the call to the appropriate device driver. The driver converts the request to a format the USB bus-class driver can understand.

As mentioned earlier, drivers communicate with each other using structures called I/O Request Packets (IRPs). For USB communications, the IRPs contain structures called USB Request Blocks (URBs) that specify protocols for the tasks of configuring devices and transferring data. The URBs are documented in the Windows 98 DDK.

If you're using an existing device driver (rather than writing your own), you need to understand how to access the driver's application-level interface, but you don't have to concern yourself with IRPs and URBs. If you're writing a device driver, you need to provide the IRPs that communicate with the system's USB drivers.

The Hub Driver's Role

The host's hub driver resides between a device-specific or USB-class driver and the USB bus-class driver. The hub driver handles the initializing of the root hub's ports and any devices downstream of the ports. This driver requires no programming by device developers. Windows 98 includes the hub driver *usbhub.sys*.

The Bus-class Driver's Role

The USB bus-class driver translates communications requests between the hub driver and the host-controller driver. It handles bus enumeration, power management, and some aspects of USB transactions. These communications require no programming by device developers. Windows 98 includes the bus-class driver *usbd.sys*.

The Host-controller Driver's Role

The host-controller driver communicates with the host-controller hardware, which in turn connects to the bus. The host-controller driver requires no programming by device developers.

Windows supports two varieties of host controllers. Controllers that conform to the Open Host Controller Interface standard use the driver *open-hci.sys*, and controllers that conform to the Universal Host Controller Interface standard use the driver *uhci.sys*. Both drivers provide a way for the USB hardware to communicate with the USB's bus-class driver. Although they differ in how they do so, any differences should be transparent to driver developers and application programmers.

The two drivers take different approaches to implementing the host-controller's functions. The UHCI places more of the communications burden on software and allows the use of simpler, cheaper hardware. The OHCI places more of the burden on the hardware and allows simpler software control. UHCI was developed by Intel and the specification is available on Intel's website. OHCI was developed by Compaq, Microsoft, and National Semiconductor and the specification is available on Compaq's website. The USB Implementers Forum's website has links to both.

The Device's Role

From the host's port, data may pass through additional hubs. Eventually the data reaches the hub that connects to the device, and this hub passes the data on to the device. The device recognizes its address, reads the incoming data, and takes appropriate action.

The Response

Many communications will require a response, which may contain data sent in response to the request or just a packet with a handshake code. This information travels back to the host in reverse order: through the device's hub, onto the bus, and to the PC's hardware and software. A device driver may pass a response on to an application, which may display the result or take other action.

Ending Communications

When an application closes or otherwise decides that it no longer needs to access the device, it uses the API function CloseHandle to free system resources.

More Examples

Communications with other USB devices follow a similar pattern, though there can be differences in how the transfer initiates and in how the device driver handles communications.

In the above example, the host ignores the device until the user takes an action. Other examples of a user initiating a transfer are clicking on a USB drive's icon to view a disk's folders in Windows Explorer's My Computer or clicking Print in an application to send a file to a USB printer. In each of these examples, nothing happens until the application requests a communication and the device driver fills a buffer with data to send or makes a buffer available for received data.

In some cases, the host continuously sends requests to the device whether or not an application has requested them. For example, a keyboard driver causes the host to make periodic requests for keypress data, whether or not the user has pressed any keys.

The host also sends requests to enumerate devices on system power-up or device attachment. The device's hub causes the host to initiate these requests when the hub notifies the host of the presence of a device. A device can use the USB's remote-wakeup feature to initiate a transfer by signaling its hub, and in turn the host, to request it to resume communications.

As mentioned earlier, some devices use class drivers instead of, or in addition to, a driver for the specific device. For an HID-class device, applications may communicate with the system's HID-class driver, which handles communications for all HIDs. Not all HIDs have a USB interface, but those that do also use a mini-driver to handle the USB-specific communications.

Some USB devices may use yet another type of driver, called a legacy virtualization driver. To communicate with the keyboard, mouse, and joystick, Windows 98 uses the virtual device drivers (VxDs) inherited from Windows 95. When one of these peripherals has a USB interface, a legacy virtualization driver translates between the device's HID interface and the VxD. The legacy virtualization driver is a VxD that knows how to talk to the HID driver.

Choosing a Driver Type

How do you decide whether to use an existing driver, a custom driver, or a combination? Sometimes the choice is limited by what's available for the device. From there it depends on a combination of the performance you need, cost, and speed of development.

Drivers Included with Windows

When it's feasible, a simple approach to accessing a USB device is to use what's available in Windows. This way, there are no drivers to write or install and any computer running Windows 98 or later can access the device.

It would be nice if Windows included generic drivers that enabled any application to request control, interrupt, bulk, and isochronous transfers. Maybe someday Windows will have this. But as of Windows 98, the included USB drivers are limited.

HID Drivers

The first class of USB peripherals suitable for a variety of applications and fully supported by Windows is the human interface device (HID) class. Applications can use API calls to identify a device, read and write generic values, and set and read the states of buttons on the device. The data is formatted in reports. The HID class has defined report formats for mice, keyboards, and joysticks, or you can define your own format.

But an HID doesn't have to be a standard peripheral type, and it doesn't even have to have a human interface. The only requirement is that the descriptors stored in the device must conform to the requirements of HID-class descriptors, and the device must send and receive data using interrupt or control transfers as defined in the HID specification.

The main limitation to HID communications is the available transfer types. For device-to-host data transfers, HIDs can use interrupt or control transfers. For host-to-device transfers, Windows 98 SE (or any host that complies with the HID 1.1 or later specification) will use interrupt transfers if an OUT interrupt pipe is available, or control transfers if not. The original release of Windows 98 complies only with the HID 1.0 specification and will use control transfers for all host-to-device transfers.

As Chapter 3 explained, interrupt transfers aren't the fastest transfer type, and they don't have the guaranteed transfer rate of isochronous transfers (though they do have guaranteed maximum latency). Control transfers have no guaranteed rate or latency. But even with these limitations, the simplicity of using the HID functions makes it attractive when the limits are acceptable.

An alternative to using API functions for accessing HIDs is to use Microsoft's DirectX components. DirectX enables control of system hardware, including HIDs. DirectX originated as a tool for game programmers, but has since expanded to enable accessing any HID. The advantage of using DirectX is that it provides faster access. Instead of having to poll an input with ReadFile, you can configure the DirectX software components to notify an application when data is available to read.

The DirectInput and DirectInput2 components of DirectX enable communications with HIDs. For Visual-Basic programmers, DirectX version 7 includes support that enables Visual-Basic programmers to use DirectX.

Point-of-Sale Driver

The Point-of-Sale USB driver is another driver that was originally intended for a specific category of devices, but may be useful to devices outside the original category. Point-of-sale (POS) devices include bar-code scanners, displays, receipt printers, and other devices used in sales transactions.

In July 1999, Microsoft released the POSUSB point-of-sale driver for USB devices. The driver enables host applications to communicate with the device as if it were connected to a conventional COM port, using Create-File, ReadFile, and WriteFile. For bidirectional communications, a device needs one IN endpoint and one OUT endpoint. A device that requires only one-way communications needs just one IN or OUT endpoint. The endpoints may be configured for bulk or interrupt transfers.

The supporting documentation includes manuals for host application and firmware programmers. The driver and documentation is available from Microsoft's website, and is scheduled to ship with future releases of Windows.

Vendor-supplied Drivers

Another way to communicate with a device is to use a driver supplied by the chip's vendor. The ideal is a ready-to-install, general-purpose driver, along with complete, commented source code in case you want to adapt it for use with a particular device. The driver should also include documentation that shows how to use API calls to open a handle to the device and read and write to it in application code.

But the usefulness of vendor-supplied drivers varies. A driver is less useful if it turns out to be buggy, doesn't include the features you need, or has sketchy documentation that makes it hard to understand and use.

Cypress Semiconductor's *ezusb.sys* is an example of a driver that you can use without modification to communicate with Cypress' EZ-USB chip using any transfer type. The driver defines a set of DeviceIOControl codes for making standard requests in control transfers, exchanging data in interrupt, bulk, and isochronous transfers, and performing other USB-related and EZ-USB-specific functions. The driver also handles the EZ-USB's unique method of having the host load the chip's firmware on power-up or attachment.

Other Generic Drivers

If the chip's vendor doesn't supply a driver, in some cases you can use a generic driver that has no device-specific features or requirements. For bulk transfers, Windows 98's DDK includes source and compiled code, documentation, and an example application for the *bulkusb.sys* driver. The driver was written for Intel's 8x930 chip, but is designed to work with just about any USB chip that supports bulk transfers. Applications use ReadFile and WriteFile for data transfers.

In a similar way, the Windows 98 DDK also includes the *isousb.sys* driver for handling isochronous transfers. This driver was also written for the 8x930 chip.

If you decide to use either of these, check the Implementers Forum's webboard for tips and fixes.

Custom Drivers

The final option is to use a custom driver. Sometimes there is no generic or vendor driver that includes the transfer types you want to use. Or you may want to define custom DeviceIOControl codes.

An example of a custom driver is Cypress' driver for its thermometer application in the Starter Kit for the CY7C63001. This driver is written to support a specific application, rather than for general use. The driver defines DeviceIOControl codes to get the temperature and button state, set LED brightness, and read and write to the controller's RAM and ports. This driver was written before the release of Windows 98. If the device doesn't need to work with hosts running Windows 95, you could instead use the HID drivers to transfer the information, without having to write a driver.

The EZ-USB is a custom driver as well. The driver supports the vendor-specific request AnchorLoad, which causes the device to store received firmware and simulate detaching and reattaching to the bus.

If a chip's vendor provides source code for a driver, even if you don't use the driver as-is, you can modify the code or use portions of it, rather than starting from scratch. Ideally, the source code will include liberal commenting to help you understand it. It should include instructions that explain how to compile and install the driver. Even making minor changes or additions to an existing driver can be difficult if the code isn't well documented.

Writing a Custom Driver

If you don't have experience writing device drivers, creating a WDM driver is not a trivial task. It requires an investment in tools, expertise in C programming, and a fair amount of knowledge about how Windows communicates with hardware and applications. However, there are resources that can simplify and speed up the process.

Requirements

The minimum requirement for writing a device driver is Microsoft's Visual C++, which is capable of compiling WDM drivers. The compiler also includes a programming environment and a debugger to help during development.

Beyond this basic requirement, other tools can help to varying degrees, including the Windows 98 Device Developer's Kit (DDK), a subscription to Microsoft's Developer's Network (MSDN), driver toolkits, and advanced debuggers.

The Windows 98 DDK includes example code and developer-level documentation for Windows 98. The USB-related documentation includes tutorials on WDM drivers and HIDs and source code for several USB drivers, including a bulk-transfer driver, an isochronous-transfer driver, a filter driver, and the *usbview* utility. The examples can be a useful starting point in developing your own drivers. You can download the Windows 98 DDK from Microsoft's website.

MSDN is Microsoft's subscription service to massive quantities of documentation, examples, and developer's tools for Microsoft products. The topics covered include WDM driver development, USB, and DirectX, with quarterly updates. There are several levels of subscription that enable you to get the documentation alone or with varying amounts of Microsoft applications and development tools. Much of the information and other tools are also downloadable from Microsoft's website.

A driver toolkit provides a way to jumpstart driver development by doing as much of the work for you as possible. Toolkits that support USB drivers are available from Bluewater Systems and DriverWorks from Compuware NuMega.

Using a Driver Toolkit

To give an idea of what's involved in creating a device driver, I'll show how it's done with BlueWater Systems' WinDK development library. In addition to code libraries, the product includes a driver Wizard, sample drivers, and excellent documentation and tutorials on related topics. WinDK creates drivers for Windows 98. An optional USB Extension enables you to use the same source code to create a driver that will run on Windows NT 4.

The Libraries

There are two libraries, depending on whether you prefer to program in C or C++.

C++ programmers can use a library of classes for carrying out the tasks common to many drivers. For example, the functions of the CUsb class handle USB-related activities, including finding a device on a system, learning its capabilities, and transferring data using control, bulk, interrupt, and isochronous transfers. The CPnPDevice class handles Plug-and-Play functions, and the CRegistry class handles saving and retrieving information from the system registry.

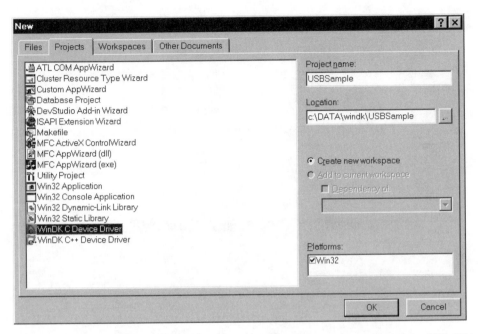

Figure 10-3: To create a driver with WinDK's Wizard, select one of the WinDK options from Visual C++'s *New* menu.

C programmers can accomplish the same things using the library of C functions.

Using the Wizard

The WinDK Wizard gets you started by creating a driver with as much code as possible filled in for you. The toolkit integrates into the Visual C++ programming environment. You start the Wizard from within Visual C++ by selecting File > New. As Figure 10-3 shows, the list of options includes WinDK C Device Driver and WinDK C++ Device Driver.

Figure 10-4 shows a few of the screens that the Wizard uses to ask you about your driver.

For a USB driver, you provide the following information to the Wizard:

- The project name and location.

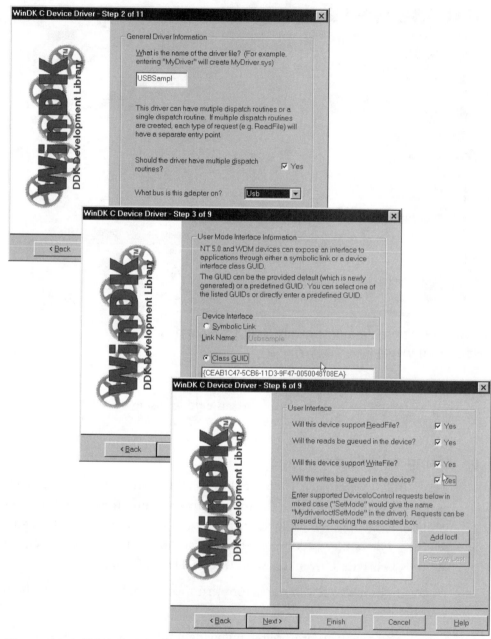

Figure 10-4: WinDK's Wizard queries you about your driver, then does as much of the work for you as possible.

- Whether to generate C or C++ code.
- Installation directories.
- Device class name.
- Driver type (WDM hardware driver).
- Bus type (USB).
- Vendor and Product IDs.
- Device Interface. This may be a GUID generated by the Wizard, an existing class GUID, or a symbolic link you specify.
- Optional registry keys for device-specific parameters and initial values for these keys.
- Whether the device will support ReadFile and WriteFile or DeviceIO-Control requests, and the names of any DeviceIOControl requests.

For USB drivers, there's no need to specify port or memory addresses or interrupts.

With this information, the Wizard creates a driver, an INF file, a test application, and a documentation file.

The driver includes default routines for power management, Plug and Play, system control, and creating and closing the device. For USB devices, these routines normally don't need modifying. After the driver's device is enumerated, the driver retrieves information about the device's configuration and endpoints.

If you specified DeviceIOControl functions for your driver, the Wizard adds skeleton code for each of these. You need to add the device-specific code that tells the driver what to do when an application calls a DeviceIOControl function. In a similar way, if the driver uses ReadFile and WriteFile, you add the device-specific code to the skeleton provided.

The INF file has the driver's filename, vendor and product IDs, and other information in the required format.

The Wizard also creates a command-line test application that opens the device with CreateFile and enables testing of the driver.

The documentation file lists each file created by the Wizard and explains its purpose.

The process is similar if you're using Compuware NuMega's DriverWorks. There's a Wizard that walks you through the process of defining your driver, then produces code to match what you've specified.

Another tool that most driver developers find essential is a debugger that enables testing of the driver code using breakpoints, single stepping, and other standard techniques. The Professional and higher levels of MSDN subscriptions include the WinDbg debugger. Compuware NuMega's Soft-ICE debugger enables debugging of WDM drivers using a single Windows 98 system.

11

How Windows Selects a Driver

When Windows detects a new USB peripheral, one of the things it has to do is figure out which device driver applications should use to communicate with the device, then load the selected driver. This is the job of Windows' Device Manager, which uses class and device installers and INF files to find the match.

This chapter explains how these components work together to select drivers for newly attached devices. I also show how to create an INF file that will cause the Device Manager to select the drivers you want.

The Process

The Device Manager is a Control-Panel applet that's responsible for installing, configuring, and removing devices. The Device Manager also adds information about each device to the system registry, which is the database that Windows maintains for storing critical information about the hardware and software installed on a system.

You can display the Device Manager by right-clicking the My Computer icon on the desktop and selecting Properties, then the Device Manager tab. Or you can get to it by selecting Start Menu > Settings > Control Panel > System > Device Manager.

The device and class installers are DLLs. Windows has default installers that the Device Manager uses to locate and load drivers for devices in the classes supported by the operating system (such as HIDs). The Device Manager and the installers together are also responsible for displaying dialog boxes as needed to prompt users for information.

The INF file is a text file containing information that helps Windows identify a device. The file tells Windows what driver or drivers to use and what information to store in the registry.

The Driver Information Database

When Windows enumerates a new USB device, the Device Manager compares the data in all of the INF files with the information in the descriptors retrieved from the device on enumerating. To prevent having to read through the files themselves each time a new device is detected, Windows maintains a driver information database with information culled from the INF files. The database files are *drvdata.bin* and *drvidx.bin*, and they're stored in the *windows\inf* folder.

You can view the contents of the files in a text editor or word processor. (Ignore the extra characters in the files.) Don't change the contents of the files, however; when you're finished viewing, just close the files without saving.

Drvidx.bin lists every Vendor and Product ID in the INF files, along with the manufacturer name, provider name, and description. *Drvdata.bin* matches manufacturers with INF files that contain information about their products. After retrieving the Vendor and Product IDs from a device, Windows uses the information in these two files to find the device's manufacturer and the INF file with information about the specific product.

The Registry's Role

The system registry stores information about all installed devices, whether or not they're attached and enumerated. When a new device is enumerated, the Device Manager stores information about the device in the registry.

To learn what kinds of information the Device Manager finds and stores, you can view (and edit) the registry's contents using the *regedit.exe* utility that comes with Windows.

A word of caution: the system registry is a vital and essential component of Windows. It's so important that Windows maintains multiple backup copies in case the current copy becomes unusable. Be extremely careful about making changes to the registry. If you goof and want to restore the registry to its previous state, boot to the DOS prompt and type *scanreg /restore.* Just viewing the registry should be safe, however.

The registry arranges its contents in a tree structure. Information about USB devices is in a couple of places:

> HKEY_LOCAL_MACHINE\Enum\USB

lists all USB devices.

HKEY indicates a registry key, or item in the registry structure. HKEY_LOCAL_MACHINE is a pointer to a data structure containing information about the system's hardware and installed software.

The devices are also listed in this branch:

> HKEY_LOCAL_MACHINE\System\CurrentControlSet\
> Services\Class

The Class branch has sub-branches for various categories. The USB branch lists the USB host controller and root hub, as Figure 11-1 shows. A USB peripheral doesn't necessary show up in the USB branch; it may be in a branch that pertains to the peripheral's function. Standard peripheral types

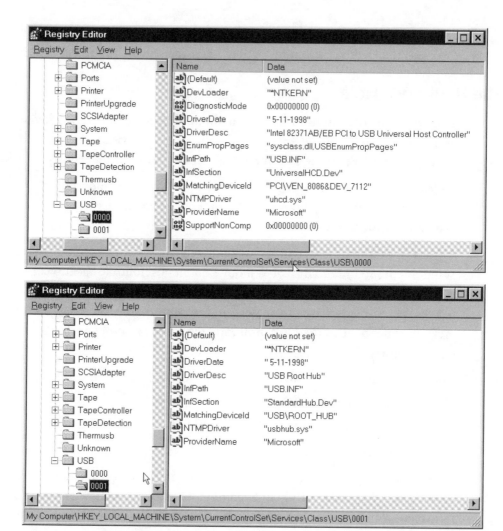

Figure 11-1: The registry's Class\USB branch has information about the system's host controller and root hub.

like keyboards, mice, and printers have their own branches, and will show up there. Many HID-class devices also have an entry in the HID branch. Other peripherals, such as digital cameras, may be in the USB branch. If the Device Manager can't quite figure out what to do with a USB device, it may call it an Unknown Device and place it in the USB branch. Some custom

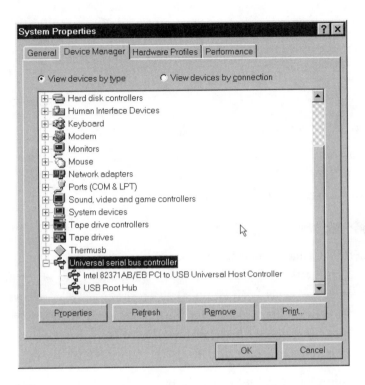

Figure 11-2: The Control Panel's Device Manager lists all attached and enumerated devices.

peripherals have their own branches. For example, the ThermUSB driver provided in Cypress' Starter Kit creates a branch called ThermUSB.

The Control Panel

The Device Manager is also responsible for adding attached devices to the Control Panel's display, under System > Device Manager, as Figure 11-2 shows.

The Device Manager's display shows only the USB devices that are currently detected. You can unplug a device while viewing the display and watch the device's listing disappear. Plug the device back in, and its listing pops back. If there was a problem communicating with the device or finding a driver, the Control Panel displays an exclamation point over the device's icon. An X over the icon means that the device is present but disabled, possibly by the user. To view additional information about a device, select the device and click Properties.

What the User Sees

What you see on the screen when you attach a new USB peripheral depends on what drivers and INF file the device uses and whether or not the device has been attached and enumerated previously.

Specific Device Listings

When you attach a device, Windows displays the messages *New Hardware Found,* and either *Unknown Device* or a name retrieved from the device. If the device has never been enumerated on the system, Windows will need to locate a driver. Chances are that the system won't already have an INF file with matching Vendor and Product IDs. If not, the product should come with a disk containing an INF file.

If Windows doesn't find a matching INF file, it runs the Add New Hardware Wizard (Figure 11-3). You see a window recommending letting the Wizard search for the best driver for the device. When you accept the recommendation and select Next, the Wizard requests a location to search.

Specify the drive containing the product's disk. When the Wizard finds the file, it displays the filename and announce that it's ready to install the driver. (To make things as easy as possible for users, vendors should store the INF file in the root directory of the product's disk!) Click Next, and the Wizard will display *Please wait while Windows builds a driver information database.*

The Wizard copies the INF file to the \windows\inf folder, loads the driver(s) specified in the file, lists the device in the Device Manager, and displays a window letting you know that it has finished installing the required software. The Device Manager's listing shows the device description, manufacturer, and provider name from the INF file.

Figure 11-3: Windows' Add New Hardware Wizard searches for and installs drivers for newly attached devices.

If the device has been enumerated previously, the system already has the information it needs, so no windows need to be displayed. The enumeration should be invisible except for a short delay that prevents the cursor from selecting items while Windows finds the correct INF file and loads any needed drivers.

Generic Device Listings

If a newly attached device uses only the standard HID drivers, it doesn't need its own INF file to identify it. On the first attachment, the Device Manager will determine that the device is HID class, and when it can't find a Vendor and Product ID match, will decide that the generic HID drivers are the best fit available.

But because there was no exact match, the Device Manager will play it safe and run the Add New Hardware Wizard to give you a chance to select a better driver (by telling Windows to look on the CD-ROM drive, for example). If you accept the default selections, Windows looks for a driver in the *windows\inf* directory, selects the INF file for the HID class *(hiddev.inf)*, and loads the HID drivers. The Device Manager lists the device as a *Standard HID Device,* with no indication of its specific function or manufacturer.

Tips for Experimenting

Here are some tips for using and experimenting with INF files:

A commercial product's Vendor ID must be an official ID assigned by the USB Implementers Forum. My examples use the Vendor ID of 0925h, which is assigned to my company, Lakeview Research.

As described above, for experimenting with HIDs, you can use Windows' generic *hiddev.inf* file, with no Vendor ID. The Device Manager will show the device as a generic HID, rather than using the name you provide in an INF file.

When experimenting with different settings in an INF file, I found that at times Windows remembered information from previous INF files, even after I had deleted the previous file and the information about the device in the registry, powered down, and rebooted. The reason is that unless you follow a specific procedure when changing the contents of an INF file, Windows may fail to rebuild the driver information database.

To ensure that Windows is aware of any changes you've made to an INF file, follow this procedure:

1. Save a copy of the new INF file that you want to use. Save it under another name (such as *mydriver.new*) or in a location other than *\windows\inf*.

2. Attach the device and allow the Device Manager to enumerate it.

3. In the Device Manager's window, select the device's entry and select Remove.

4. Deleting the entry in the Device Manager causes the device's INF file to be saved in the *windows\inf\other* folder, with the vendor's name added to the beginning of the filename. For example, Lakeview's file *mydriver.inf* would become *lakeviewmydriver.inf*. Delete this file as well. In some cases, such as the system's INF files, the *inf\other* folder won't have anything to delete.

5. Copy the INF file you want to use to the *windows\inf* folder. Be sure the file has an extension of *.inf* (such as *mydriver.inf*).

6. Unplug and re-attach the device. Windows will rebuild the driver information database using your new INF file.

Another less elegant way to accomplish the same thing is described in Microsoft's article Q139206, *Hardware List Not Updated After Installing New .inf File.* The article suggests renaming the driver information database to force Windows to build a new one. In the *windows\inf* folder, rename *drvdata.bin* to *drvdata.xxx* and rename *drvidx.bin* to *drvidx.xxx*. (By renaming the files rather than deleting them, you can get them back if necessary.) Another workaround is to use a different Product ID each time, in both the INF file and the device firmware.

If you do a lot of experimenting, and don't delete each device when you're done with it, the registry will fill with entries from your various configurations. When you no longer need a registry key, you can delete it from within *regedit.exe* (but see my cautions above about the registry).

Inside an INF File

The Device Manager looks for INF files in the system's *windows\inf* folder. By default, this is a hidden folder. If you don't see the folder in My Computer, select View > Folder Options > View, then under Hidden Files, select *Show all files.*

Examining the existing files is a good way to learn about the kinds of things contained in the files and how the information is structured. Your PC is sure to have plenty of INF files to examine. The INF file for the HID class is *hiddev.inf.* The Windows 98 DDK has some documentation on the contents and structure of INF files. INF files can be long and complicated, but the basics are fairly straightforward. In most cases, you can create an INF file by adapting one that's similar to what you need. Vendors of USB controller chips generally provide examples.

You can examine and edit INF files using the *infedit.exe* application included with Windows 98. But I find that using a text editor to view and edit the file is just as easy.

INF files for Windows 2000 have a few changes, including the need for a Services section. The Windows 2000 documentation has more about the changes.

Listing 11-1 is an INF file for a custom HID. I used *hiddev.inf* and Cypress' example INF files as models for the file. Figure 11-4 and Figure 11-5 show the information that the Device Manager displays after enumerating a device with this INF file.

Syntax

The information in an INF file must follow a few syntax rules, which will look familiar if you have experience with the *.ini* files commonly used in Windows 3.x.

- The information is arranged in sections, with each section containing one or more items. The section name is in square brackets [ ]. A carriage

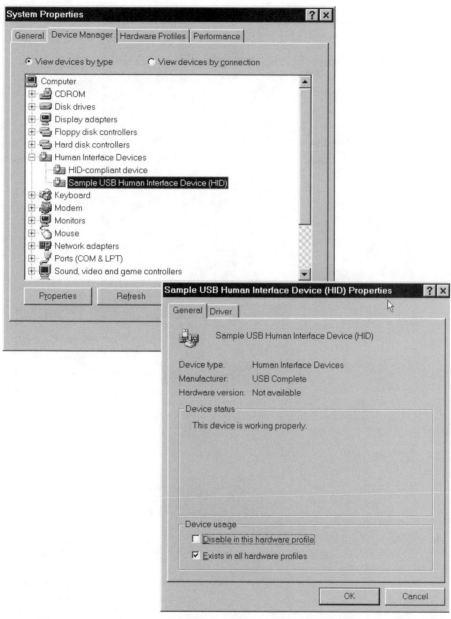

Figure 11-4: The Device Manager displays information obtained from the device's INF file. The device is listed both as an HID compliant device and as a device matching the description and Manufacturer in the INF file.

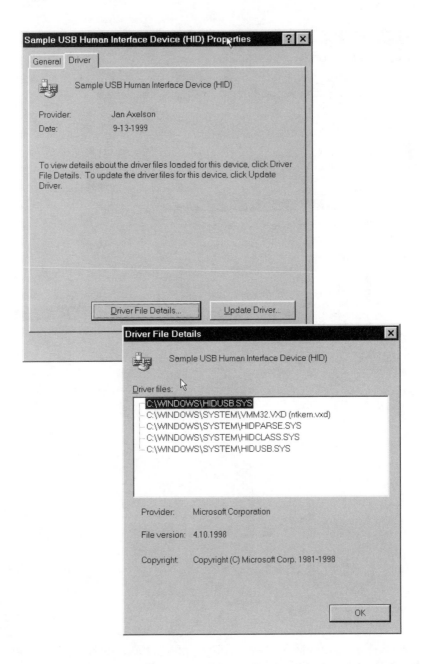

Figure 11-5: The information displayed by the Device Manager includes the Provider name and drivers specified in the device's INF file.

```
[Version]
Signature="$CHICAGO$"
Class=HID

;The GUID for HIDs
ClassGUID={745a17a0-74d3-11d0-b6fe-00a0c90f57da}

provider=%Provider%
LayoutFile=layout.inf, layout1.inf

[ClassInstall]
Addreg=Class.AddReg

[Class.AddReg]
HKR,,Installer,,mmci.dll

[Manufacturer]
%MfgName%=Lakeview

[Lakeview]
;Uses Lakeview Research's Vendor ID (0925)
;Uses the Product ID 1234
%USB\VID_0925&PID_1234.DeviceDesc%=SampleHID,
 USB\VID_0925&PID_1234

[DestinationDirs]
USBHID.CopyList = 11                ; LDID_SYS
;------------------------------------------------------------;
```

Listing 11-1: (Sheet 1 of 2) A device's INF file helps Windows locate the driver to use for the device.

```
[SampleHID]
CopyFiles=SampleHID.CopyList
AddReg=SampleHID.AddReg

[SampleHID.AddReg]
HKR,,DevLoader,,*ntkern
HKR,,NTMPDriver,,"hidusb.sys"

[SampleHID.CopyList]
hidusb.sys
hidclass.sys
hidparse.sys
;------------------------------------------------------------
  -;
[Strings]
Provider="Microsoft"
MfgName="USB Complete"
USB\VID_0925&PID_1234.DeviceDesc="Sample USB human interface
  device (HID)"
```

Listing 11-1: (Sheet 2 of 2) A device's INF file helps Windows locate the driver to use for the device.

return/line feed begins a new item. Some of the section names (Version, ClassInstall) are standard names that Windows will look for. Other sections match values specified in other sections. For example, if the Manufacturer section designates the manufacturer as Lakeview, the INF file will also have a Lakeview section. The sections can be in any order, though most follow the same convention, and the order of the items within a section can be critical. So if you're adapting an example, keep the order of items in the sections the same.

- A semicolon (;) indicates a comment.
- Text enclosed in percent symbols (%sampletext%) refers to a string. For example, you might have the following item:

```
provider=%Provider%
```

with an item in the Strings section that defines the provider string:

```
Provider="USB Complete"
```

- Some items set the value of an entry. For example, this item defines the device's class entry as HID:

```
Class=HID
```

- Some items specify information to store in the system registry:

```
HKR,,Installer,,mmci.dll
```

Sections

An INF file includes sections that help Windows identify the device, find the appropriate drivers, and store information about the device in the system registry. Here is the purpose of each section in the example INF file:

Version

The Version section is the file's header. Every INF file must have one.

The Version section in the example file has these items:

```
[Version]
Signature="$CHICAGO$"
Class=HID
;The GUID for HIDs
ClassGUID={745a17a0-74d3-11d0-b6fe-00a0c90f57da}
provider=%Provider%
LayoutFile=layout.inf, layout1.inf
```

The Signature key specifies which operating system the INF file is intended for. For devices that use WDM drivers, the value can be $Windows 98$, $Windows NT$, or $Chicago$, no matter which operating system the PC is using. Chicago was a beta name used when Windows 95 was under development and its use is still valid under Windows 98.

The Class key specifies the class for devices installed with this file. The example specifies the HID class.

The ClassGUID key specifies the GUID in the registry for devices installed with this file. A GUID is a 128-bit identifier. The example is the GUID for the HID class. It uses the standard GUID format. There's more on GUIDs later in this chapter.

The provider key names the creator of the INF file. In the example, %Provider% refers to a string defined later in the file.

The LayoutFile key names the source disks and files needed to install the driver for the device. Because the HID drivers are built into Windows 98, the example file specifies files that contain installation information for the Windows 98 setup. These files are also INF files. The information is in the SourceDisksFiles and SourceDisksNames sections of the files.

ClassInstall

The ClassInstall section installs a new class in the Class section of the registry. The Device Manager processes this section only if a device's class isn't yet installed in the operating system.

The example section has one item:

```
[ClassInstall]
Addreg=Class.AddReg
```

The Addreg key adds a class description to the system registry. In the example, the key's value refers to the Class.Addreg section, which specifies an installer file:

```
[Class.AddReg]
HKR,,Installer,,mmci.dll
```

HKR stands for HKEY_ROOT, which is the base registry key for the section that the AddReg appears in. This is typically under System\CurrentControlSet\Enum\Root, then a specific key for the device.

The installer file *mmci.dll* in the example is included with Windows 98 and is stored in the *\windows\system* folder.

Manufacturer

The Manufacturer section identifies the device (or devices) and names the Install section for each. Every INF file must have this section.

In the example, the MfgName string (defined later in the file) is set to the value *Lakeview*:

```
[Manufacturer]
%MfgName%=Lakeview
```

The Lakeview section has additional information:

```
[Lakeview]
;Uses Lakeview Research's Vendor ID (0925)
;Uses the Product ID 1234
%USB\VID_0925&PID_1234.DeviceDesc%=SampleHID,
USB\VID_0925&PID_1234
```

This section names the device's Vendor and Product IDs. When the Device Manager finds a match between these and the IDs retrieved from the device on enumerating, it knows that it has found the right INF file.

DestinationDirs

The DestinationDirs section names the folder or folders that any CopyFiles, RenFiles, and DelFiles items will use. In the example, SampleHID.CopyList is the name of a section that has a Copyfiles item. The value is a logical disk identifier (LDID) of 11, which is the system directory. The *INF File Reference* in the Windows 98 DDK lists other LDID values.

```
[DestinationDirs]
SampleHID.CopyList = 11
```

The SampleHID section has the CopyFiles item and an AddReg item:

```
[SampleHID]
CopyFiles=SampleHID.CopyList
AddReg=SampleHID.AddReg
```

These items name other sections in the file.

The SampleHID.CopyList section lists the drivers for the device:

```
[SampleHID.CopyList]
hidusb.sys
hidclass.sys
hidparse.sys
```

These are the drivers for generic HID-class devices. They're stored in the *\windows* or *\windows\system32\drivers* folder.

The SampleHID.AddReg section adds registry information for the device:

```
[SampleHID.AddReg]
HKR,,DevLoader,,*ntkern
HKR,,NTMPDriver,,"hidusb.sys"
```

DevLoader names *ntkern.vxd* as the VxD (virtual driver) that loads the drivers. *Ntkern.vxd* in turn loads the driver named in NTMPDriver. In the example, this is *hidusb.sys*. Both files are included with Windows 98. You won't find the file *ntkern.vxd* on your system because it's archived in, or bound into, the file *vmm32.vxd* for quicker loading.

Strings

The Strings section defines the strings referred to by items in other sections. Each item matches an item surrounded by percent signs in another section. So, for example, the provider in the Version section is equal to %Provider%, which equals *Microsoft* (since they are the source of the drivers).

```
[Strings]
Provider="Microsoft"
MfgName="USB Complete"
USB\VID_0925&PID_1234.DeviceDesc="Sample USB human
interface device (HID)"
```

The Generic INF File for HIDs

The INF file to use with generic HIDs is *hiddev.inf*. Every Windows 98 system should have this file. It's similar in many ways to the sample file in Listing 11-1. The Device Manager will use this file to install any HID that doesn't have its own INF file. The file also has IDs and descriptions for several manufacturers' audio and monitor-control devices, so these devices don't need their own INF files.

12

Human Interface Devices: Firmware Basics

The human interface device (HID) class is one of the first USB device types to have full support in Windows. On PCs running Windows 98 or later, applications can communicate with HIDs using the drivers built into the operating system. For this reason, USB devices that fit into the HID class are some of the easiest to get up and running.

This chapter shows how to determine whether a peripheral will fit into the human-interface class, explains the firmware requirements that define a device as a HID and enable it to exchange data with its host, and introduces the six HID-specific control requests. The next two chapters describe the reports that HIDs use to exchange information and how to access HIDs from Visual-Basic applications.

What is a HID?

Before you can know whether or not you can use Windows' HID drivers to communicate with a device, you need to know whether your device fits in the HID class.

The designation *human interface* suggests that the device interacts directly with people. A device may detect when someone presses a key or moves a mouse or joystick, or the host may send a joystick effect for the user to experience. The classic examples of HIDs are in fact keyboards, mice, and joysticks. Other HIDs include front panels with knobs, switches, buttons, and sliders; remote controls; telephone keypads; and game controls such as data gloves and steering wheels.

But a HID doesn't have to have a human interface at all. It just needs to be able to function within the limits of the class's specification. These are the major abilities and limitations of HID-class devices:

- The data exchanged resides in structures called reports. The device's firmware must support the HID report format. The host sends and receives data by sending and requesting reports in control or interrupt transfers. The report format is flexible, however, and can handle just about any type of data. A single report can contain up to 255 bytes.

- Each transaction can contain a small to moderate amount of data. For a full-speed device, the maximum is 64 bytes per transaction. For a low-speed device, the maximum is 8 bytes per transaction. Sending or receiving a report can take multiple transactions.

- A device may send information to the computer at unpredictable times. For example, there's no way for the computer to know when the user will press a key on the keyboard, so the host's driver polls the device periodically to obtain new data.

- The maximum speed of transfers is limited. A full-speed device can have no more than 1 transaction per millisecond, which works out to 64,000 bytes per second. A low-speed device can have no more than 1 transaction per 10 milliseconds, or 800 bytes per second.

- There is no guaranteed rate of transfer. If the device is configured for 10-millisecond intervals, the time between transactions may be any period equal to or less than this. The exception is devices configured to do one transaction per millisecond. Since this is the fastest possible polling rate, the device is guaranteed this rate.

Although many HIDs mostly send data from the device to the host, a HID can also receive data from the host. The classic example of host-to-device HID communications is the force-feedback joystick, where users experiences effects that match their actions, such as greater resistance when pulling the stick to cause a simulated airplane to climb or when getting a bite on a simulated fishing rod.

But any device that can live within the class's limits is a candidate to be a HID. The specification mentions bar-code readers, thermometers, and voltmeters as examples of HIDs that may not have a conventional human interface. Each of these sends data to the computer and may also receive requests that configure the device. Examples of devices that mostly receive data are remote displays, control panels for remote devices, robots, and machines of any kind that receive occasional or periodic commands from the host.

The HID interface may be only one of multiple USB interfaces supported by a device. A video display may have a HID interface for software control of brightness, contrast, and refresh rates, while using the conventional video interface to send the data to be displayed. A USB speaker that uses isochronous transfers for audio may also have a HID interface for controlling volume, balance, treble, and bass. A HID interface is often cheaper than traditional physical controls.

Two essential documents for working with HIDs are *Device Class Definition for Human Interface Devices*, which defines the HID class, and *HID Usage Tables*, which defines tables of values that help the host understand and use the HID data. Both documents are developed by members of the USB Device Working Group. The members are affiliated with the member companies of the USB Implementers Forum. The documents are published by the Implementers Forum and available on the Forum's website.

Hardware Requirements

A HID must conform to the requirements of the HID class as defined in the specification. The document describes the required descriptors, the amount of data in each transfer, the frequency of transfers, and the transfer types available.

To comply with the specification, the device's endpoints and descriptors must meet several requirements.

Endpoints

All HID transfers use either the default control pipe or an interrupt pipe. A HID must have an interrupt IN endpoint for sending data to the host. An interrupt OUT endpoint is optional.

The specification defines uses for each pipe. Table 12-1 shows the transfer types and their uses in HIDs.

You can think of the data that the host and device exchange as being of two types: low-latency data that must get to its destination quickly, and configuration data or other data that doesn't have critical timing requirements. (By configuration data, I'm referring to data sent in HID reports, not the host's requesting and selecting of device configurations on enumerating.)

The Control Pipe

The control pipe for a HID carries the eleven standard USB requests as well as six class-specific requests defined in the HID specification. Two of the HID-specific requests, Set_Report and Get_Report, provide a way for the host and device to transfer a block of any kind of data to or from the device. The host uses Set_Report to send reports and Get_Report to receive reports.

The other four requests relate to configuring the device. Set_Idle and Get_Idle set and read the Idle rate, which determines whether or not a device resends data that hasn't changed since the last poll. Set_Protocol and Get_Protocol set and read a protocol value, which can enable a device to function with a simplified protocol when the HID drivers aren't loaded.

Table 12-1: The transfer type used in a HID transfer depends on the chip's abilities and the requirements of the data being sent.

Transfer Type	Source of Data	Type of Data	Required Pipe?	OS Support
Control	Device (IN transfer)	Data that doesn't have critical timing requirements.	yes	Windows 98 and later
	Host (OUT transfer)	Data that doesn't have critical timing requirements, or any data if there is no OUT interrupt pipe.		
Interrupt	Device (IN transfer)	Periodic or low-latency data.	yes	
	Host (OUT transfer)	Periodic or low-latency data.	no	Windows 98 SE and later

The Interrupt Pipe(s)

The interrupt pipe or pipes provide an alternate way of exchanging device data, especially when the receiver must get the data quickly or periodically. An interrupt IN pipe carries data to the host, and an interrupt OUT pipe carries data to the device. Control transfers can be delayed if the bus is very busy, but once the device is configured, interrupt-transfer requests are guaranteed to meet the pipe's latency requirement. HIDs aren't required to have interrupt OUT pipes. If there is no interrupt OUT pipe, the host sends all reports on the control pipe, using Set_Report requests.

The option to use an interrupt OUT pipe was added to version 1.1 of the HID specification. A HID driver that complies only with version 1.0 won't support interrupt OUT transfers.

Firmware Requirements

For the host's drivers to communicate with a HID, the device's firmware must meet certain requirements. The device's descriptors must identify the device as having a HID interface, and the firmware must support an interrupt IN endpoint in addition to the default control pipe. The firmware must also contain a report descriptor that defines the format for transmitted and received device data.

To send data, the firmware must support Get_Report control transfers and interrupt IN transfers, and to receive data, the firmware must support Set_Report control transfers and may also support interrupt OUT transfers.

All device data transferred by a HID must use a defined report format that describes the size and contents of the data in the report. Devices may support one or more reports. A report descriptor in the device's firmware describes the reports, and may include information about how the receiver of the data should use it.

A value in each report defines the report as an Input, Output, or Feature report. Input reports send data to the host. Output reports receive data from the host. Feature reports may be in either direction.

For Input reports, the HID driver in all releases of Windows 98 uses interrupt transfers. For Output reports, the transfer type depends on what endpoints the device supports and which release of Windows 98 is installed. The original release of Windows 98 complies only with version 1.0 of the HID specification, and the HID driver uses control transfers for Output reports. Windows 98 SE complies with version 1.1 of the specification and the HID driver uses interrupt transfers for Output reports if the device has an interrupt OUT endpoint. Otherwise it uses control transfers. A device can support both transfer types.

Feature reports always use control transfers.

A report format can be simple or complex. The rest of this chapter and Chapter 13 have much more about report formats.

Identifying a Device as a HID

As with any USB device, a HID's descriptors tell the host what it needs to know in order to communicate with the device. Listing 12-1 shows example device, configuration, interface, class, and endpoint descriptors for a HID-class joystick. The host learns about the HID interface when it sends a Get_Descriptor request for the configuration containing the HID interface. The configuration's interface descriptor identifies the device as a HID. The HID class descriptor specifies the number of report descriptors supported by

```
device_desc_table:
    db 12h              ; Descriptor length (18 bytes)
    db 01h              ; Descriptor type (Device)
    db 00h,01h          ; Complies to USB Spec. Release (1.00)
    db 00h              ; Class code (0)
    db 00h              ; Subclass code (0)
    db 00h              ; Protocol (No specific protocol)
    db 08h              ; Max. packet size for EP0 (8 bytes)
    db B4h,04h          ; Vendor ID (Cypress)
    db 1Fh,0Fh          ; Product ID (joystick = 0x0F1F)
    db 88h,02h          ; Device release number (2.88)
    db 00h              ; Mfr string descriptor index (None)
    db 00h              ; Product string descriptor index (None)
    db 00h              ; Serial No. string descriptor index (None)
    db 01h              ; Number of possible configurations (1)
end_device_desc_table:

config_desc_table:
    db 09h              ; Descriptor length (9 bytes)
    db 02h              ; Descriptor type (Configuration)
    db 22h,00h          ; Total data length (34 bytes)
    db 01h              ; Interface supported (1)
    db 01h              ; Configuration value (1)
    db 00h              ; Index of string descriptor (None)
    db 80h              ; Configuration (Bus powered)
    db 32h              ; Maximum power consumption (100mA)

Interface_Descriptor:
    db 09h              ; Descriptor length (9 bytes)
    db 04h              ; Descriptor type (Interface)
    db 00h              ; Number of interface (0)
    db 00h              ; Alternate setting (0)
    db 01h              ; Number of endpoints supported
    db 03h              ; Class code ()
    db 00h              ; Subclass code ()
    db 00h              ; Protocol code ()
    db 00h              ; Index of string ()
```

Listing 12-1: Descriptors for a HID-class joystick (Sheet 1 of 2)

```
Class_Descriptor:
    db 09h          ; Descriptor length (9 bytes)
    db 21h          ; Descriptor type (HID)
    db 00h,01h      ; HID class release number (1.00)
    db 00h          ; Localized country code (None)
    db 01h          ; # of HID class descriptors to follow (1)
    db 22h          ; Report descriptor type (HID)
                    ; Total length of report descriptor
    db (end_hid_report_desc_table - hid_report_desc_table),00h

Endpoint_Descriptor:
    db 07h          ; Descriptor length (7 bytes)
    db 05h          ; Descriptor type (Endpoint)
    db 81h          ; Encoded address (Respond to IN, 1 endpnt)
    db 03h          ; Endpoint attribute (Interrupt transfer)
    db 06h,00h      ; Maximum packet size (6 bytes)
    db 0Ah          ; Polling interval (10 ms)

end_config_desc_table:
```

Listing 12-1: Descriptors for a HID-class joystick (Sheet 2 of 2)

the interface. During enumeration, the HID driver retrieves the HID class and report descriptors.

Descriptor Contents

The device and configuration descriptors have no HID-specific information. The device descriptor contains a class code, but this isn't where the device is defined as a HID. Instead, the interface descriptor is where the host learns that a device, or more properly, a device interface, belongs to the HID class. If the class-code byte in the device's interface descriptor is 3, the interface is a HID.

Other fields in the interface descriptor that contain HID-specific information are the subclass and protocol fields, which can specify a boot interface.

Boot Interfaces

The subclass field has just one active setting. A subclass of 1 indicates that the device supports a boot interface. When a device has a boot interface, it will work even when the host's HID drivers aren't loaded. This might occur when the computer boots directly to DOS, or when viewing the system setup screens that you can access on bootup, or when using Windows' Safe mode for system troubleshooting. A keyboard or mouse with a boot interface can use a predefined, simplified protocol supported by the BIOS of many hosts. The BIOS loads from ROM or other non-volatile memory on bootup and is available in any operating-system mode. The HID specification defines boot-interface protocols for keyboards and mice.

If a device does have a boot interface, the protocol field indicates if the device supports the keyboard (1) or mouse (2) interface. A value of zero indicates no device, and values 3–255 are reserved. A subclass of zero means that the device doesn't support a boot protocol. Values 2–255 are reserved.

The HID Usage Tables document defines the keyboard and mouse boot descriptors. The BIOS doesn't need to read a descriptor from the device because it knows what the protocol is and assumes that the device will support it. So a boot device doesn't have to include a boot-interface descriptor in firmware; it just has to support the boot protocol if the host hasn't requested the report protocol. When the operating system loads, the HID drivers use the HID-specific request Set_Protocol to cause the device to switch from the boot protocol to the report protocol defined in the report descriptor.

Draft 4 Compliance

During the development of the HID 1.0 specification, a change was made to the ordering of descriptors in HID firmware. In the early versions, the descriptors were stored and retrieved in this order:

> Configuration
> Interface
> Endpoint
> HID

By Draft 4 of the specification, the order had changed to:

> Configuration
> Interface

HID

Endpoint

The HID descriptor is now associated with the interface, rather than an endpoint. If the HID has two endpoints, the device doesn't need a HID descriptor for each.

A device that complies with the HID 1.1 specification uses the Draft 4 ordering. A USB test utility (such as HIDView, described in Chapter 15) that checks for Draft 4 compliance is examining the order of the descriptors.

HID Class Descriptor

The main purpose of the HID class descriptor is to identify additional descriptors for use in HID communications. The class descriptor has seven or more fields, depending on the number of additional descriptors. Table 12-2 shows the fields.

The Descriptor

bLength. The length in bytes of the descriptor.

bDescriptorType. The value 21h indicates the HID class.

The Class

bcdHID. The HID specification number that the device and its descriptors comply with. In BCD (binary-coded decimal) format. The value is a 4-character hexadecimal value with a decimal point assumed in the middle. For example, Version 1.0 is 0100h; Version 1.1 is 0110h.

bCountryCode. If the hardware is localized for a specific country, this field is a code identifying the country. The HID specification lists the codes. If the hardware isn't localized, this field is 00h.

bNumDescriptors. The number of class descriptors that are subordinate to this descriptor.

bDescriptorType. The type (report or physical) of a descriptor that is subordinate to the HID class descriptor. Every HID must support at least one report descriptor. A device may support multiple report descriptors and one

Table 12-2: The HID class descriptor has 7 or more fields in 9 or more bytes.

Offset (decimal)	Field	Size (bytes)	Description
0	bLength	1	Descriptor size in bytes
1	bDescriptorType	1	21h indicates the HID class
2	bcdHID	2	HID specification release number (BCD)
4	bCountryCode	1	Numeric expression identifying the country for localized hardware (BCD)
5	bNumDescriptors	1	Number of subordinate class descriptors supported
6	bDescriptorType	1	The type of class descriptor
7	wDescriptorLength	2	Total length of report descriptor
9	bDescriptorType	1	Constant identifying the type of descriptor. Optional, for devices with more than one descriptor.
10	wDescriptorLength	2	Total length of descriptor. Optional, for devices with more than one descriptor. May be followed by additional wDescriptorType and wDescriptorLength fields.

or more physical descriptors. Note that this field's name (but not its contents) is identical to the bDescriptorType field that identifies the HID class.

wDescriptorLength. The length of the descriptor described in the previous field.

Additional bDescriptorType, wDescriptorLength (optional). If there are additional subordinate descriptors, the descriptor type and length for each follow in sequence.

Report Descriptors

A report descriptor defines the format and uses of the data that carries out the purpose of the device. If the device is a mouse, the data reports mouse movements and button clicks. If it's a relay controller, the data contains codes that specify which relays to open and close.

The report descriptor needs to be flexible enough to handle devices with very different purposes. The format should be concise so it doesn't waste storage space in the device or bus time when the data transmits. The HID report descriptor achieves both of these at a price of a format that's more complex than sending raw bytes. The format doesn't limit the type of data in a report, but the report descriptor must describe the size and contents of the report in advance. A report descriptor's contents and length vary with the device, and can be short and simple, long and complex, or anywhere in between.

A report descriptor is a type of class descriptor. The host retrieves the descriptor by sending a Get_Descriptor request with 22h in the high byte and the report number in the low byte of the Value field. The default report number is 00h.

One way to get a feel for what a report descriptor contains and how it's structured is to look at one. Listing 12-2 is a bare-bones report descriptor that describes an Input report that sends two bytes of data to the host and an Output report that sends two bytes of data to the device. Other report descriptors build on this basic format, so a short descriptor like this is a good place to start understanding report descriptors in general.

The items in the example descriptor are required in all descriptors. Some items apply to the entire descriptor, while others are specified separately for the input and output data. More complicated report descriptors may use additional instances of these same items along with other optional items.

Each item in the example report consists of a byte that identifies the item and one or more bytes containing the item's data. Here is what each item in the example descriptor specifies:

The **Usage Page** item is identified by the value 06h and specifies the general function of the device, such as generic desktop control, game control, or alphanumeric display (to name just a few). You can think of the Usage Page as a subset of the HID class. In the example descriptor, the Usage Page is the vendor-defined value FFA0hh. The HID specification lists values for different Usage Pages and values reserved for vendor-defined Usage Pages.

The **Usage** item is identified by the value 09h and specifies the function of the individual report. Just as the Usage Page is a subset of the class, the Usage is a subset of the Usage Page. For example, Usages available for generic desktop controls include mouse, joystick, and keyboard. Because the

```
hid_report_desc_table:

    db 06h, A0h, FFh ;          Usage Page (vendor defined)
    db 09h, A5h      ;          Usage (vendor defined)

    db A1h, 01h      ;          Collection (Application)
    db 09h, A6h      ;          Usage (vendor defined)

;The input report
    db 09h, A7h      ;          Usage (vendor defined)
    db 15h, 80h      ;          Logical Minimum (-127)
    db 25h, 7Fh      ;          Logical Maximum (128)
    db 75h, 08h      ;          Report Size (8)   (bits)
    db 95h, 02h      ;          Report Count (2)   (fields)
    db 81h, 02h      ;          Input (Data, Variable, Absolute)

;The output report
    db 09h, A9h      ;          Usage (vendor defined)
    db 15h, 80h      ;          Logical Minimum (-128)
    db 25h, 7Fh      ;          Logical Maximum (127)
    db 75h, 08h      ;          Report Size (8)   (bits)
    db 95h, 02h      ;          Report Count (2)   (fields)
    db 91h, 02h      ;          Output (Data, Variable, Absolute)

    db C0h           ;          End Collection

end_hid_report_desc_table:
```

Listing 12-2: This report descriptor enables sending and receiving of two bytes.

example's Usage Page is vendor-defined, all of the Usages in the Usage Page are vendor-defined also. In the example, the Usage is A5h.

The **Collection (Application)** item begins a group of items that together perform a function that is familiar to applications, such as keyboard or mouse. Each report descriptor must have an Application Collection to enable Windows to enumerate it properly. The Usage item that follows the Collection item names the function of the collection. In the example, it's the vendor-defined value A6.

The Logical Minimum and Maximum have values of 15h and 25h and specify the range of values that the report can contain. Negative values may be expressed as two's complements. In the example, the values 80h and 7Fh indicates a range of -128 to +127.

The Report Size item has a value of 75h and indicates how many bits are in each reported data item. In the example, each data item is eight bits.

The Report Count item has a value of 95h and indicates how many data items the report contains. In the example, each report contains two data items.

The final item specifies whether the report carries data from the host to the device (91h) or from the device to the host (81h), along with other information about the data.

The End Collection item closes the Application Collection.

HID-specific Requests

The HID specification defines six HID-specific control requests. Table 12-3 lists the requests, and the following pages describe each request in more detail.

All HIDs must support Get_Report, and all boot devices must support Get_Protocol and Set_Protocol. The other requests (Set_Report, Get_Idle, and Set_Idle) are optional. However, if a device doesn't have an Interrupt OUT endpoint or if it is communicating with Windows 98 Gold hosts, it will need to support Set_Report to receive data from the host. Devices that don't support Feature reports will send data using interrupt transfers only, and may have no use for Get_Report, but to comply with the specification, they must support the request in case a host should decide to use it. A device will enumerate and transfer data OK without supporting this request, however.

Table 12-3: In addition to the eleven standard control requests, HIDs may support up to six HID-specific requests.

Request #	Request	Data source	Value	Index	Data Length (bytes)	Data	Required ?
01h	Get_ Report	device	report type, report ID	interface	report length	report	yes
02h	Get_ Idle	device	report ID	interface	1	idle duration	no
03h	Get_ Protocol	device	0	interface	1	protocol	required for boot devices
09h	Set_ Report	host	report type, report ID	interface	report length	report	no
0Ah	Set_ Idle	host	idle duration, report ID	interface	0	none	no
0Bh	Set_ Protocol	host	protocol	interface	0	none	required for boot devices

Get_Report

Purpose: Enables the host to receive data from a device in control transfers.

Request Number: 01h

Source of Data: device

Data Length: length of the report

Contents of Value field: The high byte contains the report type (1=Input, 2=Output, 3=Feature), and the low byte contains the report ID. The default report ID is 0.

Contents of Index field: the number of the interface that supports this request.

Contents of Data field: the report

Comments: The HID specification advises that the host should not use this request to obtain periodic data. (It should use interrupt transfers instead.) The request is intended only for obtaining the state of feature items and other information that the host needs to know when it initializes the device. However, a host using a boot protocol might use Get_Report to receive keypress or mouse data.

All devices must support this request.

Set_Report

Purpose: Enables a device to receive data from the host in control transfers.

Request Number: 02h

Source of Data: host

Data Length: length of the report

Contents of Value field: The high byte contains the report type (1=Input, 2=Output, 3=Feature), and the low byte contains the report ID. The default report ID is 0.

Contents of Index field: the number of the interface that supports this request.

Contents of Data field: the report

Comments: If a device doesn't have an Interrupt OUT endpoint or if the host complies only with version 1.0 of the HID specification, this request is the only way the host can send data to the device. For other devices, the host may use this request to send Feature reports or other information that the device needs to have when it initializes. Devices aren't required to support this request.

Get_Idle

Purpose: The host reads the current Idle rate from a device.

Request Number: 03h

Source of Data: device

Data Length: 1

Contents of Value field: The high byte is 0. The low byte indicates the report ID that the request applies to. If the low byte is 0, the request applies to all of the device's Input reports.

Contents of Index field: the number of the interface that supports this request.

Contents of Data field: the Idle rate, expressed in units of 4 milliseconds per bit.

Comments: See Set_Idle for more details. Devices aren't required to support this request.

Set_Idle

Purpose: Saves bandwidth by limiting the reporting frequency of an interrupt IN endpoint when the data hasn't changed since the last report.

Request Number: 09h

Source of Data: none

Data Length: 0

Contents of Value field: The high byte sets the duration, or the maximum amount of time between reports. A value of 0 means that there is no maximum and the device will report only when the report data has changed. Otherwise, the device returns a NAK. The low byte indicates the report ID that the request applies to. If the low byte is 0, the request applies to all of the device's Input reports.

Contents of Index field: the number of the interface that supports this request.

Contents of Data field: none

Comments: The duration is in units of 4 milliseconds, which gives a range of 4 to 1,020 milliseconds. No matter what the duration value is, if the report data has changed since the last report sent, on receiving a request, the device sends a report. If the data hasn't changed and the amount of time specified in the duration value hasn't elapsed since the last report, the device sends a NAK. If the data hasn't changed and the amount of time specified in the duration value has elapsed since the last report, the device sends a report. A duration value of 0 indicates an infinite duration; the device sends a report only if the report data has changed, and responds to all other interrupt IN requests with NAK.

Devices aren't required to support this request. On enumerating a HID, Windows will attempt to set the idle rate to 0. If the device supports the request, the device will report data only if it has changed.

Get_Protocol

Purpose: The host learns whether the boot or report protocol is currently active on the device.

Request Number: 0Ah

Source of Data: device

Data Length: 1

Contents of Value field: 0

Contents of Index field: the number of the interface that supports this request.

Contents of Data field: The protocol. 0=boot protocol, 1=report protocol.

Comments: Boot devices must support this request.

Set_Protocol

Purpose: The host specifies whether to use the boot or report protocol.

Request Number: 0Bh

Source of Data: host

Data Length: 1

Contents of Value field: 0

Contents of Index field: the number of the interface that supports this request.

Contents of Data field: 0=Boot Protocol; 1=Report Protocol

Comments: Boot devices must support this request.

Transferring Data

When enumeration is complete, the host has identified the device as a human interface device, has established pipes with the supported endpoints, and knows what report formats to use to send and receive data.

The host uses control transfers to send and receive Feature reports containing additional configuration data or other data that doesn't have critical timing requirements. For example, a control-panel application for a video monitor may use control transfers to send settings to the monitor. The host uses interrupt transfers to send and receive periodic or low-latency data in Input and Output reports. The device's firmware must have the complementary code to respond to the host's requests.

Sending Data to the Host

The host receives data after requesting it in an interrupt or control transfer. To respond to an interrupt transfer, the device's firmware needs only to have the requested data in its transmit buffer and to be configured to respond to an interrupt IN request. In the Cypress CY7C63001, doing this requires writing a value to Endpoint 1's transmit configuration register to enable transmitting and to specify the number of bytes to send and the data-toggle bit's value.

Below is example code for the CY7C63001 that prepares two bytes to transmit on the next interrupt IN transfer:

```
;disable Endpoint 1 interrupts
    mov A,[interrupt_mask]
    and A, EFh
    mov [interrupt_mask],A
    iowr Global_Interrupt

;Copy values from RAM to Endpoint 1's buffer
;for transmitting to the host.
    mov A, [Data_Byte0]
    mov [Endpoint1_Byte0], A
    mov A, [Data_Byte1]
    mov [Endpoint1_Byte1], A
```

```
;Configure Endpoint 1's transmit register
;so that the bytes will transmit on the next poll.
     iord USB_EP1_TX_Config
;Don't change the Data 0/1 bit.
     and A,40h
;Bits 4 and 7 enable transmitting.
;The low nibble is the number of data bytes (2).
     or A,92h
     iowr USB_EP1_TX_Config

Select:
;Enable Endpoint 1 interrupts.
     mov A,[interrupt_mask]
     or A, 10h
     mov [interrupt_mask],A
     ipret Global_Interrupt
```

When the device has received an interrupt IN request and transmitted the bits, the chip generates an Endpoint 1 interrupt. The interrupt-service routine toggles the data-toggle bit so it's correct for the next transfer. The routine could also write new values to the transmit buffer, or this may be done elsewhere in the firmware.

```
USB_EP1_ISR:
     push A
;Toggle the data 0/1 bit so it's correct
;for the next transaction.
     iord USB_EP1_TX_Config
     xor A,40h
;The interrupt clears the EnableRespondToIN bit
;(bit 7) in the TX Config. register
;Set this bit to 1 to cause data to transmit
;on the next interrupt IN request.
;Set bit 4 to 1 to enable Endpoint 1.
;Set bits 0-3 to the number of bytes to send (2).
     or A, 92h
     iowr USB_EP1_TX_Config
;Enable interrupts and return.
     mov A, [interrupt_mask]
     ipret Global_Interrupt
```

Of course, for other chips, the details will vary. If the device has no data to send, the hardware responds to a request with a NAK.

Responding to a Get_Report request for a Feature report is much like responding to any control Read request. The device must be able to detect the request, write the requested report data to the USB output buffer for transmitting, and respond to the host's handshake.

Receiving Data from the Host

The host receives data after requesting it in an interrupt or control transfer. A host that complies with version 1.1 of the HID specification sends Output reports using an interrupt OUT pipe if one is available. Otherwise, the host uses control transfers with the HID-class request Set_Report. Hosts that comply only with version 1.0 of the HID specification always use control transfers to send OUT reports. The chip's architecture and descriptors determine whether or not the device has an interrupt OUT pipe available. The host always uses Set_Report control requests to send Feature reports.

If the device has an interrupt OUT endpoint and needs to receive low-latency data, the endpoint should be configured to receive report data. Typically, when new data arrives, an interrupt will inform the device of the event. An interrupt-service routine in the firmware then does whatever is necessary with the data, either using the data right away to perform an action or storing it for later use. The interrupt-service routine should also do whatever is needed to prepare the endpoint to receive a new report.

If the device doesn't have an interrupt OUT endpoint, the firmware must detect Set_Report control requests and handle the report data in the request. The chip must do the same to receive Feature reports. Using control requests is a little more complicated than interrupt transfers. If the chip's vendor hasn't provided sample code for this request, you can use the code for other control requests as a model. A device that has an interrupt OUT endpoint should also be able to receive reports in Set_Report control transfers so it can receive Feature reports, or other reports if it happens to communicate with a non-HID 1.1-compliant host.

A Set_Report request consists of at least three transactions. The host sends a Setup transaction that specifies the request and the number of bytes in the report, followed by one or more data transactions with the report data. The device returns a handshake transaction.

These are the steps a device typically follows to handle a Set_Report request:

1. The device receives a Setup transaction and triggers an interrupt that causes the firmware to jump to an interrupt-service routine.

2. The interrupt-service routine does the following:

• Detects the code that indicates the arrival of a Set_Report request.

• Reads the Length parameter in the Setup transaction to find out the number of bytes in the report.

• Configures Endpoint 0 to receive data.

3. When the interrupt-service routine ends, the device returns to normal operation until it receives an OUT token packet indicating that host is sending data to the default endpoint. This triggers an interrupt that causes the firmware to jump to an interrupt-service routine for the endpoint.

4. The interrupt-service routine does whatever is needed with the received data, returns a handshake in the status phase, and returns to normal operation.

5. Repeat steps 3 and 4 for any additional OUT transactions, up to the Length value in the Setup transaction.

Below is Cypress code that executes on detecting a Set_Report request. The code finds out how many bytes to read and configures Endpoint 0 to receive data in an OUT transaction. This involves setting two configuration bits.

```
SetReport:
;The CY7C63001 doesn't support interrupt-type OUT
;transfers. So the host uses Control transfers with
;Set Report requests to get data from the device.

;Find out how many bytes to read.
:This value is in WLength.
;Save the length in data_count.
    mov A, [wLength]
    mov [data_count], A
```

```
;Enable receiving data at endpoint 0 by setting
;the EnableOuts bit. The bit is cleared following
:any Setup or Out transaction.
     iord USB_Status_Control
     or A, 10h
;Clear the StatusOuts bit to disable auto-Ack
;after receiving a valid status packet in response
;to a Control read (IN) transfer.
;Otherwise, the USB engine will respond to a data
;OUT packet with a stall.
     and A, F7h
     iowr USB_Status_Control
;Now we're ready to receive the report data.
;An Endpoint 0 OUT interrupt signals the arrival
;of the report data.
ret
```

The chip then waits for the arrival of the OUT token packet. When an Endpoint 0 interrupt occurs, the code checks for an OUT packet, and if one has arrived, stores the received data and returns an empty data packet in the status phase:

```
check_for_out_packet:
     iord USB_EP0_RX_Status
;Is it an OUT packet?
     and A, 02h
;If no, ignore it.
     jz done_with_packet
;If yes, process the received data.
;Disable Endpoint 0 interrupts.
     mov A,[interrupt_mask]
     and A, 0F7h
     mov [interrupt_mask], A
     iowr Global_Interrupt

;Read the received bytes and copy them to RAM.
     push X
;data_count holds the number of bytes left to read.
;X holds the index of the address to read and
;the index of the address to store the received data.
     ;Initialize the X register.
     mov X, 0
```

```
      Get_Received_Data:
      ;Find out if there are any bytes to read.
      mov A, 0
      cmp A, [data_count]

      ;Jump if nothing to read.
      jz DoneWithReceivedData

      ;Get a byte.
      mov A, [X + Endpoint_0]
      ;Save it.
      mov [X + Data_Byte0], A
      ;Decrement the number of bytes to read.
      dec [data_count]
      ;Increment the address to read.
      inc X
      ;Do another
      jmp Get_Received_Data

      DoneWithReceivedData:
      pop X

;Handshake by sending a 0-byte data packet.
call Send0ByteDataPacket

done_with_packet:
;Re-enable Endpoint 0 interrupts.
      mov A,[interrupt_mask]
      or A, 08h
      mov [interrupt_mask], A

      ipret Global_Interrupt
```

The chip is then ready for another transfer.

This is the code for sending the zero-byte data packet in the Status phase:

```
      Send0ByteDataPacket:
      ;Send a data packet with 0 bytes.
      ;Use this handshake after receiving
      ;a valid OUT data packet.
      ;Enable responding to IN packets and
      ;set the data toggle to Data1.
            mov A, C0h
```

```
        iowr USB_EP0_TX_Config
;Enable interrupts.
     mov A, [interrupt_mask]
     iowr Global_Interrupt
WaitForDataToTransfer:
;Wait for the data to transfer.
;Clear the watchdog timer
     iowr Watchdog
;Bit 7 of USB_EP0_TX_Config is cleared
;when the host acknowledges receiving the data.
     iord USB_EP0_TX_Config
     and A, 80h
     jnz WaitForDataToTransfer
     ret
```

13

Human Interface Devices: Reports

Chapter 12 introduced the concept of using structured reports for exchanging data with devices in the human-interface class. A report can be a simple buffer of raw data, or it can be a complex assortment of items, each with assigned functions and units. This chapter shows how to design a report to fit a specific application.

Report Structure

A report descriptor may contain any of dozens of items arranged in various combinations. It can be long and complex, short and simple, or something in between. The advantage of a more complex descriptor is that the device can provide detailed information about the data it sends and expects to receive. The descriptor can specify the values' uses and what units to apply to the raw data, and it can tell applications whether or not a device supports a particular feature, such as force feedback on a joystick.

But just because the specification supports an item that applies to a device doesn't mean that the report has to include it. For custom devices that are intended for use with a single application, the application often knows in advance what the device is capable of, so there's no need to request the information from the device. For example, when the vendor of a data-acquisition unit creates an application for use with the unit, the vendor already knows what the device can do and how to access it. At most, the application might check the product ID and version number from the device descriptor to learn whether it can request a particular setting or action.

Some of the details about report structures can get tedious. You have my permission to skim through them! You can always come back to it later if you need to.

The report descriptor consists of a series of items that describe the values to be transferred. Each item has a defined scope, and some items may apply to multiple values (eliminating the need for repetition).

Using the HID Descriptor Tool

The HID Descriptor Tool (Figure 13-1) is a free utility available from the USB Implementers Forum. It helps in creating report descriptors, and will also check your descriptor's structure, reporting any errors it finds. Instead of having to look up the values that correspond to each item in your report, you can select the item from a list and enter the value you want to assign to it, and the software will add the item to the descriptor. You can also add items manually. The Parse Descriptor function displays the raw and interpreted values in your descriptor, and comments on any errors found. When you have a descriptor with no errors, you can convert it to the syntax required by your firmware. The tool has limited support for vendor-specific items, and may flag these as errors.

Predefined Values

A report descriptor can contain values that describe specific uses. There are several documents that define the Usage and other values that reports may

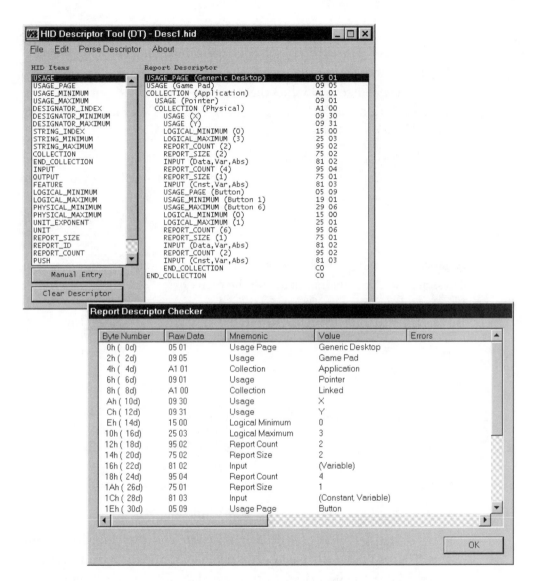

Figure 13-1: The HID Descriptor Tool helps in creating and testing HID report descriptors.

contain. The first place to look is the *HID Usage Tables* document. This has tables of values for generic desktop controls, simulation controls, game controls, LED functions, buttons, telephony devices, and more. The document also tells you where to find values that are defined elsewhere. Some are in the HID specification, while others are in the Class Definition documents for specific device types such as monitor, power, and image-class devices.

The HID specification defines two report item types: short items and long items. As of specification version 1.1, there are no defined Long items, and the type is just reserved for future use.

Short Items

A Short item's 1-byte prefix specifies the item type, item tag, and item size. These are the elements that make up the prefix byte:

Bit Number	Contents
7	Numeric value that indicates the item's function
6	
5	
4	
3	Item scope: Main, Global, or Local
2	
1	Item size
0	

The item tag (bits 4-7) indicates the item's function.

The item type (bits 3 and 2) describes the scope of the item: Main (00), Global (01), or Local (10). Main items define or group the data fields in the descriptor. Global items describe the reported data. Local items define characteristics of individual controls in the data. (This chapter has more information about these.)

The item size (bits 1 and 0) indicates how many data bytes the item contains. Note that an item size of 3 (11 in binary) corresponds to 4 data bytes:

Item Size (binary)	Number of Data Bytes
00	0
01	1
10	2
11	4

Long Items

A Long item uses multiple bytes to store the same information as the Short item's 1-byte prefix. A Long item's 1-byte prefix (FEh) identifies the item as a Long item. In addition, the item has a byte that specifies the number of data bytes, a byte containing the item tag, and up to 255 bytes of data.

The Main Item Type

A Main item defines or groups data items within a report descriptor. There are five subtypes with the Main item type. The Input, Output, and Feature items each define fields in the report. Collection and End Collection items don't define fields, but instead help to group related items within a report. The default value for all Main items is 0.

Input, Output, and Feature Items

Table 13-1 shows the supported values for the Input, Output, and Feature items, including the item tag and the meanings of the bits in the value that follows the tag.

An Input item can apply to any control, sensor reading, or other information that the device sends to the host. An Input report contains one or more Input items. The host uses interrupt IN transfers to request Input reports.

An Output item applies to information that the host sends to the device. An Output report contains one or more Output items. Output reports contain data that reports the states of controls, such as whether to open or close a

Table 13-1: The data included with Input, Output, and Feature Item Tags describes the report data.

Main Item Tag	Bit Number	Meaning if bit = 0	Meaning if bit = 1
Input (100000nn, where nn=the number of data bytes)	0	Data	Constant
	1	Array	Variable
	2	Absolute	Relative
	3	No wrap	Wrap
	4	Linear	Non-linear
	5	Preferred state	No preferred state
	6	No null position	Null state
	7	Reserved	
	8	Bit field	Buffered bytes
	9-31	Reserved	
Output (100100nn, where nn=the number of data bytes)	0	Data	Constant
	1	Array	Variable
	2	Absolute	Relative
	3	No wrap	Wrap
	4	Linear	Non-linear
	5	Preferred state	No preferred state
	6	No null position	Null state
	7	Non-volatile	Volatile
	8	Bit field	Buffered bytes
	9-31	Reserved	
Feature (101100nn, where nn=the number of data bytes)	0	Data	Constant
	1	Array	Variable
	2	Absolute	Relative
	3	No wrap	Wrap
	4	Linear	Non-linear
	5	Preferred state	No preferred state
	6	No null position	Null state
	7	Non-volatile	Volatile
	8	Bit field	Buffered bytes
	9-31	Reserved	

switch or the intensity to apply to an effect. As explained earlier, if an interrupt OUT pipe is available, a HID 1.1-compliant host host will use interrupt OUT transfers to request Output reports. Otherwise, the host will use Get_Report control requests.

A Feature item normally applies to information that the host sends to the device. However, it's also possible for the host to read Feature items from a device. A Feature report contains one or more Feature items. Feature reports contain configuration settings that affect the overall behavior of the device or one of its components. Feature reports normally control settings that you might otherwise adjust in a physical control panel. For example, the host may have a virtual (on-screen) control panel to enable users to select and control features. The host uses control transfers with Set_Report and Get_Report requests to send and receive Feature reports.

Following each item tag are 32 bits that describe the data. At most, only 9 of the bits are used, with the rest reserved. The device firmware and host software may use or ignore this information.

The bit functions are the same for Input, Output, and Feature items, except that Input items don't support the volatile/non-volatile bit. These are the uses for each bit:

Data | Constant. Data means that the contents of the item are modifiable (read/write). Constant means the contents are not modifiable (read-only).

Array | Variable. This bit specifies whether the data reports the state of every control or just reports the controls that are active. Reporting only the active controls results in a more compact report for devices such as keyboards, where there are many controls (keys) but only one or a few are active at the same time.

For example, if a keypad has eight keys, setting this bit to Variable would mean that the keypad's report would contain a bit for each key. In the report descriptor, the report size would be one bit, the report count would be eight, and the total amount of data sent would be eight bits. Setting the bit to Array would mean that each key has an assigned index, and the keypad's report would contain only the index of the keys that are active. With eight keys, the report size would be three bits, which can report a key number from 0 through 7. The report count would equal the maximum number of simultaneous keypresses that could be reported. If the user can press only one key at a time, the report count would be 1 and the total amount of data sent would be just 3 bits. If the user can press all of the keys at once, the report count would be 8 and the total amount of data sent would be 24 bits.

The specification recommends returning 0 when no controls are active, and specifying a Logical Minimum of 1 and a Logical Maximum equal to the number of controls.

Absolute | Relative. Absolute means that the value is based on a fixed origin; Relative means that the data indicates the change from the last reading. A joystick normally reports absolute data (the joystick's current position), while a mouse reports relative data (how far the mouse has moved since the last report).

No Wrap | Wrap. Wrap indicates that the value rolls over if it continues to increment after reaching its maximum or continues to decrement after reaching its minimum. A value specified as No Wrap that exceeds the limits may report a value outside the specified limits. This bit doesn't apply to Array data.

Linear | Non-linear. Linear indicates that the measured data and the reported value have a linear relationship. A graph of the reported data and the property being measured forms a straight line. In non-linear data, a graph of the reported data and the property being measured forms a curve. This bit doesn't apply to Array data.

Preferred State | No Preferred State. Preferred state indicates that the control will return to a particular state when the user isn't interacting with it. A momentary pushbutton has a preferred state (out) when no one is pressing it. A toggle switch has no preferred state; it remains in the state selected by the last user. This bit doesn't apply to Array data.

No Null Position | Null State. Null state indicates that the control supports a state where it isn't sending meaningful data. A control indicates that it's in its null state by sending a value outside the range defined by its Logical Minimum and Maximum. No Null Position indicates that the control can always be assumed to be sending meaningful data. A hat switch on a joystick is in a null position when it isn't being pressed. This bit doesn't apply to Array data.

Non-volatile | Volatile. The Volatile bit applies only to Output and Feature reports. Volatile means that the device can change the value on its own, without host interaction, as well as when the host sends a report requesting the device to change the value. For example, a control panel may have a control that users can set in two ways. They may use a mouse to click a setting in a window on the host to cause the host to send a report to the device, or they may turn a physical knob on the device. Non-volatile means that the device changes the value only when the host requests it in a report.

When the host is sending a report and doesn't want to a volatile item, the value to assign depends on whether the data is defined as relative or absolute. If a volatile item is defined as relative, a report that assigns a value of 0 will result in no change. If a volatile item is defined as absolute, a report that assigns an out-of-range value will result in no change.

This bit doesn't apply to Array data.

Bit Field | Buffered Bytes. Bit Field means that each bit or a group of bits in a byte can represent a separate piece of data and the field doesn't represent a single quantity. The application interprets the contents of the field. Buffered bytes means that the data represents a single buffer containing one or more bytes. This bit doesn't apply to Array data.

Collection and End Collection Tags

All of the report types can use Collection and End Collection items to group related items.

There are three defined types of collections: application, physical, and logical. Vendors can also define their own collection types. Collections can be nested. Table 13-2 shows the values of the Collection and End Collection tags and the defined values for the different collection types.

An application collection contains items that have a common purpose or together carry out a single function. For example, the boot descriptor for a

Table 13-2: Data values for the Collection and End Collection Main Item Tags.

Main Item Type	Value	Description
Collection (A1h)	00h	Physical
	01h	Application
	02h	Logical
	03h-7Fh	Reserved
	80h-FFh	Vendor-defined
End Collection (C0h)	None	Closes a collection

keyboard groups the keypress and LED data in an application collection. All reports must be in an application collection

A physical collection contains items that represent data at a single geometric point. A device that collects a variety of sensor readings from multiple locations might group the data for each location in a collection. The boot descriptor for a mouse groups the button and position indicators in a physical collection.

A logical collection forms a data structure consisting of items of different types that are linked by the collection. An example is the contents of a data buffer and a count of the number of bytes in the buffer.

Each collection begins with a Collection item and ends with an End Collection item. All Main items between the Collection and End Collection items are part of the collection. Each collection must have a Usage tag (described below).

If a report contains an unknown vendor-defined collection type, the host ignores all Main items in the collection. If a known collection type has an unknown Usage, the host ignores all items in the collection.

The Global Item Type

Global items identify reports and describe the data in them, including characteristics such as the data's function, maximum and minimum allowed values, and the size and number of report items. A Global item tag applies to every item that follows until the next Global tag. This saves storage space because there's no need to repeat values that don't change from one item to the next. There are 12 defined Global items, shown in Table 13-3..

Identifying the Report

Report ID is a prefix that precedes the report data in a data packet. A device can support multiple reports, with each containing different data and having its own ID. This way, a transfer doesn't have to include every piece of data every time. However, in many cases the simplicity of having a single report is more important than the need to reduce the bandwidth used by reports to the absolute minimum. A Report ID item applies to all items that follow until a new Report ID. If there is no Report ID item, an ID of 0 is assumed. A descriptor should not declare a Report ID of 0. Input, Output, and Feature reports can share a Report ID, but each report of the same type must have its own ID.

Describing the Data's Use

The items that describe how the data will be used are Usage Page, Logical and Physical Maximums and Minimums, Unit, and Unit Exponent. All of these help the receiver of the report to interpret report data. All but the Usage Page are involved with converting raw report data to values with units attached. These items make it possible for a report to contain data in a simple and compact form, with the receiver of the data having the responsibility of conversion. However, in some cases, the sender of the report data might choose to do some or all of the converting.

Usage Page. An item's Usage is a 32-bit value that describes its function. The Usage is made up of two 16-bit parts: the Usage Page, which is a Global item, and the Usage Index, which is a Local item. Multiple items may share a Usage Page while having different Usage Indexes. After a Usage Page appears in a report, all Usage Indexes that follow will use that Usage Page until a new one is declared. Re-using the Usage Page reduces the amount of data that the descriptor has to store and send.

The HID Usage Tables document lists the defined Usage Pages and their values and also names the document section or other document that

Table 13-3: There are twelve defined Global items.

Global Item Type	Value (nn indicates the number of bytes that follow)	Description
Usage Page	000001nn	Defines the data's usage or function.
Logical Minimum	000101nn	Smallest value that an item will report.
Logical Maximum	001001nn	Largest value that an item will report.
Physical Minimum	001101nn	The logical minimum expressed in physical units.
Physical Maximum	010001nn	The logical maximum expressed in physical units.
Unit exponent	010101nn	Base 10 exponent of units.
Unit	011001nn	Unit values
Report Size	011101nn	Size of an item's fields in bits.
Report ID	100001nn	Prefix that identifies a report.
Report Count	100101nn	The number of data fields for an item
Push	101001nn	Places a copy of the global item state table on the stack.
Pop	101101nn	Replaces the item state table with the last structure pushed onto the stack.
Reserved	110001nn to 111101nn	For future use.

describes each page and its indexes. There are Usage Pages for many common device types, including generic desktop controls (mouse, keyboard, joystick), digitizer, bar-code scanner, camera control, and various game controls. Specialized devices may not have a defined Usage Page that matches. In this case, a vendor can define the Usage Page. Values from FF00h to FFFFh are reserved for vendor-defined Usage Pages.

Logical Minimum and Logical Maximum. The Logical Minimum and Maximum define the limits for reported values. The limits are expressed in "logical units," which means that they use the same units as the raw values they describe. For example, if a device reports readings of up to 500 milliamperes with each bit representing 2 milliamperes, the Logical Maximum is 250.

Negative values may be expressed as two's complements. If the minimum and maximum are each one byte, 0 to 7Fh are positive values and 80h to

FFh are negative values. To convert a two's complement to the negative value it represents, complement each bit and add 1 to the result. Here are some examples:

Original Value (hexadecimal)	FF	FD	80
Complement (hexadecimal)	00	02	7F
Two's Complement (result after adding 1) (hexadecimal)	01	03	80
Value Expressed as a Negative Number (decimal)	-1	-3	-128

To convert in the opposite direction, subtract one and complement each bit.

The HID specification says that if both the Logical Minimum and Maximum are considered positive, there's no need for a sign bit. For example, a range from 0 to 255 can have a Logical Minimum of 00h and a Logical Maximum of FFh. If you use these values, the device will enumerate and transfer data without problems. But how do you know if the values are considered positive? It depends on the application. Using these values, the HID-View utility (described in Chapter 15) reports the error, "Logical Minimum must be less than the Logical Maximum." You won't get this error if you use a minimum of 80h (-128) and maximum of 7F (+127). On the other hand, the HID Descriptor Tool reports the error if you use a minimum of 80h and maximum of 7Fh, while it accepts 00h and FFh.

The Physical Minimum, Physical Maximum, Unit Exponent, and Unit items define how to convert the reported values into more meaningful units.

Physical Minimum and Physical Maximum. The Physical Minimum and Maximum define the limits for the value when expressed in the units defined by the Units tag. In the above example, the Physical Minimum would be 0 and the Physical Maximum would be 500. The receiving device uses the logical and physical limit values to obtain the value in the desired units. In the example, reporting the data in units of 2 milliamperes means that the value can transfer in a single byte, with the receiver of the data using the Physical Minimum and Maximum values to translate to milliamperes. The price is a loss in resolution, compared to reporting 1 bit per milliampere. If the report doesn't specify the values, they default to the same as the Logical Minimum and Maximum.

Unit Exponent. The Unit Exponent specifies what power of 10 to apply to the value obtained after using the logical and physical limits to translate the value into the desired units. The exponent can range from -8 to +7. A value of 0 causes the value to be multiplied by 10^0, or 1, which is the same as applying no exponent. These are the codes:

Exponent	0	1	2	3	4	5	6	7	-8	-7	-6	-5	-4	-3	-2	-1
Code	00h	01h	02h	03h	04h	05h	06h	07h	08h	09h	0Ah	0Bh	0Ch	0Dh	0Eh	0Fh

For example, if the value obtained is 1234 and the Unit Exponent is 0Eh, the final value is 12.34.

Unit. The Unit tag specifies what units to apply to the report data after it's converted using the Physical and Unit Exponent items. The HID specification defines codes for the basic units of length, mass, time, temperature, current, and luminous intensity. Most other units can be derived from these.

Specifying a Unit value can be more complicated than you might expect. Table 13-4 shows values you can work from. The value can be as long as four bytes, with each nibble having a defined function. Nibble 0 (the least significant nibble) specifies the measurement system, either English or SI (International System of Units), and whether the measurement is in linear or angular units. Each of the nibble positions that follow represents a quality to be measured, with the value of the nibble representing the exponent to apply to the value. For example, a nibble with a value of 2 means that its corresponding value is in units squared. A nibble with a value of 0Dh, which represents -3, means that the units of teh corresponding value are 1/units^3. (These exponents are separate from the Unit Exponent value, which is a power of ten applied to the data, rather than an exponent applied to the units.)

Converting Raw Data

To convert raw data to values with units attached, three things must occur. The firmware's report descriptor must contain the information needed for the conversion. The sender of the data must send data that matches the

Table 13-4: The units to apply to a reported value are a function of the measuring system and exponent values specified in the Unit item

Nibble Number	Quality Measured	Measuring System (Nibble 0 value)				
		None (0)	SI Linear (1)	SI Rotation (2)	English Linear (3)	English Rotation (4)
1	Length	None	Centimeters	Radians	Inches	Degrees
2	Mass	None	Grams		Slugs	
3	Time	None	Seconds			
4	Tempera- ture	None	Fahrenheit		Celsius	
5	Current	None	Amperes			
6	Luminous Intensity	None	Candelas			
7	Reserved	None				

specification in the descriptor. And the receiver of the data must apply the conversions specified in the descriptor.

Below are examples of descriptors and raw and converted data. Remember that just because a tag exists in the HID specification doesn't mean you have to use it. If the application knows what format and units to use for the values it's going to send or receive, the firmware doesn't have to specify it.

To measure time in seconds, up to a minute, the report descriptor might include this information:

> Logical Minimum: 0
> Logical Maximum: 60
> Physical Minimum: 0
> Physical Maximum: 60
> Unit: 1003h. Nibble 0 = 3 to select the English Linear measuring system (though in this case, any value from 1 to 4 would work). Nibble 3 = 1 to select time in seconds.
> Unit Exponent: 0

With this information, the sender and receiver both know that the value sent equals the number of seconds.

Now, what if instead you want to measure time in tenths of seconds, again up to a minute? You would need to increase the Logical and Physical Maximums and change the Unit Exponent:

> Logical Minimum: 0
>
> Logical Maximum: 600
>
> Physical Minimum: 0
>
> Physical Maximum: 600
>
> Unit: 1003h. Nibble 0 = 3 to select the English Linear measuring system. Nibble 3 = 1 to select time in seconds.
>
> Unit Exponent: 0Fh. This represents an exponent of -1, to indicate that the value is expressed in tenths of seconds rather than seconds.

Sending values as large as 600 will require 3 bytes, which the firmware specifies in the Report Size tag.

To send a temperature value using one byte to represent temperatures from -20 to 110 degrees Fahrenheit, the report descriptor might contain the following:

> Logical Minimum: -128 (80h expressed as a two's complement)
>
> Logical Maximum: 127 (7Fh)
>
> Physical Minimum: -20 (ECh expressed as a two's complement)
>
> Physical Maximum: 110 (6Eh)
>
> Unit: 10003h. Nibble 0 is 3 to select the English Linear measuring system, though in this case, any value from 1 to 4 is OK. Nibble 4 is 1 to select degrees Fahrenheit.
>
> Unit Exponent: 0

These values ensure the highest resolution possible, because the transmitted values can span the full range from 0 to 255.

In this case the logical and physical limits differ, so converting is required. To find the resolution, or number of bits per unit, use this equation:

```
Resolution = _
  (Logical_Maximum - Logical_Minimum) / _
  ((Physical_Maximum - Physical_Minimum) * _
  (10 ^ Unit_Exponent ))
```

With the example values, this works out to 1.96 bits per degree, or 0.51 degree per bit.

To convert a value to the specified units, use this equation:

```
Value = _
  Value_In_Logical_Units *
  ((Physical_Maximum - Physical_Minimum) * _
  (10 ^ Unit_Exponent )) /
  (Logical_Maximum - Logical_Minimum)
```

If the value in logical units (the raw data) is 63, the converted value in the specified units is 32 degrees Fahrenheit.

Specifying velocity in centimeters per second requires a Unit value that contains units of both centimeters and seconds. From Table 13-4, the Unit value to use is 1011h. Nibble 0 = 1 to select the SI measuring system, nibble 1 = 1 to select length in centimeters, and nibble 3 = 1 to select time in seconds.

To illustrate how complicated it can get, the Unit value for volts is F0D121, which indicates the SI Linear measuring system in units of $(cm^2)*(gm)/(sec^{-3})*(amp^{-1})$. However, remember that the Unit value only specifies the units. All the receiver has to do is identify the Units value and assign the units to received data; there's no need to do the calculations implied in the Units value.

Describing the Data's Size and Format

Two Global items describe the size and format of the report data.

Report Size specifies the size in bits of an Input, Output, or Feature item's fields. Each field contains one piece of data.

Report Count specifies how many fields an Input, Output, or Feature item contains. For example, for two 8-bit fields, Report Size is 8 and Report Count is 2. For ten 4-bit fields, Report Size is 4 and Report Count is 10. For one 16-bit field, Report Size is 16 and Report Count is 1.

A single Input, Output, or Feature report can have multiple items, each with its own Report Size and Report Count, up to the maximum 255 bytes per report.

Saving and Restoring Global Items

The final two Global items enable saving and restoring sets of Global items. These allow flexibility in the report formats while using minimum storage space in the device.

Push places a copy of the Global-item state table on the CPU's stack. The Global-item state table contains the current settings for all previously defined Global items.

Pop is the complement to Push. It restores the saved states of the previously pushed Global item states.

The Local Item Type

Local items define characteristics of the knobs, switches, buttons, and other controls that a report returns data for. A Local item applies to all controls that follow within the Main item, until a new value is assigned. Local items don't carry over to the next Main item. Each Main item begins fresh, with no Local items defined.

Local items relate to general usages, body-part designators, and strings. A Delimiter item enables grouping of sets of Local items. Table 13-5 shows the values and meaning of each of the items.

Usage. The Local Usage item is the Usage Index that works together with the Global Usage Page to describe the function of an item or collection. As with the Usage Page, the HID Usage Tables document lists many Usage Indexes. For example, the Buttons Usage Page uses Local Usage Indexes from 1 to FFFFh to specify individual buttons, with a value of 0 meaning no button pressed.

A report may assign one Usage to multiple controls, or it may assign a different Usage to each control. If a report item is preceded by a single Usage, that

Table 13-5: There are ten defined Local items.

Local Item Type	Value (nn indicates the number of bytes that follow)	Description
Usage	000010nn	An index that describes the use for an item or collection.
Usage Minimum	000110nn	The starting Usage associated with an array or bitmap.
Usage Maximum	001010nn	The ending Usage associated with an array or bitmap.
Designator Index	001110nn	Designates the body part used for a control.
Designator Minimum	010010nn	The starting Designator associated with an array or bitmap.
Designator Maximum	010110nn	The ending Designator associated with an array or bitmap.
String Index	011110nn	Associates a string with an item or control.
String Minimum	100010nn	The first string index when assigning a group of sequential strings to controls in an array or bitmap.
String Maximum	100110nn	The last string index when assigning a group of sequential strings to controls in an array or bitmap.
Delimiter	101010nn	The beginning (1) or end (0) of a set of Local items.
Reserved	101011nn to 111110nn	For future use.

Usage applies to all of the item's controls. If a report item is preceded by more than one Usage, and the number of controls equals the number of Usages, each Usage applies to one control, with the Usages and controls pairing up in sequence. In the following example, the report contains two bytes. The first byte's Usage is X, and the second byte's Usage is Y.

```
Report Size (8),
Report Count (2),
Usage (X),
Usage (Y),
Input (Data, Variable, Absolute),
```

If a report item is preceded by more than one Usage and the number of controls is greater than the number of Usages, each Usage pairs up with one control, and the final Usage applies to all of the remaining controls. In the following example, the report is 16 bytes. Usage X applies to the first byte, Usage Y applies to the second byte, and a vendor-defined Usage applies to the third through 16th bytes.

```
Usage (X)
Usage (Y)
Usage (vendor defined)
Report Count (16),
Report Size (8),
Input (Data, Variable, Absolute)
```

Usage Minimum and Maximum. The Usage Minimum and Maximum can assign a single Usage to multiple controls. The following example reports the state (0 or 1) of each of three buttons. The Usage Minimum and Maximum assign the Button Usage Page to all three items. The item uses one bit per button.

```
Logical Minimum (0)
Logical Maximum (1)
Report Count (3)
Report Size (1)
Usage Page (Button Page)
Usage Minimum (1)
Usage Maximum (3)
Input (Data, Variable, Absolute)
```

The Usage Minimum and Maximum can also assign a single Usage to a series of array items.

Designator Index. For items with a Physical descriptor, the Designator Index specifies the body part the control uses.

Designator Minimum and Maximum. When a report contains multiple controls with the same Designator, the Designator Minimum and Maximum can specify which controls the Usage applies to.

String Index. An item or control can include a string index to associate a string with that item or control. The strings are stored in the same format described in Chapter 5 for product, manufacturer, and serial-number strings.

String Minimum and Maximum. When a report contains multiple controls with the same String Index, the String Minimum and Maximum can specify which controls the Usage applies to.

Delimiter. The Delimiter defines the beginning (1) or end (0) of a local item. A delimited local item may contain alternate usages for a control. This enables different applications to define a device's controls in different ways. For example, a button may have a generic use (Button1) and a specific use (Send, Quit, etc.).

Physical Descriptors

A physical descriptor describes the part or parts of the body intended to activate a control. For example, each finger might have its own assigned control.

A physical descriptor is a type of class descriptor. The host can retrieve a physical descriptor by sending a Get_Descriptor request with 23h in the high byte of the Value field and 00h in the low byte of the Value field.

Physical descriptors are always optional. For most devices, they either don't apply at all or the information they could provide has no practical use. The HID specification has more information on how to use physical descriptors, for those devices that need them.

Padding

To pad a descriptor so it contains a multiple of eight bits, the descriptor may include a Main item with no assigned Usage. The following example describes an Input report that transfers three bits with data and five bits of padding:

```
Report Count (3)
Report Size (1)
Usage Page (Button Page)
Usage Minimum (1)
Usage Maximum (3)
Input (Data, Variable, Absolute)
```

```
Report Size (5),
Input (Constant)
```

14

Human Interface Devices: Host Applications

Chapter 12 and Chapter 13 described human-interface-device communications from the device's perspective and the report format that HIDs use to exchange data with the host. This chapter shows how to communicate with HIDs from applications. The application may use any programming language that can call API functions. Example code shows how to communicate with a device from a Visual-Basic application.

Host Communications Overview

Windows 98 includes everything applications need to communicate with HIDs. There's no need to install drivers because Windows has them built in.

Later editions of Windows, including Windows 2000, will also include HID support.

How the Host Finds a Device

Communicating with a HID isn't as simple as opening a port, setting a few parameters, and then reading and writing data. Before an application can exchange data with a HID, it has to find the device and get information about its reports. To do this, the application has to jump through a few hoops by calling a series of API functions. The application first finds out what HIDs are attached to the system. It then examines information about each until it finds one with the desired attributes. For a custom device, the application can search for a specific vendor and product ID. Or the application can search for a device of a particular type, such as a mouse or joystick.

After finding a device, the application can exchange information with it by sending and receiving reports.

Table 14-1 lists the API functions used in establishing communications and exchanging data with a HID. The functions are listed in a typical order that an application might call them. Some of the functions are required in order to gain access to the device, while others provide optional information.

Documentation

The documentation for the functions is spread among several areas in the MSDN library and Windows 98 DDK. The functions that relate only to HID communications are in the Windows 98 DDK, in the WDM documentation section under *WDM HID and USB Client Drivers*. Functions related to detecting devices are in the Windows Platform SDK, under *Hardware > Device Management* and repeated in the NT 4 DDK, under *Setup Functions*. Functions relating to exchanging data are in the Windows Platform SDK, under *Files and I/O*.

Table 14-1: Communicating with HIDs uses a variety of API functions.

API Function	DDK	DLL	Purpose
HidD_GetHidGuid	Win98	hid.dll	Obtains GUID for the HID class
SetupDiGetClassDevs	NT	setupapi.dll	Returns a device information set containing all of the devices in a specified class.
SetupDiEnumDevice-Interfaces	NT	setupapi.dll	Returns information about a device in the device information set.
SetupDiGetDeviceInter-faceDetail	NT	setupapi.dll	Returns a device pathname.
CreateFile	NT	kernel32.dll	Open communications with a device.
HidD_GetAttributes	W98	hid.dll	Returns Vendor ID, Product ID, and Version.
HidD_GetPreparsedData	W98	hid.dll	Returns a handle to a buffer with information about the device's capabilities
HidP_GetCaps	W98	hid.dll	Returns a structure describing the device's capabilities.
HidP_GetValueCaps	W98	hid.dll	Returns a structure describing the capabilities of the device's values.
HidP_GetButtonCaps	W98	hid.dll	Returns a structure describing the capabilities of the device's buttons.
WriteFile	NT	kernel32.dll	Sends a report to the device.
ReadFile	NT	kernel32.dll	Reads a report from the device.
CloseHandle	NT	kernel32.dll	Frees resources used by CreateFile.
SetupDiDestroyDevice-InfoList	NT	setupapi.dll	Frees resources used by SetupDiGet-ClassDevs.
HidD_FreePreparsedData	W98	hid.dll	Frees resources used by HidD_GetPreparsedData.

Calling API Functions from Visual Basic

The examples in this chapter use Microsoft's Visual Basic. You can write a lot of Visual-Basic applications without ever coding an API call, because Visual Basic provides its own syntax and controls for performing common functions. For example, to print a file, you can use Visual Basic's Printer Object instead of API functions. The Printer Object provides a simpler and more bullet-proof way to access printers. When you run the application, the code that executes may call API functions, but Visual-Basic programmers are insulated from having to make the calls directly.

But sometimes you may want to do something that Visual Basic doesn't support explicitly. In these cases, which include communicating with HIDs, Visual-Basic applications can call API functions.

As explained in Chapter 10, an API function is a part of Windows' Application Programmer's Interface, which contains thousands of functions that applications can use to communicate with the operating system. The executable code for the functions resides in dynamic linked library (DLL) files provided with Windows.

In a Visual-Basic application, the code to call an API function follows the same syntax rules as the code to call any function. But instead of placing the function's executable code in a routine within the application, the API function requires only a declaration that enables Windows to find and use the DLL containing the function's code.

Calling API functions in Visual Basic requires some extra programming knowledge. The documentation included with Visual Basic doesn't offer much guidance. The documentation for the API functions themselves uses C syntax to show how to declare and call the functions. To use an API function in Visual Basic, you need to translate from C to Visual Basic.

The process is more complicated than a simple word-for-word translation, mainly because Visual Basic doesn't support all of C's structures and uses a different format for string variables. Before you can translate, you need to understand exactly what the function is passing and returning. Even if you have an example to work from, understanding what the function is doing will help you in using it.

This chapter introduces the basics of calling API functions in Visual Basic and shows how to do the API calls needed for HID communications. For greater detail on API calls and Visual Basic in general, I recommend Dan Appleman's books, especially *Dan Appleman's Win32 API Puzzle Book and Tutorial for Visual Basic Programmers*. This is the book I used as a reference in figuring out how to call the API functions in this chapter. If you're already familiar with API calls, or if you want to get right to the HID-specific functions, you can skip over the these introductory sections and return to them later if needed.

To use an API function in a Visual Basic program, you need two things: a declaration that enables the application to use the function and a call that causes the function to execute.

The Declaration

This is a Visual-Basic declaration for the API function WriteFile, which you can use to write data to a HID (as well as files and other devices):

```
Public Declare Function WriteFile _
    Lib "kernel32" _
    (ByVal hFile As Long, _
    ByRef lpBuffer As Byte, _
    ByVal nNumberOfBytesToWrite As Long, _
    ByRef lpNumberOfBytesWritten As Long, _
    ByVal lpOverlapped As Long) _
As Long
```

The declaration includes several pieces of information:

- The function's name (WriteFile).
- The values the function will pass to the operating system (hFile, lpBuffer, nNumberOfBytesToWrite, lpNumberOfBytesWritten, and lpOverlapped). The names use the convention of adding a prefix to indicate the type of data the variable contains: h=handle, lp=long pointer, etc.
- The data types of the values passed (Long, Byte).
- Whether the values will be passed by value (ByVal) or by reference (ByRef).
- The name of the file that contains the executable code for the function (*kernel32.dll*).
- The data type of the value returned for the function (Long). A few API calls have no return value and may be declared as subroutines rather than functions.

The declaration must be in the declarations section of a module. You might want to place the declarations for API functions and the user-defined types they pass in a separate module (a *.bas* file) in your project. This will make them easy to add to multiple projects.

Visual Basic's documentation includes the file *win32api.txt*, which contains declarations for many API calls. You can add this file as a module to your project, or you can cut and paste the declarations you need into another module in your project. However, the file doesn't include every API call, and isn't likely to include newer ones like those that relate to HID communications.

To declare a function not included in *win32api.txt*, the starting point is Microsoft's documentation, which includes a declaration in C, comments, and sometimes an example. You can also find example C declarations in the header files included in the Windows 98 and Platform DDKs. Sometimes these header files have useful comments as well. The header files are text files that you can view in any word processor.

These are header files that have HID-related declarations:

File Name	Contents
hid.h	HID user-mode declarations and functions
hidpi.h	Public interface to the HID parsing library
hidsdi.h	Public definitions for the code that implements the HID DLL
hidusage.h	HID usages
setupapi.h	Windows NT/98 setup services

Sometimes the function's documentation names the header file. If not, a simple way to find it is to use the *Find > Files or Folders* utility available from Windows' *Start* menu. In the *Named* text box, enter **.h*, and in the *Containing Text* text box, enter the name of the function whose declaration you want to find. Be sure that *Include Subfolders* is checked, and let Windows go to work finding the file for you.

In some cases, the translation from C to Visual-Basic syntax is fairly straightforward. In others, the C parameters don't correspond in a simple way to the alternatives in Visual Basic.

These are some general guidelines for creating Visual-Basic declarations:

Variable Types

C and Visual Basic each use different terms to specify variable types, and C supports more variable types than Visual Basic. However, to specify a variable type for an API call, all you really have to do is determine the variable's length, then use a Visual-Basic type that matches. These are some of the C types and their Visual-Basic equivalents:

C Type	Visual-Basic Type
CHAR	Byte
USHORT USAGE	Integer
ULONG HWND BOOLEAN DWORD LP_ (long pointer prefix) P_ (long pointer prefix)	Long
PCTSTR	String

To avoid problems that can result from passing the wrong variable type, an API declaration should declare variables as specific types if possible. In some cases, an application may use a variable in multiple ways, each requiring a different type. There are two ways to handle this. You can create multiple declarations, using the Alias keyword to give each a different name, or you can declare the variable As Any and specify the variable type in the function call.

ByRef and ByVal

For each variable, you have a choice of passing it by reference (ByRef) or by value (ByVal). These parameters have the same meanings as when you use them in Visual-Basic functions and subroutines. For many functions written in Visual Basic, either will work. But the concept is important to understand when calling API functions, because many of the functions have variables that must be passed a specific way.

ByRef and ByVal determine what information the call passes to enable the function to access the variable. Every variable has an address in memory where its value is stored. When an application passes a variable to a function, it can pass the variable's address, or the value itself.

The information is passed by placing it on the stack, which in this case refers to a temporary storage location used (among other things) to pass values to functions.

Passing a variable ByRef means that the function call places the address of the variable on the stack. If the function changes the value by writing a new value to the address, the new value will be available to the calling application, because the value will be stored at the address where the application expects to find it. The address passed is called a pointer, because it points to, or indicates, the address where the value is stored.

Passing a variable ByVal means that the function places the value of the variable on the stack. The value at the variable's address in memory is unchanged. If the function changes the value, the calling application won't know about it because the function has no way to pass the new value back to the application.

Passing ByRef is the default, but you can include the ByRef parameter in declarations if you wish. This way, you can quickly see if you've forgotten to assign the parameter to a value. If the declaration doesn't include ByVal or ByRef, you can specify either when you call the function.

For all variable types except strings, there are two situations where you must pass a variable ByRef:

- The function changes the value and the calling application needs to use the new value. Passing ByRef enables the calling application to access the new value.

- The variable is a user-defined type. You can't pass user-defined types ByVal in Visual Basic.

String variables are a special case. Visual Basic uses a string format called BSTR for storing strings in memory. The BSTR format differs from the format expected by API calls. In memory, a BSTR string consists of four bytes containing the string's length in bytes followed by the string's characters in Unicode (2 bytes per character). But most Windows 98 API functions expect a string to consist of a series of ANSI character codes (1 byte per character), followed by a null (0) termination.

Fortunately, there is a solution that doesn't require the application code to translate between formats. If the string is declared ByVal, Visual Basic creates a copy of the string in ANSI format and passes a pointer to the string. In other words, declaring a Visual-Basic string ByVal actually causes the string to be passed ByRef in the expected format. If the function will change the contents of the string, the application should initialize the string to be at least as long as the longest expected returned string.

For various reasons, some structures can't be passed either ByRef or ByVal. In these cases, there is an alternate way. It requires creating a byte array equal to the structure's size, then using Visual Basic's undocumented VarPtr operator to pass the byte array's address ByVal. When the function returns, the application can copy the data from the byte array into a structure, which is a user-defined variable type.

Functions and Subroutines

Most API calls are functions, which have a return value that the declaration must also specify. A few are subroutines, with no return value. You can declare these as subroutines, or as functions with the returned value ignored.

Providing the DLL's Name

Each declaration must also name the file that contains the function's executable code. The file is a DLL. When the application runs, Windows loads the named DLLs into memory (unless they're already loaded).

In most cases, the declaration only has to include the file name (the *.dll* extension is optional) and not the location. The DLLs used for HID communications are included with Windows. When Windows is installed, the DLLs are stored in standard locations (such as *\windows\system*) that the operating system will search automatically. The operating system will also search the application's working directory for a DLL. In the Visual-Basic environment, the working directory is Visual Basic's directory, not your application's directory. If you use a DLL that isn't stored in a standard Windows directory or the application's working directory, the declaration must specify the location.

These are DLL files that contain functions used in HID communications:

Filename	Type of Functions Included
hid.dll	HID communications.
setupapi.dll	Finding and identifying devices
kernel32.dll	Exchanging data, other general functions

Strings

Windows 98 and Windows NT differ in how they store strings. Windows 98 stores each character as an 8-bit ANSI code, while NT stores each character as a 16-bit Unicode. To handle the difference, there are two versions of API calls that pass string variables. The Windows 98 version ends in A (ANSI), and the NT version ends in W (wide). For example, there is a SetupDiGetClassDevsA function and a SetupDiGetClassDevsW function.

A declaration can include an Alias that enables applications to call the name without the A or W suffix (SetupDiGetClassDevs, for example). This way, only the declaration, not the code that calls the function, needs to change with the operating system. The examples in this book are for Windows 98 and use the -A versions.

Structures

Some of the API functions used in HID applications pass and return structures, which contains multiple items that may be of different types. The Windows 98 and Platform documentation for the API calls documents the structures used by the calls. The structures are also declared in the header files, using C syntax. C programmers typically define the structures needed by an application by including their header files in the project.

Here again, Visual Basic uses different syntax and translating is required. In Visual Basic, you can declare a structure as a user-defined type. Some of the structures translate in a straightforward way. For example, the Visual-Basic declaration for the HIDD_ATTRIBUTES structure consists of Long and

Integer variables that translate directly from the USHORT and ULONG types in the C declaration:

```
Public Type HIDD_ATTRIBUTES
    Size As Long
    VendorID As Integer
    ProductID As Integer
    VersionNumber As Integer
End Type
```

You can then declare a variable of the user-defined type:

```
Dim DeviceAttributes As HIDD_ATTRIBUTES
```

Before passing the structure in an API call, the Size property must be set to the size of the structure in bytes. The LenB operator will do this:

```
DeviceAttributes.Size = LenB(DeviceAttributes)
```

The HidD_GetAttributes API function can then pass the structure ByRef:

```
Public Declare Function HidD_GetAttributes _
    Lib "hid.dll" _
    (ByVal HidDeviceObject As Long, _
    ByRef Attributes As HIDD_ATTRIBUTES) _
As Long
```

When an application calls the function, the function can change the values in the structure, and the application will see the new values.

Calling API Functions

After the code has declared a function and any user-defined types it passes, the application may call the function.

Here is a call to the HidD_GetAttributes function declared above:

```
Dim Result as Long
Result = HidD_GetAttributes _
    (HidDevice, _
    DeviceAttributes)
```

HidDevice is a Long value returned by a previous API call. Result is non-zero on success. DeviceAttributes is a structure containing the Vendor ID, Product ID, and product version number retrieved from the device.

Two Useful Routines

In addition to the basic API functions for USB communications, there are a couple of other API functions that I've found useful in HID communications. One copies data in memory, and the other returns text describing the last error detected by the operating system.

Moving Data in Memory

The API function RtlMoveMemory transfers a series of bytes from one location in memory to another. This function is useful copying raw data between byte arrays and structures. This is the declaration:

```
Public Declare Function RtlMoveMemory _
    Lib "kernel32" _
    (dest As Any, _
    src As Any, _
    ByVal Count As Long) _
As Long
```

With this declaration, anything goes. Rather than declaring the data address's (src) and destination (dest) as specific types, the values are declared As Any to allow flexibility in using the function. Count is the number of bytes to copy.

Here RtlMoveMemory copies four bytes from a structure into a byte array whose address will be passed in a call to the SetupDiGetDeviceInterfaceDetail function.

```
Call RtlMoveMemory _
    (DetailDataBuffer(0), _
    MyDeviceInterfaceDetailData, _
    4)
```

Viewing Errors

The second useful function is FormatMessage, which returns text describing the last error that Windows detected.

This is the function's declaration:

```
Public Declare Function FormatMessage _
    Lib "kernel32" _
```

```
    Alias "FormatMessageA" _
    (ByVal dwFlags As Long, _
    ByRef lpSource As Any, _
    ByVal dwMessageId As Long, _
    ByVal dwLanguageId As Long, _
    ByVal lpBuffer As String, _
    ByVal nSize As Long, _
    ByVal Arguments As Long) _
As Long
```

The function also uses the following system constant:

```
Public Const FORMAT_MESSAGE_FROM_SYSTEM = &H1000
```

I call FormatMessage from within a Visual-Basic function that returns the string containing the error message. This code is adapted from an example in Dan Appleman's *Win32 API Puzzle Book:*

```
Private Function GetErrorString _
    (ByVal LastError As Long) _
As String

'Returns the error message for the last error.

Dim Bytes As Long
Dim ErrorString As String
ErrorString = String$(129, 0)
Bytes = FormatMessage _
    (FORMAT_MESSAGE_FROM_SYSTEM, _
    0&, _
    LastError, _
    0, _
    ErrorString$, _
    128, _
    0)

'Subtract two characters from the message to
'strip the CR and LF.
If Bytes > 2 Then
    GetErrorString = Left$(ErrorString, Bytes - 2)
End If

End Function
```

The last error is returned in ErrorString$. During debugging, I call this function after making an API call and display the error, either in a list box or using a debug.print statement in the immediate window.

Finding a Device

Now that you have some background in calling API functions, it's time to look at the functions involved in communicating with a HID. The first task is to find the device you want to communicate with. This involves examining properties of the HIDs that a system has available and looking for a match, either in Vendor and Product IDs or in device capabilities. A series of API calls will accomplish this.

Obtain the GUID for all HIDs

Before an application can communicate with a HID, it must obtain the globally unique identifier (GUID) for the HID class. Chapter 10 introduced GUIDs, which are 128-bit values that each uniquely identify an object. In this case, the object is the HID class. The GUID value is defined by Microsoft, and is included in the file *hidclass.h*, so in theory you could hard-code it into the application. But you can also obtain the GUID by using an API function that reads the value from the system. Doing it this way, you'll be sure to have the correct value in the expected format.

The API call to retrieve the GUID for the HID class is HidD_GetHidGuid.

The declaration is:

```
Public Declare Sub HidD_GetHidGuid _
    Lib "hid.dll" _
    (ByRef HidGuid As GUID)
```

This routine has no return value, so it can be declared as a subroutine, as above. Or you can declare it as a function, with a return value of type Long, and ignore the returned value:

```
Public Declare Function HidD_GetHidGuid _
    Lib "hid.dll" _
    (ByRef HidGuid As GUID)
    as Long
```

The GUID is returned in the variable HidGuid, which has the following user-defined type:

```
Public Type GUID
    Data1 As Long
    Data2 As Integer
    Data3 As Integer
    Data4(7) As Byte
End Type
```

HidGuid is declared byRef because Visual Basic requires user-defined types to be passed byRef.

The call to get the GUID is:

```
Call HidD_GetHidGuid(HidGuid)
```

or

```
Dim Result as Long
Result = HidD_GetHidGuid(HidGuid)
```

The application doesn't have to do anything with the individual elements that make up the GUID; it just needs to pass the address of the GUID to other API functions.

Get an Array of Structures with Information about the HIDs

The GUID enables the application to get information about the HIDs on a system. The functions to do this are Windows Device Management Functions. There are two sets of essentially identical documentation for these in MSDN's NT DDK and Platform SDK.

The SetupDiGetClassDevs function returns the address of an array of structures containing information about all attached and enumerated HIDs. This is the function's declaration:

```
Public Declare Function SetupDiGetClassDevs _
    Lib "setupapi.dll" _
    Alias "SetupDiGetClassDevsA" _
    (ByRef ClassGuid As GUID, _
    ByVal Enumerator As String, _
    ByVal hwndParent As Long, _
    ByVal Flags As Long) _
```

```
As Long
```

The code to call the function is:

```
DeviceInfoSet = SetupDiGetClassDevs _
    (HidGuid, _
    vbNullString, _
    0, _
    (DIGCF_PRESENT Or DIGCF_DEVICEINTERFACE))
```

The ClassGuid is HidGuid, the value returned in the last call. Enumerator and hwndParent are unused. The flags are two system constants defined in the file *setupapi.h*. The Visual-Basic declarations for them are:

```
Public Const DIGCF_PRESENT = &H2
Public Const DIGCF_DEVICEINTERFACE = &H10
```

These flags tell the function to look only for device interfaces that are currently present (attached and enumerated) and that are members of the HID class, as specified in the ClassGuid parameter.

The value returned, DeviceInfoSet, is the address of an array of structures containing information about all attached and enumerated HIDs. Again, there's no need to access the individual elements in the collection. You need the value only so you can pass it on in the next API call.

When the application is finished using the DeviceInfoSet, it should free the resources used by calling the API function SetupDiDestroyDeviceInfoList, as described later in this chapter.

Identify Each HID Interface

The next call is SetupDiEnumDeviceInterfaces, which retrieves a pointer to a structure that identifies an interface in the previously retrieved DeviceInfoSet array. Each call must specify one interface by passing an array index. To retrieve information about all of the interfaces, an application can step through the array, incrementing the array index until the function returns zero, indicating that there are no more interfaces. The GetLastError API call will then return *No more data is available*.

How do you know if an interface is the one you're looking for? You don't, yet. The application needs more information before it can decide if it wants to use an interface. If the function returns multiple interfaces, the application will need to investigate each in turn, until it either finds what it's looking for or determines that the desired interface isn't present.

Again, the use for any returned pointers is to pass them on to the next function so we can learn more about the interfaces.

This is the declaration:

```
Public Declare Function SetupDiEnumDeviceInterfaces _
    Lib "setupapi.dll" _
    (ByVal DeviceInfoSet As Long, _
    ByVal DeviceInfoData As Long, _
    ByRef InterfaceClassGuid As GUID, _
    ByVal MemberIndex As Long, _
    ByRef DeviceInterfaceData _
        As SP_DEVICE_INTERFACE_DATA) _
As Long
```

DeviceInterfaceData is a user-defined type with this structure:

```
Public Type SP_DEVICE_INTERFACE_DATA
    cbSize As Long
    InterfaceClassGuid As GUID
    Flags As Long
    Reserved As Long
End Type
```

The parameter cbSize is the size of the structure in bytes. Before calling SetupDiEnumDeviceInterfaces, the size must be stored in the structure that the function will pass. The LenB operator can retrieve the size, which is 28 bytes: 4 for each Long and 16 for the GUID, which contains one Long (4 bytes), two Integers (4 bytes), and eight Bytes. The other values in the SP_DEVICE_INTERFACE_DATA structure should be zero.

The code to identify all HIDs is:

```
Dim Result as Long
Dim MemberIndex as Long
Dim MyDeviceInterfaceData As SP_DEVICE_INTERFACE_DATA
'Store the size of the structure
MyDeviceInterfaceData.cbSize = _
    LenB(MyDeviceInterfaceData)
MemberIndex = 0
```

```
Do
    Result = SetupDiEnumDeviceInterfaces _
        (DeviceInfoSet, _
        0, _
        HidGuid, _
        MemberIndex, _
        MyDeviceInterfaceData)
    MemberIndex = MemberIndex + 1
    'Add code here to find out if this is the
    'desired device.
Loop until Result = 0
```

Two of the values passed to this function are values returned previously: HidGuid and DeviceInfoSet. DeviceInfoData is an optional pointer to an SP_DEVINFO_DATA structure that limits the search to interfaces of a particular device, and is unused here because we're getting all of the interfaces. MemberIndex is the index of the DeviceInfoSet array. MyDeviceInterfaceData is the returned structure that identifies an interface of the requested type, which in this case is a HID.

Get the Device Pathname

The next API call, SetupDiGetDeviceInterfaceDetail, returns yet another structure. This time the structure relates to a device interface identified in the previous call. The structure contains a device pathname that the application can use to open communications with the device.

The declaration is:

```
Public Declare Function _
    SetupDiGetDeviceInterfaceDetail _
    Lib "setupapi.dll" _
    Alias "SetupDiGetDeviceInterfaceDetailA" _
    (ByVal DeviceInfoSet As Long, _
    ByRef DeviceInterfaceData _
        As SP_DEVICE_INTERFACE_DATA, _
    ByVal DeviceInterfaceDetailData As Long, _
    ByVal DeviceInterfaceDetailDataSize As Long, _
    ByRef RequiredSize As Long, _
    ByVal DeviceInfoData As Long) _
    As Long
```

The structure returned in DeviceInterfaceDetailData is a user-defined type:

```
Public Type SP_DEVICE_INTERFACE_DETAIL_DATA
    cbSize As Long
    DevicePath As String
End Type
```

Because of the different string formats used by Visual Basic and C, you can't pass this structure in the usual way, using ByRef to pass the structure's address. But there is a way around the problem. The first step is to allocate a buffer in memory to hold the structure. Then you can use the VarPtr operator to get the starting address of the buffer, and pass the address ByVal. When the function returns, you can copy the data in the buffer into a DeviceInterfaceDetailData structure, or just extract the data of interest, which is the device pathname.

Before calling this function for the first time, there's no way to know the value of DeviceInterfaceDetailDataSize, which must contain the size in bytes of the DeviceInterfaceDetailData structure. Yet the call won't return the structure unless it has this information. The solution is to call the function twice. The first time, GetLastError will return the error *The data area passed to a system call is too small,* but the RequiredSize parameter will contain the correct value for DeviceInterfaceDetailDataSize. The second time, you pass the returned value and the function succeeds.

This is the code for the first call:

```
Dim Needed as Long
Result = SetupDiGetDeviceInterfaceDetail _
    (DeviceInfoSet, _
    MyDeviceInterfaceData, _
    0, _
    0, _
    Needed, _
    0)
```

DeviceInfoSet and MyDeviceInterfaceData are structures returned by previous calls. After calling this function, Needed contains the buffer size to pass in the next call.

Before calling the function again, we need to take care of a few things.

The DetailData variable to be passed in the next call is set to equal the value returned in Needed:

```
Dim DetailData as Long
DetailData = Needed
Dim DetailDataBuffer() as Byte
```

The size of the structure to be returned is stored in its cbSize parameter:

```
'Store the structure's size.
MyDeviceInterfaceDetailData.cbSize = _
Len(MyDeviceInterfaceDetailData)
```

Because we're going to pass only the address of a byte array for the returned structure, we need to allocate enough memory in the array to hold the structure:

```
ReDim DetailDataBuffer(Needed)
```

The first four bytes of the byte array hold the array's size, which can be copied from the cbSize property in the MyDeviceInterfaceDetailData structure:

```
Call RtlMoveMemory _
    (DetailDataBuffer(0), _
    MyDeviceInterfaceDetailData, _
    4)
```

Now we're ready to call SetupDiGetDeviceInterfaceDetail again:

```
'Call SetupDiGetDeviceInterfaceDetail again.
'This time, pass the address
'of the first element of DetailDataBuffer
'and the returned required buffer size in DetailData.
Result = SetupDiGetDeviceInterfaceDetail _
            (DeviceInfoSet, _
            MyDeviceInterfaceData, _
            VarPtr(DetailDataBuffer(0)), _
            DetailData, _
            Needed, _
            0)
```

VarPtr(DetailDataBuffer(0)) is the starting address of the byte array that will contain the MyDeviceInterfaceDetailData structure. DetailData holds the size returned by the previous call.

The item of interest in the returned structure is the device pathname to be used in additional API calls. To extract the pathname from the byte array, convert the byte array to a string, convert the result to Unicode for compatibility with Visual Basic, and strip the cbSize characters from the beginning of the string.

```
'Convert the byte array to a string.
DevicePathName = CStr(DetailDataBuffer())
'Convert to Unicode.
DevicePathName = StrConv(DevicePathName, vbUnicode)
'Strip cbSize (4 characters) from the beginning.
DevicePathName = _
    Right$(DevicePathName, Len(DevicePathName) - 4)
```

Get a Handle for the Device

Now that we have a device pathname, we're ready to open communications with the device itself. The first step is the all-purpose function CreateFile, which can open a file or any device whose driver supports CreateFile. HID-class devices are among these.

On success, the value returned by CreateFile is a handle that other API functions can use to exchange data with the device.

This is the declaration for CreateFile:

```
Public Declare Function CreateFile _
    Lib "kernel32" _
    Alias "CreateFileA" _
    (ByVal lpFileName As String, _
    ByVal dwDesiredAccess As Long, _
    ByVal dwShareMode As Long, _
    ByRef lpSecurityAttributes As Long, _
    ByVal dwCreationDisposition As Long, _
    ByVal dwFlagsAndAttributes As Long, _
    ByVal hTemplateFile As Long) _
    As Long
```

And this is the call to open a HID:

```
Dim HidDevice As Long
HidDevice = CreateFile _
    (DevicePathName, _
```

```
GENERIC_READ Or GENERIC_WRITE, _
(FILE_SHARE_READ Or FILE_SHARE_WRITE), _
0, _
OPEN_EXISTING, _
0, _
0)
```

The function passes a pointer to the DevicePathName string returned in the previous call. The parameter is declared as a String to be passed ByVal, because of Visual-Basic's different string format, as explained earlier.

The constants passed by the call are defined in several locations, including *winnt.h* and *wdm.h*, and must be declared in a declarations section of a module in the Visual-Basic application:

```
Public Const GENERIC_READ = &H80000000
Public Const GENERIC_WRITE = &H40000000
Public Const FILE_SHARE_READ = &H1
Public Const FILE_SHARE_WRITE = &H2
Public Const OPEN_EXISTING = 3
```

The other three parameters don't apply, and the function passes zero for each.

When the application no longer needs to access the device, it should free system resources by calling the CloseHandle API function, as described later in this chapter.

Read the Vendor and Product IDs

One way to identify whether or not a device is the one you want is to get its Vendor and Product IDs and see if they match the product you're looking for. This is the way to find custom devices that don't fit standard usages. For other devices, this information may not be important, and if not, you can skip this step.

The API function HidD_GetAttributes will retrieve the Vendor and Product IDs and the product's version number. This is the declaration for the function:

```
Public Declare Function HidD_GetAttributes _
    Lib "hid.dll" _
```

```
        (ByVal HidDeviceObject As Long, _
         ByRef Attributes As HIDD_ATTRIBUTES) _
    As Long
```

The information is returned in a HIDD_ATTRIBUTES structure:

```
Public Type HIDD_ATTRIBUTES
    Size As Long
    VendorID As Integer
    ProductID As Integer
    VersionNumber As Integer
End Type
```

This is the call that retrieves the structure:

```
Dim DeviceAttributes As HIDD_ATTRIBUTES
Result = HidD_GetAttributes _
            (HidDevice, _
             DeviceAttributes)
```

HidDevice is the device pathname returned by CreateFile. If Result is non-zero, the DeviceAttributes structure filled without error.

You can then find out if the Vendor and Product IDs (and version number) match what you're looking for:

```
'Example values:
Const MyVendorID = &H0925
Const MyProductID = &H1234

Dim MyDeviceDetected As Boolean
If (DeviceAttributes.VendorID = MyVendorID) And _
    (DeviceAttributes.ProductID = MyProductID) Then
        MyDeviceDetected = True
Else
    MyDeviceDetected = False
    'Close the handle to the device.
    Result = CloseHandle _
        (HidDevice)
    End If
```

If it isn't a match, the application should use the CloseHandle API call (covered later in this chapter) to close the handle to the device. The application can then move on to test the next HID detected by SetupDiEnumDevice-Interfaces (if any).

Get a Pointer to a Buffer with Device Capabilities

Another way to find out more about a device is to examine its capabilities. You can do this for a device whose Vendor and Product IDs matched the values you were looking for, or you can examine the capabilities for an unknown device.

The first task is to get a pointer to a buffer with information about the device's capabilities. The API call to do this is HidD_GetPreparsedData. This is the declaration:

```
Public Declare Function HidD_GetPreparsedData _
    Lib "hid.dll" _
    (ByVal HidDeviceObject As Long, _
    ByRef PreparsedData As Long) _
As Long
```

This is the function call:

```
Result = HidD_GetPreparsedData _
    (HidDevice, _
    PreparsedData)
```

HidDevice is the handle returned by CreateFile. PreparsedData contains the starting address of the buffer. The application doesn't need to access the data in the array; it just needs to pass its starting address to another API function.

When the application no longer needs to access the PreparsedData, it should free system resources by calling the API function HidD_FreePreparsedData, as described later in this chapter.

Get the Device's Capabilities

The HidP_GetCaps function returns a structure that contains information about the device's capabilities. The structure contains the device's Usage, Usage Page, report lengths, and the number of button capabilities, value capabilities, and data indices for Input, Output, and Feature reports, as stored in the device's firmware. If you didn't use the Vendor and Product IDs to identify the device, the capabilities information can help you decide if you want to continue communicating with the device. Even if you know that you have the device you're looking for, the report lengths and other information are useful in determining what kinds of data you can transfer. Not every item in the structure applies to all devices.

This is the declaration for the function:

```
Public Declare Function HidP_GetCaps _
    Lib "hid.dll" _
    (ByVal PreparsedData As Long, _
    ByRef Capabilities As HIDP_CAPS) _
As Long
```

The information is returned in a HIDP_CAPS structure:

```
Public Type HIDP_CAPS
    Usage As Integer
    UsagePage As Integer
    InputReportByteLength As Integer
    OutputReportByteLength As Integer
    FeatureReportByteLength As Integer
    Reserved(16) As Integer
    NumberLinkCollectionNodes As Integer
    NumberInputButtonCaps As Integer
    NumberInputValueCaps As Integer
    NumberInputDataIndices As Integer
    NumberOutputButtonCaps As Integer
    NumberOutputValueCaps As Integer
    NumberOutputDataIndices As Integer
    NumberFeatureButtonCaps As Integer
    NumberFeatureValueCaps As Integer
    NumberFeatureDataIndices As Integer
End Type
```

This is a call for the function:

```
Result = HidP_GetCaps _
    (PreparsedData, _
    Capabilities)
```

PreparsedData is the pointer returned by HidD_GetPreparsedData. When the function returns, you can examine and use whatever values are of interest in the Capabilities structure. For example, if you're looking for a mouse, you can look for a Usage Page of 01h and a Usage of 02h.

The report lengths are useful for setting buffer sizes for sending and receiving reports.

An application designed for use with a custom device may know all about the device's capabilities in advance. In this case, if the application identifies the device by its Vendor and Product IDs, it can skip examining the capabilities because it has no need for the information.

Get the Capabilities of the Values

The device capabilities aren't all that an application can retrieve from the device. It can also get the capabilities of each value and button in a report.

HidP_GetValueCaps returns a pointer to an array of structures containing information about each value in a report. The NumberInputValueCaps property of the HIDP_CAPS structure gives the number of values. This is the declaration for the function:

```
Public Declare Function HidP_GetValueCaps _
    Lib "hid.dll" _
    (ByVal ReportType As Integer, _
    ByRef ValueCaps As Byte, _
    ByRef ValueCapsLength As Integer, _
    ByVal PreparsedData As Long) _
As Long
```

This is the declaration for the HidP_Value_Caps structure:

```
Public Type HidP_Value_Caps
    UsagePage As Integer
    ReportID As Byte
    IsAlias As Long
    BitField As Integer
    LinkCollection As Integer
    LinkUsage As Integer
    LinkUsagePage As Integer
    IsRange As Long
    IsStringRange As Long
    IsDesignatorRange As Long
    IsAbsolute As Long
    HasNull As Long
    Reserved As Byte
    BitSize As Integer
    ReportCount As Integer
    Reserved2 As Integer
    Reserved3 As Integer
```

```
        Reserved4 As Integer
        Reserved5 As Integer
        Reserved6 As Integer
        LogicalMin As Long
        LogicalMax As Long
        PhysicalMin As Long
        PhysicalMax As Long
        UsageMin As Integer
        UsageMax As Integer
        StringMin As Integer
        StringMax As Integer
        DesignatorMin As Integer
        DesignatorMax As Integer
        DataIndexMin As Integer
        DataIndexMax As Integer
    End Type
```

The items in the structure include many familiar values from the device's report descriptor, as described in Chapter 13.

The IsRange, IsStringRange, and IsDesignatorRange values indicate whether or not the device uses minimum and maximum values for the indicated property. If IsRange is false, UsageMin is the Usage and UsageMax is unused. If IsStringRange is false, StringMin is the string index and String-Max is unused. If IsDesignatorRange is false, DesignatorMin is the designator index and DesignatorMax is unused.

This is a call to retrieve the data in a byte array:

```
    Dim ValueCaps(1023) As Byte

    Result = HidP_GetValueCaps _
        (HidP_Input, _
        ValueCaps(0), _
        Capabilities.NumberInputValueCaps, _
        PreparsedData)
```

The byte array is initialized to a size at least as large as the amount of data expected. From there, an application can copy the individual items into an array of structures.

In a similar way, you can use the `HidP_GetButtonCaps` function and `HidP_ButtonCaps` structure to retrieve information about buttons in a report.

Reading and Writing Data

All of the previous API calls are concerned with finding a device that matches what the application is looking for. When this is accomplished, the application and a device are finally ready to exchange data in reports, using the ReadFile and WriteFile API functions.

Write Data to the Device

An application can send data to a device when it has a handle to the device and knows the number of bytes in the device's Output report. To write data, the application copies the data to send to a buffer and calls WriteFile. The buffer size should equal the size reported in the OutputReportByteLength property of the HIDP_CAPS structure returned by HidP_GetCaps.

Like CreateFile, WriteFile is a generic API call that can be used with a file or any device whose driver supports the function. This is the function's declaration:

```
Public Declare Function WriteFile _
    Lib "kernel32" _
    (ByVal hFile As Long, _
    ByRef lpBuffer As Byte, _
    ByVal nNumberOfBytesToWrite As Long, _
    ByRef lpNumberOfBytesWritten As Long, _
    ByVal lpOverlapped As Long) _
As Long
```

The data to send is in a Byte array that contains the report ID in the first byte, followed by the report data. This code creates and fills a SendBuffer Byte array:

```
Dim Count As Integer
Dim SendBuffer() As Byte
'The SendBuffer array begins at 0,
'so subtract 1 from OutputReportByteLength.
```

```
ReDim SendBuffer _
    (Capabilities.OutputReportByteLength - 1)
'The first byte is the Report ID
SendBuffer(0) = 0
'The next bytes are data.
'This example copies the data from an OutputReportData
'Byte array filled earlier by the application.
For Count = _
        1 To Capabilities.OutputReportByteLength - 1
    SendBuffer(Count) = OutputReportData(Count - 1)
Next Count
```

This is the code to call WriteFile to send a report to the device:

```
Dim NumberOfBytesWritten As Long

NumberOfBytesWritten = 0
Result = WriteFile _
    (HidDevice, _
    SendBuffer(0), _
    CLng(Capabilities.OutputReportByteLength), _
    NumberOfBytesWritten, _
    0)
```

HidDevice is the handle returned by CreateFile. SendBuffer(0) is the first element in the Byte array containing the report. The parameter is passed ByRef to cause the function to pass the byte's address. CLng(Capabilities.OutputReportByteLength) is the size of the output report returned by HidP_GetCaps, converted to a Long to match the declaration. NumberOfBytesWritten returns the number of bytes the function successfully wrote to the device. If Result is non-zero, the function succeeded.

Read Data from the Device

The complement to WriteFile is ReadFile. When the application has a handle to the device and knows the number of bytes in the device's Input report, the application can use ReadFile to read data from a device.

To read data, the application declares a buffer to hold the data and calls ReadFile. The buffer size should equal the size reported in the InputReportByteLength property of the HIDP_CAPS structure returned by HidP_GetCaps.

Like CreateFile and WriteFile, ReadFile is a generic API call that can be used with a file or any device whose driver supports the function. This is the function's declaration:

```
Public Declare Function ReadFile _
    Lib "kernel32" _
    (ByVal hFile As Long, _
    ByRef lpBuffer As Byte, _
    ByVal nNumberOfBytesToRead As Long, _
    ByRef lpNumberOfBytesRead As Long, _
    ByVal lpOverlapped As Long) _
As Long
```

The data read is in a Byte array that contains the report ID in the first byte and the report data in the following bytes. This code creates and fills a Read-Buffer Byte array:

```
Dim NumberOfBytesRead As Long
'Allocate a buffer for the report.
Dim ReadBuffer() As Byte
Dim NumberOfBytesRead As Long

'The ReadBuffer array begins at 0,
'so subtract 1 from the number of bytes to read.
ReDim ReadBuffer _
    (Capabilities.InputReportByteLength - 1)

Result = ReadFile _
    (HidDevice, _
    ReadBuffer(0), _
    CLng(Capabilities.InputReportByteLength), _
    NumberOfBytesRead, _
    0)
```

HidDevice is the handle returned by CreateFile. ReadBuffer(0) is the first element in the Byte array that will contain the report. The parameter is passed ByRef, so the function passes the address of the byte. CLng(Capabilities.InputReportByteLength) is the size of the input report returned by HidP_GetCaps, converted to a Long to match the declaration. NumberOfBytesRead will return the number of bytes the function successfully read from the device.

If Result is non-zero, the function was successful. Byte 0 of ReadBuffer will contain the report ID, and the following bytes will contain the data read from the device.

There is one big caution about using ReadFile in Visual-Basic applications. ReadFile is blocking call. If an application calls ReadFile when the device has no data to send, the application hangs until you either close the application with Control-Alt-Delete or unplug the device from the bus. There are two ways to prevent this from happening: be sure the device always has data to send, or place the ReadFile call in a separate program thread. (Using ReadFileEx or Overlapped I/O doesn't help.)

To ensure that the device always has data to send, you can write the firmware so that the IN endpoint is always enabled and ready to respond to a request for data. If there is no new data to send, the device can send the same data as last time. The sample firmware included with this book uses this method. Another approach requires cooperation from the application that accesses the device. Before each ReadFile, the application can call a WriteFile that sends a report. The report contains a vendor-defined bit that tells the firmware to get ready to send data. Then when the application calls ReadFile, the device's endpoint is enabled, with data ready to transmit. These solutions aren't ideal, but they're workable.

A more elegant solution uses multiple program threads. A thread is program code that executes independently. If ReadFile is in its own thread, the main application can continue to respond even if ReadFile hangs. But in Visual Basic, simple applications are always single-threaded.

If you want to use multithreading, one solution is to write a multi-threaded application using C++, Delphi, or another compiler that supports multi-threading.

What about Visual Basic's support for multi-threading? As of version 6, applications can't use the CreateThread API function. Visual Basic does support multi-threading in ActiveX EXE servers, but there is apparently no way to kill a thread if a ReadFile can't complete because a device isn't sending the requested amount of data. One way around this is to define a report item that enables the device to tell the server to stop reading from the device. The server can then continuously attempt to read from the device, notifying an application when data has been received, without blocking the application while it waits. When the application is finished communicating with the device, it can send a report to the device, using a vendor-defined report item to tell the device to notify the server that there will be no more data. The server can then stop reading from the device and the application can close gracefully. For more about ActiveX EXE servers, see Dan Appleman's book *Developing ActiveX Components in Visual Basic.*

Another possibility is the Visual-Basic support included in DirectX7 for communicating with HIDs. Microsoft has promised to add Visual-Basic examples to its DirectX documentation.

Or you can write a multi-threaded DLL that performs the ReadFiles, though here again the device will have to send something in response to every ReadFile to enable the call to complete. PowerBasic's PB/DLL compiler enables you to write a multi-threaded DLL in Basic. PowerBasic's website (www.powerbasic.com) has a good tutorial on multi-threaded programming.

Closing Communications

When an application is finished communicating with a device, it should free the resources previously reserved for it. Three of the API functions used earlier have complementary functions for freeing resources.

The declarations and calls are short. Each passes a single parameter obtained from its complementary function.

The complement to CreateFile is CloseHandle:

```
Public Declare Function CloseHandle _
    Lib "kernel32" _
    (ByVal hObject As Long) _
As Long

Result = CloseHandle _
    (HidDevice)
```

The complement to SetupDiGetClassDevs is SetupDiDestroyDeviceInfoList:

```
Public Declare Function SetupDiDestroyDeviceInfoList _
    Lib "setupapi.dll" _
    (ByVal DeviceInfoSet As Long) _
As Long

Result = SetupDiDestroyDeviceInfoList _
    (DeviceInfoSet)
```

And the complement to HidD_GetPreparsedData is HidD_FreePreparsedData:

```
Public Declare Function HidD_FreePreparsedData _
    Lib "hid.dll" _
    (ByRef PreparsedData As Long) _
As Long

Result = HidD_FreePreparsedData _
    (PreparsedData)
```

For each, a non-zero Result indicates success. Be sure to include each of these in your code that executes before the application closes.

15

Device Testing

Users expect installing and using USB peripherals to be painless. The burden is on the developer to make it so. USB is a complex interface, and misbehaving software or firmware can make a peripheral irritating or impossible to use. Don't skimp on testing!

The peripheral's firmware and the host's applications must of course know what data to send and what to do with the data they receive. But that's not the end of it. In addition, the installation must be as invisible as possible for users. Attachment and removal must be able to occur at any time. And the device must transfer data efficiently while co-existing peacefully with whatever other peripherals happen to be sharing the bus. Anything short of this and users will look elsewhere for their products.

Fortunately, there are many tools that help in testing new peripheral designs. This chapter introduces a variety of these, including the free software and other resources available from the USB Implementers Forum and protocol analyzers available from several sources. These are in addition to the development boards and monitor programs available from chip vendors and described in Chapter 9.

USBCheck

USBCheck is a suite of five test applications for USB devices. The applications enable you to view descriptors, send control requests, view the results, and run further tests on hubs, communication-class devices, and HIDs. You can download USBCheck for free from the Implementers Forum's website.

Detecting a Device

When you run USBCheck, the software identifies the device to test by displaying a window asking you to plug in the device (or unplug and re-attach if it's already plugged in). When you do this, your device's normal listing in the Device Manager disappears and is replaced with a listing under *Other Detected Devices,* described as a *USB Diagnostic Device.* This is because USBCheck uses its own driver, *usbdiag.sys,* which replaces the driver normally used by the device.

In order for this step to work, the device has to be functional enough to respond to the standard requests. However, not all commercial products pass even this step without problems or quirks. One printer-port adapter I tried wasn't detected at all by USBCheck, for unknown reasons, even though the adapter worked. When I attached one camera, Windows tried to locate and reload drivers for the camera, although USBCheck was able to run its tests in spite of this.

When you want to use the device in its intended way, you *must* close the USBCheck application and again unplug and re-attach your device, so that Windows can restore the device's normal drivers. The device listing will also return to its proper location in the Device Manager's window.

The Tests

The first set of tests is called Chapter 9, which refers to that chapter in the USB specification. The tests read the descriptors and send standard requests.

These tests are extremely useful as an initial check that Windows is retrieving the expected information from your device.

To start, it's interesting to view the descriptors for whatever USB peripherals you may have on your system. Figure 15-1 shows a hub's descriptors, which tell you several things. The device descriptor identifies the device as a hub. The configuration descriptor says that the hub may be self- or bus-powered and that is draws no more than 100 milliamperes from the bus. The interface descriptor says that the hub has one endpoint (in addition to Endpoint 0). And the endpoint descriptor describes the hub's required interrupt endpoint, which has an interval of 255 milliseconds and a maximum packet size of 1 byte.

In a similar way, you can use the Chapter 9 tests to retrieve descriptors from devices you develop, to verify that Windows is reading the expected information from the device. Once you have that working, you can move on to the other tests.

Listing 15-1 is a report for the complete set of Chapter 9 tests on a custom HID. You can run individual tests, such as sending a Get_Descriptor or Set_Interface request, or run all of the tests at once and view the results. If your device supports remote wakeup, the test will ask you to send a Remote Wakeup signal to the host. You can skip this test if you're not set up to trigger a remote wakeup.

The other tests are for devices in specific classes. Chapter 11 of the specification is about hubs, and USBCheck's Chapter 11 test sends hub-specific requests. The CDC (communications device class) test retrieves and analyzes descriptors specific to CDCs. The fifth test is HIDView, which I'll cover in more detail.

HIDView

After running USBCheck's Chapter 9 tests on an HID-class device, a window will appear advising you to run HIDView. Figure 15-2 shows the options for testing.

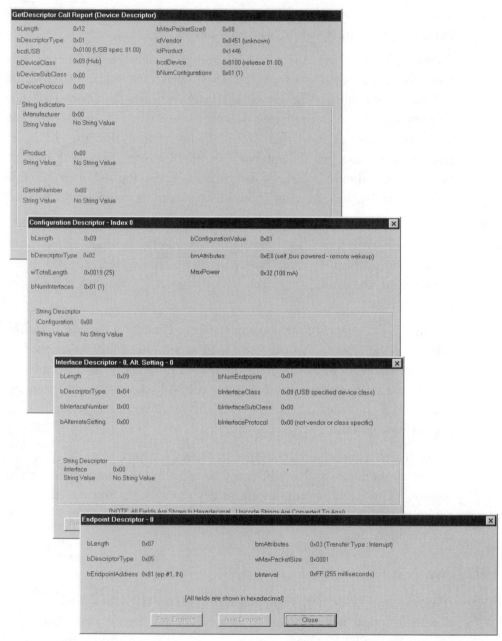

Figure 15-1: These windows from USBCheck show the contents of a hub's descriptors.

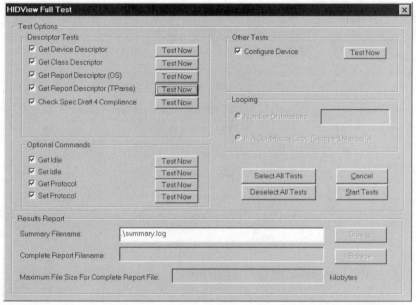

Figure 15-2: The HIDView utility enables you to test HID-class devices.

If you run all of the tests, you'll see a display like Figure 15-3's. From the Full Test window you can also run individual tests and view the results. Figure 15-4 shows the result of retrieving a device's report descriptor.

A Get Data from Device button displays the result of reading data from the device, either one time or continuously. This enables you to test the ability of the host to receive Input reports from the device.

When a HID passes the HIDView tests and you're able to read data from the device, you're well on your way to having a functioning HID. On the other hand, failing one or more tests gives an indication of where the problem lies.

After closing HIDView, don't forget to unplug and re-attach your device, to cause Windows to replace the diagnostic driver with the device's normal drivers.

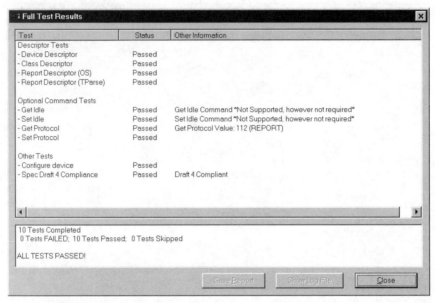

Figure 15-3: HIDView examines the device's report descriptors and sends other requests related to HID functions.

Protocol Analyzers

The ultimate tool for USB development is a protocol analyzer. The analyzer is a combination of hardware and software that enables you to view every detail of USB traffic. The analyzer does the work for you, collecting the data you request, then decoding and displaying it in a variety of formats. You can watch what happens during enumeration, detect and examine protocol and signaling errors, view the data being transferred during control, interrupt, bulk, and isochronous transfers, or focus on any aspect of a communication that you wish.

For developing a commercial product, a protocol analyzer is essential. For experimenting and learning, you can do a lot with the tools provided by chip vendors and the free utilities from the Implementers Forum, but a protocol analyzer will make things easier and will open your eyes to many new

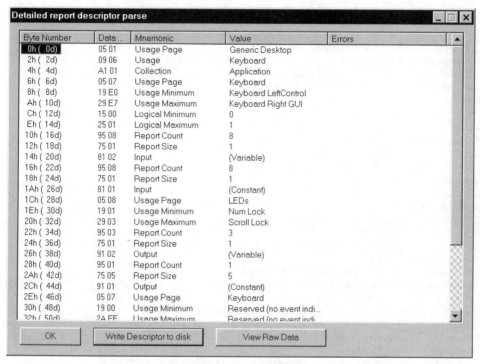

Detailed report descriptor parse

Byte Number	Data ...	Mnemonic	Value	Errors
0h (0d)	05 01	Usage Page	Generic Desktop	
2h (2d)	09 06	Usage	Keyboard	
4h (4d)	A1 01	Collection	Application	
6h (6d)	05 07	Usage Page	Keyboard	
8h (8d)	19 E0	Usage Minimum	Keyboard LeftControl	
Ah (10d)	29 E7	Usage Maximum	Keyboard Right GUI	
Ch (12d)	15 00	Logical Minimum	0	
Eh (14d)	25 01	Logical Maximum	1	
10h (16d)	95 08	Report Count	8	
12h (18d)	75 01	Report Size	1	
14h (20d)	81 02	Input	(Variable)	
16h (22d)	95 08	Report Count	8	
18h (24d)	75 01	Report Size	1	
1Ah (26d)	81 01	Input	(Constant)	
1Ch (28d)	05 08	Usage Page	LEDs	
1Eh (30d)	19 01	Usage Minimum	Num Lock	
20h (32d)	29 03	Usage Maximum	Scroll Lock	
22h (34d)	95 03	Report Count	3	
24h (36d)	75 01	Report Size	1	
26h (38d)	91 02	Output	(Variable)	
28h (40d)	95 01	Report Count	1	
2Ah (42d)	75 05	Report Size	5	
2Ch (44d)	91 01	Output	(Constant)	
2Eh (46d)	05 07	Usage Page	Keyboard	
30h (48d)	19 00	Usage Minimum	Reserved (no event indi...	
32h (50d)	2A FF	Usage Maximum	Reserved (no event indi...	

OK   Write Descriptor to disk   View Raw Data

Figure 15-4: HIDView also enables you to examine your device's report descriptor. This example shows a keyboard descriptor.

things. I developed the sample HID firmware included with this book using only Cypress' tools and USBCheck, but the developing would have gone faster with a protocol analyzer.

Protocol analyzers are complex pieces of equipment. Even though there are many developers working on USB designs, the market for analyzers is limited in comparison to, for example, the market for generic PCs. The result is that analyzers aren't inexpensive. However, as with most things electronic, prices will come down in time, especially as USB becomes more popular. Three vendors of USB protocol analyzers are CATC, Hitex Development Tools, and QualityLogic (formerly Genoa Technology).

As an example of what you can do with a protocol analyzer, I'll describe QualityLogic's USB Expert. Other analyzers have similar abilities, and

DEVICE 00 Vid (0x0925) Pid (0x1234) Tests:

- Get Device Descriptor Passed.
Returned Device Descriptor:
0x12 0x01 0x10 0x01 0x00 0x00 0x00 0x08
0x25 0x09 0x34 0x12 0x01 0x00 0x01 0x02
0x00 0x01
Descriptor Fields:
bLength   : 0x12
bDescriptorType   : 0x01 (Dev. Descriptor)
bcdUSB   : 0x0110 (USB spec. 01.10)
bDeviceClass   : 0x00 (ifc's specify own)
bDeviceSubClass   : 0x00
bDeviceProtocol   : 0x00
bMaxPacketSize0   : 0x08
idVendor   : 0x0925 (unknown)
idProduct   : 0x1234
bcdDevice   : 0x0001 (release 00.01)
iManufacturer   : 0x01
- Get String Descriptor 0 (Language ID's) Passed.
- Checking Language ID's Passed.
Language ID   : 0x0409
- Get String Descriptor Index 1, Language ID 0x0409 Passed.
USB C
iProduct   : 0x02
Language ID   : 0x0409
- Get String Descriptor Index 2, Language ID 0x0409 Passed.
HID
iSerialNumber   : 0x00
bNumConfigurations : 0x01 (1)
CONFIGURATION Index 0 Tests:

- Get Configuration Descriptor Passed. Configuration Value = 0x01

Configuration Descriptor:
0x09 0x02 0x22 0x00 0x01 0x01 0x00 0x80
0x32 0x09 0x04 0x00 0x00 0x01 0x03 0x00
0x00 0x00 0x09 0x21 0x00 0x01 0x00 0x01
0x22 0x34 0x00 0x07 0x05 0x81 0x03 0x06
0x00 0x0a

Listing 15-1: (Sheet 1 of 3) USBCheck's Chapter 9 test report shows the result of the tests, which retrieve descriptors and send other control requests. This report is for a custom HID.

Get Configuration Descriptor with Transfer size 0x22 for Config# 0x0

Descriptor Fields:
bLength   : 0x09
bDescriptorType   : 0x02
wTotalLength   : 0x0022 (34)
bNumInterfaces   : 0x01 (1)
bConfigurationValue : 0x01
iConfiguration   : 0x00
bmAttributes   : 0x80 (bus powered)
MaxPower   : 0x32 (100 mA)
- Get Configuration Passed. Device Is Unconfigured

- Set Configuration Passed. Set To 0x01

- Get Configuration Passed. Returned 0x01.

- Unconfigure Device Passed. Set To 0x00

- Get Configuration Passed. Device Is Unconfigured

- Set Configuration Passed. Set To 0x01

- Get Configuration Passed. Returned 0x01.

- Check If Alt. Setting For Ifc 0 is 0 Passed. Single interface responded with STALL

INTERFACE 0x0 Tests:

INTERFACE Number 0x00, Alt. Setting 0x00 Tests:

bLength   : 0x09
bDescriptorType   : 0x04
bInterfaceNumber   : 0x00
bAlternateSetting : 0x00
bNumEndpoints   : 0x01
bInterfaceClass   : 0x03 (USB specified device class)
bInterfaceSubClass : 0x00
bInterfaceProtocol : 0x00 (not vendor or class specific)
iInterface   : 0x00
- Set Interface Passed. Single interface responded with STALL

- Get Interface Passed. Single interface responded with STALL

Listing 15-1: (Sheet 2 of 3) USBCheck's Chapter 9 test report shows the result of the tests, which retrieve descriptors and send other control requests. This report is for a custom HID.

```
Descriptor (Endpoint 0x00) Fields:
bLength        : 0x07
bDescriptorType   : 0x05
bEndpointAddress  : 0x81 (ep #1, IN)
bmAttributes     : 0x03 (Transfer Type : Interrupt)
wMaxPacketSize   : 0x0006
bInterval       : 0x0A (10 milliseconds)
ENDPOINT With Address 0x81 Tests:

- GetStatus Passed. Endpoint NOT Stalled

- Set Feature (STALL) Passed.

- GetStatus Passed. Set Stall Confirmed

- Clear Feature (STALL) Passed.

- GetStatus Passed. Clear Stall Confirmed

NonStandard Descriptor
Size : 0x09 Bytes
Type : 0x21
Data : 0x00 0x01 0x00 0x01 0x22 0x34 0x00

More DEVICE Tests For Current Configuration:
- Get Status Passed. Remote Wakeup Not Supported - Remote Wakeup Disabled,
Bus-Powered


00 Vid (0x0925) Pid (0x1234): All Selected Test(s) PASSED!
DEVICE IS CHAPTER 9 COMPLIANT
bcdDevice: 0x0001 (release 00.01)
```

Listing 15-1: (Sheet 3 of 3) USBCheck's Chapter 9 test report shows the result of the tests, which retrieve descriptors and send other control requests. This report is for a custom HID.

everyone's products are constantly being improved, so be sure to check for the latest information when you're ready to buy.

Hardware

The USB Expert's hardware consists of two pieces: the main unit and the probe (Figure 15-5). The main unit contains the buffer that stores the USB traffic and an embedded PC to manage the storage and transferring of the analyzer's data to a desktop or portable PC. The probe connects in series with the USB segment to be monitored, with an additional parallel connection that carries the segment's data to the Expert's main unit for analyzing. The parallel connection enables the Expert to monitor the USB traffic without affecting it. The probe also has a connector for hardware triggering and a manual trigger button.

The Expert communicates with a PC via a TCP/IP Network connection. To use the Expert, you must have a PC with an Ethernet interface configured for TCP/IP. An Ethernet interface is fast, and it's inexpensive to add an Ethernet interface if your PC doesn't already have one. If the PC connects to a network, both the PC and USB Expert can connect to the same 10 BaseT

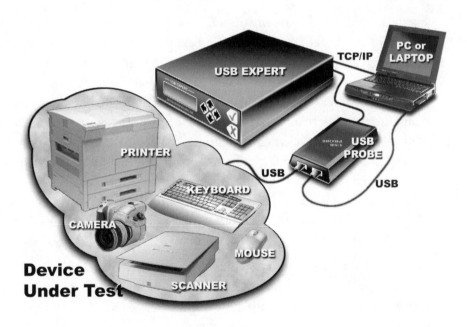

Figure 15-5: QualityLogic's USB Expert protocol analyzer collects USB data and sends it to a PC over a TCP/IP connection. An application on the PC displays the data in a variety of formats.

Ethernet hub. If the PC doesn't have a network connection, the Expert can use the provided Direct-Connect 10-BaseT cable to connect to the PC. The same PC that connects to the Expert can serve as the host of the bus being tested. The TCP/IP interface also enables remote testing.

Other protocol analyzers use different interfaces. Some, including Quality-Logic's USB Protocol Analyzer, connect to an ISA expansion board in a PC. Analyzers with this type of interface tend to be less expensive, but aren't as portable. Other options are the PC's parallel port or, not surprisingly, the USB itself.

Software

The USB Expert's software application enables you to begin and stop data logging and view, save, and print the results.

Figure 15-6 shows the screen you use to begin capturing data. Data logging can begin on detecting any of a number of event types: a particular USB event (such as a Setup packet or STALL), a programmed trigger in an application, or an external signal. Or you can just start collecting data immediately. If you want to see what happens during enumeration, you can configure the Expert to trigger on the first Setup packet sent to the device's address, initiate data logging, then attach the device. The Expert will begin storing traffic on detecting the first Setup packet in the enumeration process. If you want to see what happens when your application sends a Write-File to the device's driver, you can add a call to the Expert's trigger function just before calling WriteFile in your application. If you want to see if your device is responding to any requests with STALL, you can trigger on this.

When the data collection is complete, you can view the results in just about any imaginable format. You can use filtering to display only the items you're interested in. I'll mention only some of the available screens and reports.

The Transactions tab (Figure 15-7) displays each occurrence of the transaction types you specify. Right-clicking on a transaction displays additional information about it. In a similar way, the Events and Data tabs display the information formatted by event (including Idle, Reset, and Resume states,

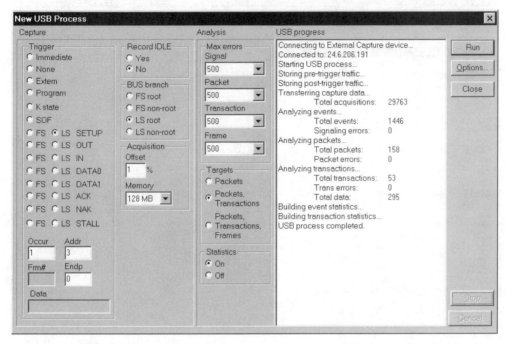

Figure 15-6: The USB Expert gives you many options for triggering and recording data.

End-of-Packet signals, and errors) or focusing on the data transferred, rather than on the events. You can search for invalid packets or other errors, then see exactly where they occurred and view details about each error.

You can also view all of the information that transferred in any control request. Figure 15-8 shows a Set_Address request. The Expert decodes class-specific requests, including those for hubs, HIDs, and printers. A Signal-Layer display shows data as you would see it on a logic analyzer, and a Transfer-Layer display shows all transactions associated with a transfer.

Implementers Forum Resources

One advantage of USB that other interfaces don't have is that the developers of the specification didn't stop with the release of the specification docu-

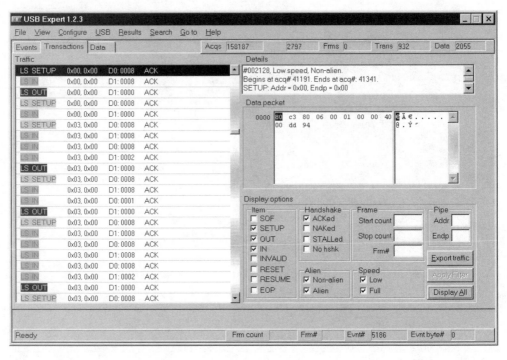

Figure 15-7: You can view each transaction by type, and right-click for more information.

ment. The Forum remains very much involved in helping developers design and test USB products. I've already mentioned that the Forum's website has documents and tools, including USBCheck, available to everyone. In addition, joining the Implementers Forum gives you access to resources that will help ensure that your product complies with the specification and causes no problems for users.

The Compliance Program

For a thorough testing of your product under a variety of conditions, Forum members can enroll a device in the Implementers Forum's Compliance Program. When a device meets the program's three criteria, the Forum deems it to have "reasonable measures of acceptability" and adds it to its Integrators List.

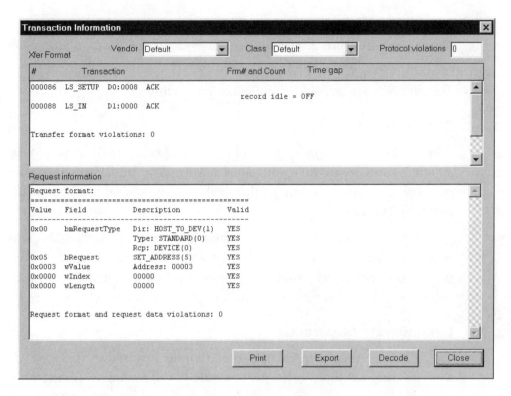

Figure 15-8: This display of a Set_Address request shows that the host assigned an address of 03h to the device.

The three criteria are checklists, compliance testing, and demonstrated operation.

Checklists

The checklists contain questions relating to your product and its behavior. Filling out the appropriate checklists is the first step in achieving compliance. You do this step on your own.

There are checklists for vendors of peripherals, hubs, systems with USB hosts, and cables. Some products require multiple checklists. I'll focus on peripheral testing.

The Peripheral checklist is nine pages of questions about your device. They cover mechanical design, device states and signals, and operating voltages and power consumption. You should be able to answer yes to everything. Accompanying each is a reference to a page in the specification where you can find more information.

The checklists are available from the Forum's website.

Compliance Testing

When you can answer yes to everything on the checklists that apply to your product, you're ready for compliance testing. The Implementers Forum sponsors compliance workshops that enable you to test your device with a variety of hardware.

Before attending a workshop, the Forum recommends performing the tests as fully as possible on your own. The Forum's website has detailed descriptions of the tests, which cover responding to standard requests, power consumption and distribution, and signal quality.

Demonstrated Operation

The final test is demonstrated operation. In other words, does the device do what it's designed to do in its normal mode of operation? A printer must print the documents sent to it, a keyboard must send keystrokes in a format that the operating system understands, and a camera must transfer images to the host.

But that's not all...an additional part of demonstrated operation is passing a series of interoperability tests. This is where you emulate the user's experience using your product on a system with a variety of other USB peripherals attached and in use with a variety of software. The goal is "an enjoyable end-user experience." These tests are important!

The USB Interoperability Guidelines document spells out what should be self-evident: your device should function without ever causing a device-not-detected error or a system crash, hang, or reboot.

The following are the minimal situations that you must test. In each case, the specified actions shouldn't interfere with the operation of the device being tested (except in the case of device removal, of course) or any other attached devices.

- With the system powered, attach the device. If your device has an associated application, attach the device before installing or loading the application. The operating system must identify the device and load the appropriate drivers.

- With the device attached, power up the system (cold boot). The device, device driver, and application software must operate after powering up.

- With the device attached, reboot without powering off (warm reboot). The device, device driver, and application software must operate after the reboot.

- With the system powered, detach and re-attach the device at any time. The device, device driver, and application software must operate normally after re-attaching.

- With the system powered, detach the device and attach it to a different port. The device, device driver, and application software must operate normally after re-attaching.

- Suspend and resume. The device, device driver, and application software must operate normally after resuming.

- If remote wakeup is supported, suspend and initiate a remote wakeup event. The device, device driver, and application software must operate normally after the remote wakeup.

- With the system powered and the device attached, install the application software associated with the device. The application must be able to communicate with the device after installing.

- Remove the application software associated with the device.

The device must pass these tests not only on a bus with just your device, but also on a bus that connects a variety of hubs and other common peripherals. (The Forum's website lists devices that are verified to have no interopability problems of their own.) The Guidelines document calls this topology the Gold Tree. The minimum configuration has two of your devices, one other similar device, five hubs, a keyboard, mouse, speakers, scanner, and a printer! The device should be tested with both UHCI and OHCI controllers. The Interoperability document has more specifics about the tests.

If your device has one or more isochronous endpoints, you must also test what happens when the host can't configure a device because there isn't enough bandwidth for the requested pipe. When the device can't be configured, it must inform the user of what has happened and advise the user to stop using other devices that use isochronous transfers in order to enable the device to be configured.

For this test, you can use the Bandwidth Load Application available from the Implementers Forum. The application requires a dummy device that will receive isochronous OUT data. The device doesn't have to have any isochronous endpoints. The application uses a replacement driver that configures the device with isochronous endpoints and causes the data to be sent. Because there are no handshakes, it doesn't matter that the device never sees the data.

If your device supports a boot interface, you must test this as well, to ensure, for example, that a keyboard with a boot interface will work with BIOSes that have keyboard support.

Testing Opportunities

Compliance workshops offer various opportunities to test your device with hosts and peripherals from other vendors. Every workshop has plenty of vendors and products available. You can schedule private tests with vendors of host hardware. And you can participate in a Plugfest, where as many vendors as possible connect their devices to a single host to find out if all can co-exist peacefully.

16

Hubs: the Link between Devices and the Host

Every USB device must connect to a hub. As Chapter 2 explained, a hub is an intelligent device that provides attachment points for devices and manages each device's connection to the bus. Devices that plug directly into the PC connect to the root hub. Other devices connect to external hubs downstream from the root hub.

The hub's two main jobs are repeating USB traffic and managing its devices' connections. Managing the connections includes getting newly attached devices up and communicating as well as detecting and blocking communications from misbehaving devices that could interfere with other devices' use of the bus.

This chapter presents essentials about hub communications. You don't need to know every detail about hubs in order to design a USB peripheral, but

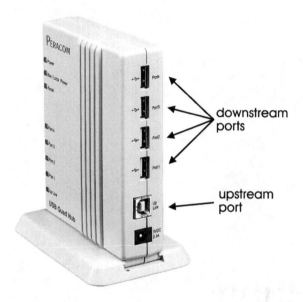

downstream
ports

upstream
port

Figure 16-1: A hub has one upstream port and one or more downstream ports.
(Photo of Peracom hub courtesy of B & B Electronics.)

some understanding of what the hub must do will help understanding how
your device communicates with the host.

Hub Basics

Each hub has one port, or attachment point, that connects in the upstream
direction (toward the host) (Figure 16-1). This upstream port may connect
directly to the host's root hub, or it may connect to another hub. Each hub
also has one or more ports downstream from the host. Most downstream
ports have a connector for attaching cables. An exception is a hub that is
part of a compound device whose ports connect to functions embedded in
the device. Hubs with one, two, four, and seven downstream ports are common.

Each hub has two main components: a hub repeater and a hub controller.
The hub repeater is responsible for passing USB traffic between the host's
root hub or another upstream hub and whatever downstream devices are

attached and enabled. The hub repeater also detects when a device is attached and removed, establishes the connection of a device to the bus, detects bus faults such as over-current conditions, and manages power to the device. The hub controller manages communications between the host and the hub repeater.

The Repeater

As appropriate, a hub re-transmits, or repeats, the packets it receives, sending them on their way either upstream or downstream. If any low-speed devices are attached, the hub must detect low-speed data received from upstream and repeat only this data to the low-speed devices. The hub also converts between low-speed and full-speed edge rates and signal polarities in both directions.

The hub repeats all full-speed packets received from the host (including data that has passed through one or more additional hubs) to all enabled, full-speed, downstream ports. Enabled ports include all ports with attached devices that are ready to receive communications from the hub. Exceptions would include a device that the host controller has stopped communicating with due to errors or other problems, a device in the Suspend state, or a device that isn't yet ready to communicate because it has just been attached or is in the process of exiting the Suspend state.

Low-speed devices never see full-speed traffic. The hub repeats only low-speed packets to low-speed devices. The hub identifies a low-speed packet by the PRE packet identifier that precedes it. The hub repeats the low-speed packets, and only these packets, to any enabled low-speed devices. The hub also sends the low-speed packets to its full-speed downstream ports, because any of these might connect to a hub that connect to the packet's destination device. The host adds a delay of at least four full-speed bit widths between the PRE packet and the low-speed packet to give the hubs time to make their low-speed ports ready to receive data.

Low-speed traffic from the host uses the low-speed bit rate, but with full-speed data's polarity and faster edge rates. A low-speed device sends and receives data using the slower low-speed edge rates and an inverted signal polarity, compared to full-speed data. Chapter 18 has more on the signal polarities, and Chapter 19 has more about edge rates.

In the full-speed upstream and downstream directions, the hub doesn't translate or process the traffic in any way. It just regenerates the edges of the signal transitions. In transmitting to a low-speed device, the hub converts the received full-speed transitions to the slower edge rate required by the low-speed device. In receiving data from the low-speed device, the hub converts the received low-speed transitions to the faster edge rate used by full-speed devices. The hub also inverts all data sent to and received from a low-speed device, to match the full-speed polarity.

Managing Communications

The responsibilities of the hub controller relate to managing communications between the host and the device.

As it does for all devices, the host enumerates a newly detected hub to find out its abilities. The hub descriptor retrieved during enumeration tells the host how many ports the hub has. After enumerating the hub, the host requests the hub to tell it whether there are any devices attached and if so, the host enumerates these as well.

The host finds out if a device is attached to a port by sending a Get_Port_Status request. This is a Get_Status request sent to the hub with a port number in the Index field. The hub returns two 16-bit values that indicate whether a device is attached as well as other information, such as whether the device is low power or in the Suspended state.

Hubs are also responsible for disabling any port responsible for loss of bus activity or babble. Loss of bus activity occurs when a packet doesn't end with the expected End-of-Packet signal. Babble occurs when a device continues to transmit beyond the End-of-Packet signal.

Endpoints

In addition to Endpoint 0, which all devices must have for control transfers, hubs must have a Status Change endpoint configured for interrupt IN transfers. The host polls this endpoint to find out if there have been any changes at the hub. On each poll, the hub returns either a NAK if there have been no changes, or data that indicates which port (or the hub itself) has a change. If there is a change, the host sends requests to find out more about the change and take whatever action is needed. For example, if the hub reports the attachment of a new device, the host will attempt to enumerate it.

Speed

The hub's upstream port must be full speed. All downstream ports with connectors must support both full- and low-speed communications. However, an embedded or permanently attached device may be low speed, and in this case the port doesn't have to support full-speed communications.

Because low-speed devices aren't capable of receiving full-speed data, the hub doesn't repeat full-speed traffic to low-speed devices. A low-speed device would try to interpret the full-speed traffic as low-speed data and might even mistakenly see what it thinks is valid data. Full-speed data on an unshielded, low-speed cable would also cause radiated electromagnetic interference (EMI). In the other direction, there is no valid low-speed data that a full-speed device could interpret as valid full-speed data, so it's OK for a full-speed cable to carry low-speed data.

When there is no data on a full-speed bus, the host continues to send Start-of-Frame packets once per frame, and all hubs pass these packets on to their full-speed devices. These packets keep full-speed devices from entering the Suspend state on an otherwise idle bus.

Low-speed devices don't see the Start-of-Frame packets. Instead, at least once per frame hubs must send their low-speed devices a low-speed End-of-Packet (EOP) signal (defined in Chapter 19). This functions as a keep-alive signal that keeps a device from entering the Suspend state on a bus with no low-speed activity. Chapter 17 has more on how hubs manage the Suspend state.

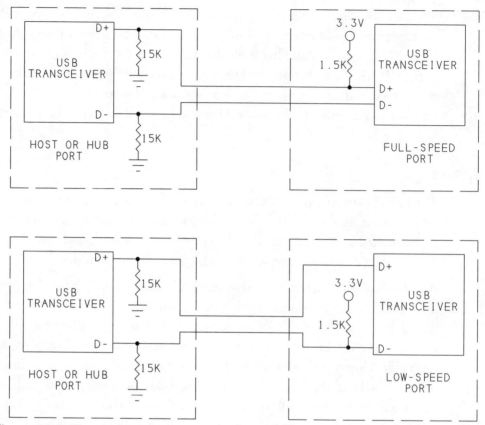

Figure 16-2: The device's port has a stronger pull-up than the hub's. The location of the pull-up tells the hub whether the device is low- or full-speed.

The hub detects the speed of an attached device by determining which signal line is more positive on an idle line. Figure 16-2 illustrates. As Chapter 5 explained, the hub has a 15-kilohm pull-down resistor on each of the port's two signal lines, D+ and D-. A device has a 1.5-kilohm pull-up resistor on either D+ (for a full-speed device) or D- (for a low-speed device). When a device plugs into a port, the device's pull-up is stronger than the hub's pull-down, so the line is pulled high. When the voltage on one of the lines is more positive than the hub's logic-high input threshold, the hub assumes a device is attached, and detects the speed by which line it is.

How Many Hubs in Series?

USB was designed as a desktop bus. It's not intended for long-distance links. But that hasn't stopped people from wondering just how far a USB peripheral can be from its host.

The specification limits the length of each USB cable segment to about five meters. (The specification doesn't specify a length, but instead lists requirements that together limit the maximum length.) You can increase the total length of a link by stringing together a series of hubs, with 5-meter cables between. But how many hubs in series can you use?

The number of hubs that you can connect in series is limited by the hubs' and cables' electronics and the delays that result from propagating the signals along the cable and through the hub. The specification requires the delays to be minimal. The limit is five hubs in series, with each hub and the final device each using a 5-meter cable. This means that a USB peripheral can be 30 meters (96 feet) from its host.

The Hub Class

Hubs are members of the Hub class, which is the only class defined in the main USB specification. Each hub supports the standard descriptors as well as descriptors that are specific to hubs.

Hub Values for the Standard Descriptors

The specification assigns values for some parameters in the device, interface, and configuration descriptors, as well as the endpoint descriptor for the status-change endpoint:

Device Descriptor

bDeviceClass = HUB_CLASSCODE (09H)
bDeviceSubClass =0

Interface Descriptor

bNumEndpoints =1

bInterfaceClass = HUB_CLASSCODE (09H)

bInterfaceSubClass =0

bInterfaceProtocol =0

Configuration Descriptor

MaxPower = The maximum amount of bus power the hub will consume in this configuration

Endpoint Descriptor (for Status Change Endpoint)

bEndpointAddress = Implementation-dependent; Bit 7: Direction = In(1)

wMaxPacketSize = Implementation-dependent

bmAttributes = Transfer Type = Interrupt

bInterval = FFH (Maximum allowable interval)

The Hub Descriptor

Each hub must also have a hub descriptor. The hub descriptor contains the following fields:

Identifying the Descriptor

bDescLength. The number of bytes in the descriptor.

bDescriptorType. Hub Descriptor, 29h.

Hub Description

bNbrPorts. The number of downstream ports the hub supports.

wHubCharacteristics:

Bits 1 and 0 specify the power-switching mode. 00=Ganged; all ports are powered together. 01=Ports are powered individually. 10, 11=Reserved.

Bit 2 indicates whether the hub is part of a compound device (1) or not (0).

Bits 4 and 3 are the Overcurrent Protection mode. 00=Global protection and reporting. 01=Protection and reporting for each port. 1X=No protection and reporting (for bus-powered hubs only).

Bits 5 through 15 are reserved.

bPwrOn2PwrGood. The maximum delay between beginning the power-on sequence on a port and when power is good on the port. The value is in 2-millisecond units. (Set to 100 for a 200-millisecond delay.)

bHubContrCurrent. The maximum current required by the Hub Controller's electronics only, in milliamperes.

DeviceRemovable. Indicates whether the device(s) attached to the hub are removable (0) or not (1). The number of bits in this value equals the number of the highest port with an attached device (0 through 255) + 1. Bit 0 is reserved. Bit 1 is for Port 1, bit 2 is for Port 2, and so on up to bit 254.

PortPowerCtrlMask. All bits should be 1s. This field is only for compatibility with V1.0 software. It has 1 bit for each port that requires extra pad bits.

Hub-class Requests

Hubs accept or return data for seven of the USB's eleven standard requests. Of the others, one request is optional and the other three are undefined for hubs. Like other devices, hubs must return STALL for unsupported requests. The Hub Class defines eight specific requests within the standard requests. For example, a Get_Status request with an Index value of 0 causes the hub to return its status. The Hub Class also defines one entirely new request, Get_Bus_State.

Table 16-1 shows the hub-specific requests

Hubs respond in the standard way to Clear_Feature, Get_Configuration, Get_Descriptor, Get_Status, Set_Address, Set_Configuration, and Set_Feature. Set_Descriptor is optional and should return STALL if not supported. A hub can support only one interface, so Get_Interface and Set_Interface are undefined. A hub can't have an isochronous endpoint, so Synch_Frame is undefined.

Table 16-1: The Hub class has nine class-specific requests. All but Get_State use the USB's standard request codes.

Specific Request	Request #	Request	Data source	Value	Index	Data Length (bytes)	Data
Get Hub Status	00h	Get_Status	Hub	0	0	4	hub status and change indicators
Get Port Status	00h	Get_Status	Hub	0	Port	4	port status and change indicators
Clear Hub Feature	01h	Clear_ Feature	none	feature	0	0	none
Clear Port Feature	01h	Clear_ Feature	none	feature	Port	0	none
Set Hub Feature	03h	Set_ Feature	none	feature	0	0	none
Set Port Feature	03h	Set_ Feature	none	feature	Port	0	none
Get Hub Descriptor	06h	Get_ Descriptor	Hub	descriptor type & index	0 or language ID	descriptor length	descriptor
Set Hub Descriptor (optional)	07h	Set_ Descriptor	host	descriptor type & index	0 or language ID	descriptor length	descriptor length
Get Bus State	02h	Get_State	Hub	0	Port	1	per-port bus state

17

Managing Power

One of the most convenient features of USB is the ability for peripherals to draw power from the bus. Although many peripherals can be entirely bus powered, there are limitations that make bus power unsuitable for some.

This chapter will help you decide whether or not your design can use bus power. Whether your design is bus-powered or self-powered, you'll find out how to ensure that your design follows the specification's requirements for power management and conservation.

Powering Options

Inside a typical PC, and available to a typical self-powered hub, is a power supply with amperes to spare. USB peripherals can take advantage of this existing capability rather than having to provide their own individual and redundant supplies.

The ability to draw power from the same cable that carries data to and from the PC is a huge convenience. Most computer rooms have a large assortment of "wall wart" power supplies, each hanging across multiple slots in its outlet strip and contributing to a tangle of wires. Some peripherals have internal power supplies, but these just make the peripherals bigger and heavier and again require redundant components.

Using the PC's supply often saves energy as well, because power supplies in PCs use efficient switching regulators rather than the cheap linear regulators used in wall warts. Not having to include a power supply also means that peripherals are cheaper to manufacture.

Before USB, most peripherals used the PC's RS-232 serial and printer ports, which don't include a power-supply line. The ability to use bus power is so compelling that the designers of some peripherals that connect to these ports have used schemes that borrow the small amount of current available from unused data lines in the interface. With a super-efficient regulator, you can get a few milliamperes from a serial or parallel port to power a device. Another approach used by some peripherals is to kludge onto the keyboard connector, which does have access to the PC's power supply. With USB, you don't have to resort to these tricks.

Voltages

The nominal voltage between the VBUS and GND wires in a USB cable is 5V, but the actual value can be a little more or quite a bit less. A device that's using bus power must be able to handle the variations and still comply with the specification.

These are the minimum and maximum voltages allowed at a hub's downstream ports:

Hub Type	Minimum Voltage	Maximum Voltage
High Power	4.75	5.25
Low Power	4.4	5.25

To allow for cable and other losses, devices should be able to function with supply voltages a few tenths of a volt less than the minimum available at the hub's connector. In addition, transient conditions can cause the voltage at a low-power hub's port to drop briefly to as low as 4.07V.

If components in the device need a higher voltage, the device can contain a step-up switching regulator. Most USB controller chips require a +5V or +3.3V supply. Components that use 3.3V supplies are handy because the device can use an inexpensive, low-dropout linear regulator to obtain 3.3V.

Which Peripherals Can Use Bus Power?

Not every peripheral can take advantage of bus power. Although the USB can provide generous amounts of current in comparison to other interfaces, the current available from the PC's power supply or an external hub does have limits. Figure 17-1 is a chart that will help you decide whether a device can use bus power.

Advances in semiconductor technology have reduced the power required by electronic devices. This is good news for designers of bus-powered devices. Thanks to CMOS processes used in chip manufacturing, lower supply voltages for components, and power-conserving modes in CPUs, you can do a lot with 100 milliamperes.

A peripheral that requires up to 100 milliamperes can be bus powered and will work when attached to any host or hub. A peripheral that requires up to 500 milliamperes can use bus power with one limitation: not every battery-powered computer and no bus-powered hub supports peripherals that draw more than 100 milliamperes from the bus. Also remember that the peripheral must draw no more than these amounts even when the bus voltage is at its limits.

Of course, some devices need to function when they're not attached to the host at all. A digital camera is an example. These will need their own supplies. Self power can use batteries or power from a wall socket. To save battery power without requiring users to plug in a supply, a device can be designed to be bus-powered when connected to the bus and self-powered otherwise.

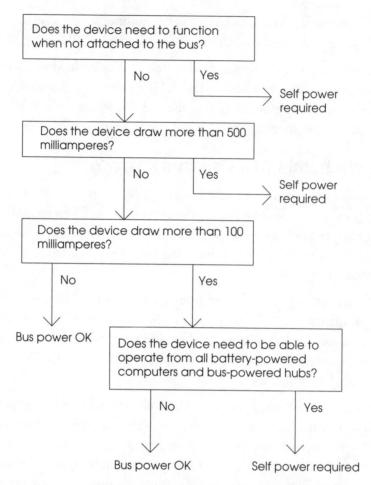

Figure 17-1: Not every device can use bus power alone. However, a device that has its own supply may also be capable of being bus-powered.

A device in the Suspend state can draw very little current from the bus, so some devices will need their own supplies to enable operating when the host has put the device in the Suspend state.

Power Needs

The specification defines a low-power device as one that draws up to 100 milliamperes from the bus, and a high-power device as one that draws up to

500 milliamperes from the bus. A self-powered device has its own power supply and can draw as much power as its supply is capable of.

On power-up, any device can draw up to 100 milliamperes from the bus until the device is configured. This enables self-powered devices to be configured even if the user hasn't yet attached or switched on an external supply.

A high-power device can't draw more than 100 milliamperes until the host has said it's OK to do so. This typically happens this during enumeration. After retrieving a configuration descriptor, the host examines the amount of current requested in MaxPower, and if the current is available, it sends a Set_Configuration request specifying that configuration.

A self-powered device may also draw up to 100 milliamperes from the bus at any time. This enables the device's USB interface to function when the device's power supply is off.

These limits are absolute maximums, not averages. And again, remember that the bus's power-supply voltage may be as high as 5.25V, which may result in greater current consumption.

A device never provides upstream power. Even the pull-up resistor must remain unpowered until VBUS is present.

Informing the Host

During the configuration process, the host learns whether the device is self powered or bus powered and the maximum current the device will draw from the bus.

As Chapter 5 explained, each device's configuration descriptor holds a Max-Power value that specifies the maximum bus current the device requires. All hubs have over-current protection that prevents excessive currents from flowing to a device.

A peripheral can support both bus-powered and self-powered options, using self power when available and bus power (possibly with limited abilities) otherwise. When the power source changes, the host must re-enumerate the hub. To enable forcing a re-enumeration, power to the device's bus pull-up resistor may be controlled by a FET. Switching the FET off briefly, then back on, simulates a disconnect and re-connect. If the device doesn't have this feature, users will need to remove the device from the bus before attaching or removing the power supply. The device reports its use of bus or self power in response to a Get_Status (Device) request from the host.

Hub Power

Powering options for hubs are similar to those for other devices, but hubs have some special considerations. A hub must also control power to its devices and monitor power consumption, taking action when the devices are using too much current and presenting a safety hazard.

Power Sources

Like other devices, all hubs except the root hub are self-powered or bus-powered. The root-port hub gets its power from the host.

If the host's power is AC power from a wall socket or another external source, the root-port hub must be high power and capable of supplying 500 milliamperes to each port on the hub. If the host is battery-powered, the hub may supply either 500 or 100 milliamperes to each port on the hub. If it supplies 100 milliamperes, the hub is defined as a low-power hub.

Bus-powered hubs are limited. All of a bus-powered hub's downstream devices must be low power. This is because the hub can draw no more than 500 milliamperes and the hub itself will use some of this, leaving less than 500 milliamperes for all attached devices combined. However, there are many peripherals that can function with 100 milliamperes or less.

Like other high-power, bus-powered devices, a bus-powered hub can draw up to 100 milliamperes until it's configured, and up to 500 milliamperes after being configured. During configuration, the hub must manage the available current so that its devices and the hub combined don't exceed the allowed current. A possible use for a bus-powered hub would be a hub with an embedded keyboard and pointing device. The keyboard and mouse use little power, so the hub can easily use bus power.

Like other self-powered devices, a self-powered hub may also draw up to 100 milliamperes from the bus so the hub interface can continue to function when the hub's power supply is off. If the hub's power is from an external source, such as AC power from a wall socket, the hub is full power and must be capable of supplying 500 milliamperes to each port on the hub. If the hub uses battery power, the hub may supply 500 or 100 milliamperes to each port on the hub.

Over-current Protection

As a safety precaution, hubs must be able to detect an over-current condition, which occurs when the current used by the total of all devices attached to the hub exceeds a preset value. When the port circuits on a hub detect an over-current condition, they limit the current at the port and the hub informs the host of the problem.

The specification doesn't name a value to trigger the over-current actions, but it must be less than 5 amperes. To allow for transient currents, the over-current value should be greater than the total of the maximum allowed currents for the devices. In the worst case, seven high-power, bus-powered downstream devices can legally draw up to 3.5 amperes. So a supply for a self-powered hub with up to seven downstream ports would provide much less than 5 amperes at all times unless something goes very wrong.

The specification allows a device to draw larger inrush currents when it attaches to the bus. However, this current is typically provided by the stored energy in a capacitor downstream from the over-current protection circuits.

Power Switching

A bus-powered hub must have circuits that can provide and cut off power to its downstream ports. A single switch may control all ports, or the ports may switch individually. A self-powered hub must support switching to the Powered Off state, and may also support power switching to its downstream ports.

Saving Power

The USB's Suspend state ensures that a device doesn't consume power from the bus when the host has no reason to communicate with it. A device enters the Suspend state when there is no activity on the bus for a time, or when the host sends a request to suspend to the device's hub.

The amount of current that a suspended device can draw from the bus is limited to a few milliamperes if the device supports remote wakeup, or much less if not. A device that needs to function even when the host has ceased communicating may need to be self-powered. However, most USB chips can shut down, consuming very little power, but still detect when there is activity requiring attention on an I/O pin.

Global and Selective Suspends

Most suspends are global, where the host stops communicating with the entire bus. When a PC running Windows 98 detects no activity for a period of time, the PC enters a low-power state and stops sending Start-of-Frame packets on the USB. When a full-speed device detects that no Start-of-Frame packet has arrived for 3 milliseconds, it enters the Suspend state. Low-speed devices do the same when they haven't received a low-speed keep-alive signal for 3 milliseconds. The Cypress CY7C63000 low-speed chips have a bus-activity bit that the firmware can monitor to find out if it needs to enter the Suspend state. Other chips have similar features.

A host may also suspend an individual device by sending a Set_Port_Feature request to the device's hub with the Index field set to the port number and the Value field set to Port_Suspend. (See Chapter 16.) This instructs the hub to stop sending any traffic, including Start-of-Frames or low-speed keep-alives, to the named port. The specification defines this as a selective suspend. However, on some early host controllers in PCs, the remote wakeup for selectively suspended devices isn't reliable.

Current Limits for Suspended Devices

A low-power device can draw no more than 500 microamperes from the bus when in the Suspend state. This is a very small amount, and includes the current through the device's bus pull-up resistor. The pull-up current flows from the device's pull-up supply, which must be between 3.0 and 3.6V, through the 1.5-kilohm pullup and the hub's 15-kilohm pull-down to ground. In the worst case, with a pull-up voltage of 3.6V and resistors that are 5% less than their nominal values, the pull-up current is 230 microamperes, leaving just 220 microamperes for anything else.

A high-power device that supports remote wakeup and has had its remote-wakeup feature enabled by the host can draw up to 2.5 milliamperes from the bus. This also includes current through the pull-up resistor. The limit is an average over intervals of up to 1 second, so brief peak currents can be greater. For example, a flashing LED that draws 20 milliamperes for one tenth of each second draws an average of 2 milliamperes per second.

A device should begin to enter the Suspend state after being in the Idle state for 3 milliseconds. The device must be in the Suspend state after being Idle for 10 milliseconds.

Resuming Communications

When a device is in the Suspend state, two actions can cause it to enter the Resume state and restart communications. Any activity on the bus will cause the device to enter the Resume state. And if the device's remote wakeup feature is enabled by the host, the device itself may request a resume at any time.

To resume, the host places the bus in the Resume state (the K state, defined in Chapter 19) for at least 20 milliseconds. It follows the Resume with a low-speed End-of-Packet signal. (Some BIOSes incorrectly send the End-of-Packet after just a few hundred microseconds.) The host then resumes sending Start-of-Frame packets and any other communications requested by the device driver.

A device causes a Resume by driving the bus in the Resume state for between 1 and 15 milliseconds. The device then places its drivers in a high-impedance state to enable the host to drive the bus. A device may send the Resume at any time on a Suspended bus, as long as the bus has been suspended for at least 5 milliseconds. The host controller software must allow all devices at least 10 milliseconds to recover from a Resume.

18

The Electrical Interface

All of the protocols and program code in the world are of no use if the signals don't make it down the cable in good shape. The electrical interface plays an important part in making USB a reliable way to transfer information.

From a practical point of view, if you're using cables and components that others have designed, you don't need to know much about the electrical interface. You can just use the products you have and trust that the hardware designers have done their job. But if you're designing USB transceivers or cables, printed-circuit boards with USB interfaces, or a protocol analyzer that must unobtrusively monitor the bus, you do need to understand the electrical interface and how it applies to your project.

This chapter presents the essentials about the electrical interface of the USB's drivers and receivers and details about the cables that carry the signals.

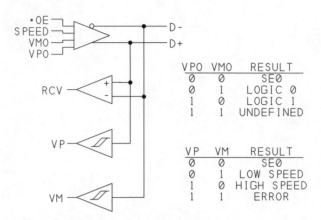

Figure 18-1: Philips' PDIUSBP11 transceiver includes a differential driver and receiver as well as two single-ended receivers for detecting bus speed and Single-Ended Zeros.

Signal Voltages

Figure 18-1 shows the circuits inside a Philips' PDIUSB11 USB transceiver. The chip converts between the signals on the bus and TTL logic levels. Any USB controller chip contains similar circuits.

The transceiver contains the differential driver and receiver required to send and receive data on the bus. When transmitting data, the driver has two outputs that are 180 degrees out of phase. When one output is high, the other is low. The receiver detects the voltage difference between the two lines. When D+ is more positive than D-, the signal is defined as a differential 1, and when D- is more positive than D+, the signal is a differential 0. This type of link is called a balanced line.

The differential receiver's output can interface directly to a TTL-compatible input.

The differential driver has four TTL-compatible inputs. When *OE is a logic high, the driver is disabled and the transceiver is able to receive data. Whe *OE is a logic low, the driver is enabled. When the driver is enabled, the VPO and VMO inputs together determine the output's state, as shown by the truth table in the figure. The Speed input determines the edge rate (rise and fall times) of the driver's outputs, with a logic low causing the driver to use the slower edge rates required for transmissions to low-speed devices.

The chip also has two single-ended receivers that detect the D+ and D- voltages with reference to signal ground. The logic states of the receivers' outputs indicate whether the bus is low speed or full speed, and whether the bus is in the Single-Ended-Zero state (described below).

The components that connect to any USB cable must be able to withstand the shorting of any line to any other line without component damage.

Differential 1 and 0

When transferring data, the USB's two logic states are differential 1 and differential 0. Other differential interfaces, such as RS-485, define these states strictly as the difference between the voltages on the two lines, with no reference to a signal ground. USB differs because it specifies absolute voltages in addition to the voltage difference.

A differential 1 exists at the driver when the D+ output is at least 2.8V and the D- output is no greater than 0.3V, referenced to the driver's signal ground. A differential 0 exists at the driver when D- is at least 2.8V and D+ is no greater than 0.3V, referenced to the driver's signal ground. All drivers must comply with these definitions.

At the receiver, a differential 1 exists when D+ is at least 2V, referenced to the receiver's signal ground, and the difference between D+ and D- is greater than 200 millivolts. A differential 0 exists when D- is at least 2V, referenced to the receiver's signal ground, and the difference between D- and D+ is greater than 200 millivolts. However, a receiver may optionally have less stringent definitions that require only a differential voltage greater than 200 millivolts, ignoring the requirement for one line to be at least 2V.

In either case, the difference between the minimum transmitted and received voltages means that a signal can have some noise or attenuation, and the receiver will still see the correct logic level.

The differential 1s and 0s don't translate directly into 1s and 0s in the transmitted data, but instead indicate either a change or no change in logic level or a bit stuff, as explained in Chapter 19.

Other Valid States

Besides the differential 1s and 0s of transmitted data, the USB defines two other valid states indicated by voltages on D+ and D-.

Idle

Voltages that indicate an idle line are similar to the voltages for differential 1 and 0. The Idle voltages differ depending on whether the interface is low or full speed. This enables a hub to easily detect the speed of a newly attached device.

In the Idle state, when no drivers are active, D+ is more positive on a full-speed line and D- is more positive on a low-speed line.

On a full-speed line in the Idle state, D+ must be greater than 2.7V, and D- must be less than 0.8V. A device may optionally use a less stringent definition for the lower voltage, with a limit of 2V instead of 0.8V.

Single-Ended Zero

The Single-Ended-Zero state occurs when both D+ and D- are 0.3V or less at the driver and 0.8V or less at the receiver. The definitions for entering the End-of-Packet, Disconnect, and Reset states (described in Chapter 19) use Single-Ended Zeros.

The complement of the Single-Ended Zero is the Single-Ended 1. This occurs when both D+ and D- are greater than 2.8V at the driver and greater than 2V at the receiver. This is an invalid state on the bus, and should never occur.

Cables

The USB specification includes detailed requirements for cables. The requirements help to ensure that any compliant cable will be able to carry

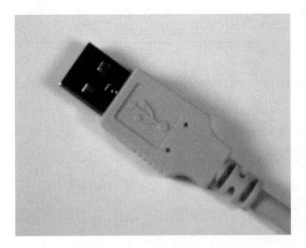

Figure 18-2: The USB icon identifies a USB cable and also indicates the top surface of the plug when attached.

the bus's fast digital signals without errors due to noise in the cable or large amounts of noise radiating from the cable.

Conductors

USB cables have four conductors: VBUS, GND, D+ and D-.

VBUS is the +5V supply.

GND is the ground reference for VBUS as well as for D+ and D-.

D+ and D- are the differential signal pair.

Chapter 17 described the voltage and current limits for VBUS.

The USB icon embossed on the plug connector identifies a USB cable (Figure 18-2).

Cables to be used in full-speed and low-speed segments have different requirements, compared in Table 18-1.

A full-speed cable must be shielded, and the two signal wires must be a twisted pair. Low-speed cables don't require shielding or twisted pairs. This enables low-speed cables to be very flexible, so you can move a mouse or other low-speed device easily, without resistance from a stiff cable. For some

Table 18-1: Comparison of full-speed and low-speed cables

Specification	Low Speed	Full Speed
Maximum length (meters)	3	5
Shield required?	no	yes
Twisted pair required?	no	yes
Slew rate of drivers (nanoseconds)	75–300	4–20
Characteristic impedance (ohms)	unspecified	90
Wire gauge (AWG#)	28 or lower	28 or lower
Pull-up location at the port	D-	D+
Detachable cable OK?	no	yes
Captive cable OK?	yes	yes

devices, the need for a flexible cable is reason enough to require a low-speed interface.

In a full-speed cable, the signal wires must have a characteristic impedance of 90 ohms. This value is a measure of the input impedance of an infinite, open line and determines the initial current on the lines when the outputs switch. The characteristic impedance for the signal wires in low-speed cable isn't defined because the slower edge rates mean that the initial current doesn't affect the logic states seen by the receiver.

The specification lists requirements for the cable's conductors, shielding, and insulation. These are the major requirements for full-speed cables:

Data wires: twisted pair, #28 AWG.

Power and ground: non-twisted, #20 to #28 AWG.

Drain wire: stranded, tinned copper wire, #28 AWG

Inner shield: aluminum metallized polyester

Outer shield: braided, tinned copper

The specification also lists requirements for the cable's durability and performance.

The specification requires the following colors and connections for the conductors:

pin	Conductor	Color
1	VBUS (+5V)	red
2	D-	white
3	D+	green
4	GND	black
shell	shield	drain wire

Connectors

The specification describes two connector types: the series-A plug for the upstream end of the cable and the series-B plug for the downstream end of the cable (Figure 18-3). Every cable must have a series-A plug, but not all cables require a series-B plug.

A typical hub will have a series-B receptacle on its upstream side. This accepts the downstream end of the cable that connects to the root hub or another upstream hub. A hub with external ports will also have one or more series-A receptacles. These accept the upstream ends of the cables that connect to devices or other downstream hubs.

The connectors are keyed so you can't plug them in upsidedown. The logo is on the top side of the plug as you attach it.

Detachable and Captive Cables

The specification defines cables as being either detachable or captive. From the names, you might think that a detachable cable is one that can be removed from its device, while a captive cable is permanently attached to its downstream device. But in fact, a captive cable can be removable, as long as its downstream connector is *not* a series-B (or series-A) type.

A detachable cable must be full speed, with a series-A plug for the upstream connection and a series-B connector for the downstream connection. The generic USB cables offered by various vendors are of this type.

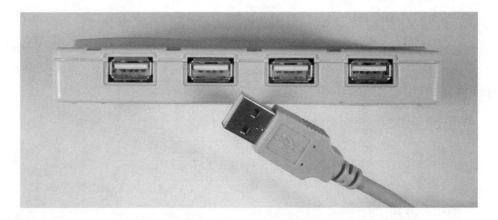

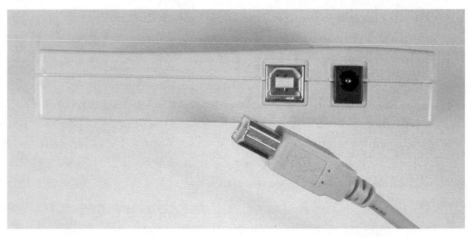

Figure 18-3: The series-A plug (top) is on the upstream end of the cable, and the series-B plug (bottom) is on the downstream end. On a hub, the downstream ports use series-A receptacles and the upstream port uses a series-B receptacle.

A captive cable may be low- or full-speed. It has a series-A plug for the upstream connection. For the downstream connection, the cable can be permanently attached, or removable with a different connector type. The non-standard connector doesn't have to be hot pluggable, but the series-A plug must be hot pluggable. Requiring low-speed cables to be captive eliminates the problem of users trying to use low-speed cables in full-speed segments.

USB Complete

Cable Length

Version 1.0 of the USB specification included maximum lengths for cable segments. A full-speed segment could be up to 5 meters and a low-speed segment could be up to 3 meters. Version 1.1 dropped the length specifications in favor of a discussion of characteristics that limit a cable's ability to meet the specification. On full-speed cables, the limits are due to signal attenuation, cable propagation delay (the amount of time it takes for a signal to travel from driver to receiver), and the voltage drops on the VBUS and GND wires. On low-speed cables, the length is limited by the rise and fall times of the signals, the capacitive load presented by the segment, and the voltage drops on the VBUS and GND wires.

The original limits of 3 and 5 meters are still good general guidelines. Cables of these lengths that meet the specifications are readily available. Longer segments may be feasible with careful attention to cable design and testing. Chapter 17 explained how the length limits translate to a maximum distance of 30 meters between a host and its peripheral, assuming the use of five hubs and six 5-meter cable segments.

The USB specification prohibits extension cables, which would extend the length of a segment by adding a second cable in series. An extension cable for the upstream side of a cable would have a series A plug on one end and a series-A receptacle on the other, while an extension cable for the downstream side would have a series-B plug and receptacle.

The prohibition against extension cables eliminates the temptation to stretch a segment beyond the interface's physical limits. USB extension cables are available, but just because you can buy one doesn't mean that it's a good idea or that it will work. Instead, buy a single cable of the length you need, and add hubs as necessary.

There is one exception: an *active* extension cable consists of a hub, a downstream port, and a cable. This will work fine, because it contains the required hub. An active extension cable will cost more than a passive cable, but it's the right way to do it.

Ensuring Signal Quality

The USB's specifications for drivers, receivers, and cable design ensure that virtually all data transfers occur without errors (with error-checking protocols to catch the ones that don't).

The hardware interface has several requirements that help to ensure signal quality. These include balanced lines, shielded cables and twisted pairs required for full-speed cables, and slower edge rates required for low-speed drivers.

Sources of Noise

Noise can enter a wire in many ways, including by conductive, common-impedance, magnetic, capacitive, and electromagnetic coupling. If a noise voltage is large enough, and if it's present when the receiver is detecting a transmitted bit, the noise can cause the receiver to misread the logic level. Very large noise voltages can damage components.

Conductive and common-impedance coupling require ohmic contact between the signal wire and the wire that is the source of the noise. Conductive coupling occurs when a wire brings noise from another source into a circuit. For example, a noisy power-supply line carries noise into the circuit it powers. Common-impedance coupling occurs when two circuits share a wire, such as a ground return.

The other types of noise coupling result from interactions between the electric and magnetic fields of the wires themselves and of signals that couple into the wires from outside sources, including other wires in the interface.

Capacitive and inductive coupling can cause crosstalk, where signals on one wire enter another wire. Capacitive coupling, also called electric coupling, occurs when two wires carry charges at different potentials, resulting in an electric field between the wires. The strength of the field, and of the resulting capacitive coupling, varies with the distance between the wires. Inductive, or magnetic, coupling occurs because current in a wire causes the wire to emanate a magnetic field. When the magnetic fields of two wires overlap, the energy in each wire's field induces a current in the other wire.

When wires are greater then 1/6 wavelength apart, the captive and inductive coupling is considered together as electromagnetic coupling. An example of electromagnetic coupling is when a wire acts as a receiving antenna for radio waves.

The USB's interface uses a variety of techniques to limit noise from these sources.

Balanced Lines

One way that the USB eliminates noise is with the balanced lines that carry the bus's differential signals. The advantage of using balanced lines is that they are electrically quiet. Any noise that couples into the interface is likely to couple equally into both signal wires. Because the receiver detects only the difference between the two wires' voltages, any noise that is common to both cancels out.

In contrast, in the unbalanced, single-ended lines used by RS-232 and other interfaces, the receiver detects the difference between a signal wire and a ground line shared by other circuits. The ground line is likely to be carrying noise from a number of sources, and the receiver sees this noise when it detects the difference between the signal voltage and ground.

Twisted Pairs

In a full-speed USB cable, the two signal lines must form a twisted pair. A twisted pair is two insulated conductors that spiral around each other with a twist every few inches (Figure 18-4). The twisting reduces noise in two ways, by reducing the amount of noise in the wires and by canceling whatever noise does enter the wires. Twisting is most effective at eliminating low-frequency, magnetically coupled signals such as 60-Hz power-line noise.

Twisting reduces noise by minimizing the area between the conductors. The magnetic field that emanates from a circuit is proportional to the area between the conductors. When the conductors twist around each other, the total area between them is minimized. The tighter the twists, the smaller the

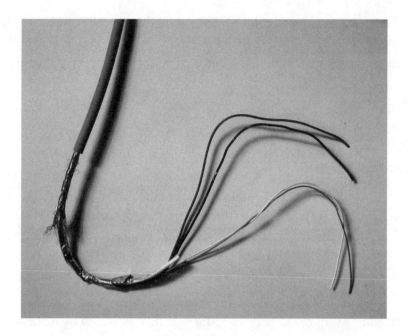

Figure 18-4: A full-speed USB cable contains a twisted pair for data, plus VBUS and GND lines, plus aluminum metallized polyester and braided copper shields.

area. Reducing the area shrinks the magnetic field that emanates from the wires and thus reduces the amount of noise coupling into the field.

A twisted pair cancels noise that enters the wires because the conductors swap physical positions with each twist. Any noise that magnetically couples into the wires reverses polarity with each twist. The result is that the noise present in one twist is cancelled by a nearly equal, opposite noise signal in the next twist. Of course, the twists aren't perfectly uniform, so the canceling isn't perfect, but the noise is much reduced.

Shielding

Metal shielding prevents noise from entering or emanating from a cable. Shielding is most effective at blocking noise due to capacitive, electromagnetic, and high-frequency magnetic coupling.

Full-speed cables have specific shielding requirements, while low-speed cables require no shielding.

In a full-speed cable, an aluminum metallized polyester shield surrounds the four conductors. Surrounding this is a shield of braided, tinned copper wire. Between the shields and contacting both is a copper drain wire. The outside layer is a polyvinyl chloride jacket. The shield terminates at the connector plug.

In a low-speed cable, the drivers' slower rise and fall times make shielding unnecessary.

The specification leaves the grounding details to the user, with the warning that the grounding method must be consistent with accepted industry practices and regulations with respect to safety, electromagnetic interference (EMI), radio-frequency interference (RFI), and electrostatic discharge (ESD).

Edge Rates

Low-speed cables aren't required to use twisted pairs or shielding. But the lower data rate enables the drivers to use slower transitions, or edge rates, that reduce both the reflected voltages seen by receivers and the noise that emanates from the cable.

When a digital output switches, a mismatch between the line's characteristic impedance and the load presented by the receiver will cause reflected voltages that briefly affect the voltage seen by the receiver. If the reflections are large enough and last long enough, the receiver may misread a transmitted bit.

In a low-speed cable, the slower edge rates ensure that any reflections have died out by the time the output has finished switching. (High-speed cables use a different approach that actually makes use of the first reflection.) The slow edge rates also mean that the signals contain less high-frequency energy and thus the noise emanated by the cables is less.

19

Signals and Encoding

You can design a USB peripheral without knowing all of the details about how the data being transferred is encoded on the bus. But understanding something about these helps in understanding USB's abilities and limits.

This chapter presents the essentials of the USB's encoding and data formats. For more details, I recommend the book *USB Hardware and Software* by John Garney and others involved with USB's development.

Bus States

Chapter 18 introduced four bus states that correspond to voltages on the two signal wires: Differential 1 and 0, Idle, and Single-Ended-Zero. The specification describes eight additional bus states that describe conditions that the voltages can signify, either alone or in combination, at a port. The additional bus states are J, K, Resume, Connect, Start-of-Packet, End-of-Packet, Disconnect, and Reset.

J and K

The differential 1s and 0s are a measure of the voltages on the lines. But the data states indicated by the differential 1s and 0s differ, depending on whether the interface is low speed or full speed:

bus voltage	data state, low-speed device	data state, full-speed device
differential 0	K	J
differential 1	J	K

Defining the J and K states like this enables using a single terminology to describe an event, even though the voltages on low- and full-speed lines differ. For example, a Start-of-Packet exists when the bus changes from Idle to the K state. On a full-speed segment, this means that D- becomes more positive than D+, while on a low-speed segment, it means that D+ becomes more positive than D-.

On a full-speed interface, a J data state is a differential 0 and a K data state is a differential 1. On a low-speed interface, it's the opposite: a J data state is a differential 1 and a K data state is a differential 0. As we'll see, however, the data is encoded, and the J and K data states don't correspond to the transmitted 0s and 1s in the transmitted data.

Resume

When a device is suspended, the K data state signifies a resume from the suspended state.

Connect

A downstream port is in the Connect state when the bus has been in the Idle state for between 2.5 microseconds and 2.0 milliseconds.

Start-of-Packet

The Start-of-Packet bus state exists when the bus has changed from an Idle State to the K data state.

End-of-Packet State

The bus is in the End-of-Packet state when a receiver has been in the Single-Ended-Zero state for at least one bit time, followed by a J data state for at least one bit time. A receiver may optionally define a shorter minimum time for the J data state. At the driver, the Single-Ended Zero is approximately two bit widths.

Disconnect State

A downstream port is in the Disconnect state when a Single-Ended Zero has lasted for at least 2.5 microseconds.

Reset State

When a Single-Ended Zero lasts for 10 milliseconds, the device must be in the Reset state. A device may enter the Reset state after as little as 2.5 microseconds.

Data Encoding

All data on the USB is encoded. The encoding format, called *Non-Return to Zero Inverted (NRZI) with bit stuffing*, ensures that the receiver remains synchronized with the transmitter without the overhead of sending a separate clock signal or Start and Stop bits with each byte.

If you use an oscilloscope or logic analyzer to view USB data on the bus, you'll find that unlike other interfaces, reading the bits isn't as easy as matching voltage levels to logic levels.

Instead of defining logic 0s and 1s as voltages, the USB defines logic 0 as a voltage change, and logic 1 as a voltage that remains the same. Figure 19-1 shows an example. Each logic 0 results in a change from the previous state. Each logic 1 results in no change in the voltages. The bits transmit least-significant-bit (LSB) first.

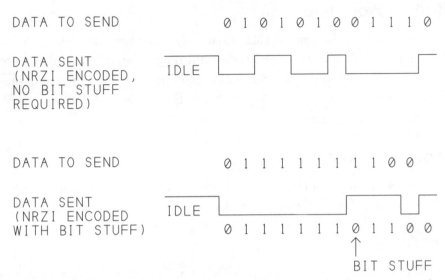

Figure 19-1: In NRZI encoding, a 0 causes a change and a 1 causes no change. Bit stuffing adds a 0 after six consecutive 1s.

Staying Synchronized

When two devices exchange data, the receiving device needs a way to know when each bit is available to be read. With RS-232 and similar interfaces, the transmitter and receiver each have their own clock reference, and both must agree on the frequency. Each transmitted word begins with a transition from the idle state to a Start bit. The receiver synchronizes to this transition and then uses timing circuits and the agreed-on bit rate to read each bit in the calculated middle of each bit time. The Stop bit returns the link to the idle state so the next Start bit can be detected.

If the transmitter's and receiver's clocks differ by up to a few percent, the receiver will still be able to read ten or eleven bits before the timing gets so far off that bits are misread. Each new transmitted word has a Start bit that resynchronizes the clocks.

But adding a Start and Stop bit to each data byte adds 25 percent overhead. A 9600-bps link with 8 data bits and one Start and Stop bit transmits only 7680 data bits (960 bytes) per second. There are 1920 Start and Stop bits!

Another approach used by SPI, I²C, and Microwire interfaces is to send a clock signal along with the data. The protocol defines when to read the bits, either on detecting a rising or falling edge or a high or low logic level. Sending a clock requires an extra signal line, however, and a noise glitch on the clock line can cause misread data.

NRZI requires no Start and Stop bits or clock line. The USB uses two other techniques to remain synchronized: bit stuffing and Sync fields. Each adds some overhead to each transaction, but especially with larger packet sizes, the amount of overhead is minimal.

Fortunately, the USB hardware does all of the encoding and decoding automatically, so device developers and programmers don't have to worry about it. But the encoded data does make it difficult to see the bits on an oscilloscope or logic analyzer. The solution is to use a protocol analyzer that decodes the data for you.

Bit Stuffing

Bit stuffing is required because the receiver synchronizes on the transitions of the data bits. If the data is all 0s, there are plenty of transitions. But if the data contains a long string of 1s, the lack of transitions could cause the receiver to get out of sync.

If the data has six consecutive 1s, the transmitter stuffs, or inserts, a 0 (represented by a transition) after the sixth 1. This ensures at least one transition for every seven bit widths. The receiver detects and discards any bit that follows six consecutive 1s.

Considering just the data bytes, there are only three values with six consecutive 1s:

    00111111
    01111110
    11111100

Including both the data and control and status information, bit stuffing can increase the number of transmitted bits by up to 17%. In reality the average is much less.

Sync Field

Bit stuffing alone isn't enough to ensure that the transmitting and receiving clocks in a transfer are synchronized.

Because devices and host don't share a clock signal, the receiving device has no way of knowing exactly when a transmitting device will send a transition that marks the beginning of a new packet. Although devices can detect a transition that signals a new transmission, a single transition isn't enough to ensure that the receiver will remain synchronized for the duration of a packet, even with bit stuffing.

To keep things synchronized, each packet begins with a sync field to enable the receiving device to align, or synchronize, its clock to the transmitted data. The sync field is eight bits: KJKJKJKK. The transition from the Idle to the first K serves as a sort of Start bit that indicates the arrival of a new packet, but there's just one sync field per packet, rather than a Start bit for each byte.

The alternating Ks and Js provide the transitions for synchronizing, and the final two Ks mark the end of the field. By the end of the sync field, the receiving device knows precisely when each bit in the packet will arrive. The price to pay for synchronizing is the addition of eight bit times to each packet. Larger packets are more efficient than smaller ones!

An End-of-Packet signal returns the bus to the Idle (J) state in preparation for the next sync field.

Timing Accuracy

The USB's full-speed rate of 12 Megabits per second enables fast communications but results in more critical requirements for devices' cables and timing components. Where the fast data rate isn't needed, the low-speed rate of 1.5 Megabits per second can allow the use of less expensive components and cables (although the need for slower edge rates actually increases the manufacturing cost of low-speed chips).

The timing requirements for full-speed devices are strict. The data rate can vary no more than 0.25%. The data rate is typically derived from a timing crystal. Many factors can affect the crystal's frequency, including the initial accuracy, capacitive loading, and aging of the crystal, as well as the supply voltage and temperature. Crystal accuracy is often specified as parts per million (ppm), which is the maximum number of cycles the crystal may vary from its rated value, in the time required for 1 million cycles at the rated frequency. The rating required for 0.25% accuracy is 2500 ppm.

In contrast, a low-speed device's data rate can vary up to 1.5% (15,000 ppm). This enables low-speed devices to use low-cost ceramic resonators in place of quartz crystals.

The host's data rate must be extremely accurate, within 0.05%, or 500 ppm. The frame intervals must be accurate as well, at 1 millisecond +/-500nsec. To maintain this accuracy, hubs must be able to adjust their frame intervals to match the host's.

The specification also defines limits for data jitter, or small variations in the timing of the individual bit transitions. The jitter allows for differences in the rise and fall times of the drivers as well as clock jitter and other random noise.

Packet Format

As Chapter 3 explained, all USB data travels in packets, which are blocks of information with a defined format. The packets in turn contain fields, with each field type holding a particular type of information. The field types are sync, PID, address, endpoint, frame number, data, and CRC. Table 19-1 illustrates.

Sync Field

Each packet begins with an 8-bit sync field, as described earlier. The sync Field serves as the Start-of-Packet delimiter. This field may transmit only on an idle bus.

Table 19-1: All USB traffic is in packets. Packets are made up of fields. The field type determines its contents.

Name	SIze (bits)	Packet Types	Purpose
Sync	8	all	Start-of-packet and synchronization
PID	8	all	Identify the packet type
Address	7	In, Out, Setup	Identify the function address
Endpoint	4	In, Out, Setup	Identify the endpoint
Frame Number	11	SOF	Identify the frame
Data	0 to 1023	In, Out, Setup	Data
CRC	5 or 16	In, Out, Setup	Detect errors

Packet Identifier Field

The Packet Identifier Field (PID) is 8 bits. Bits 0 through 3 identify the type of packet and bits 4 through 7 are the one's complement of these bits, for use in error checking.

There are ten defined PID codes for Token, Data, and Handshake and Preamble packets. Chapter 3 introduced these codes. The lower two bits identify the PID type, and the upper two bits identify the specific PID.

Address Field

The address field is seven bits that identify the function that the host is communicating with. The function is a device (which may be a hub), or a specific function in a compound device.

Endpoint Field

The endpoint field is four bits that identify an endpoint number within a function. A low-speed function can have no more than 3 endpoint numbers, but a full-speed function can have up to 16.

Frame Number Field

The frame-number field is eleven bits that identify the specific frame. The host sends this field in each start-of-frame packet. The number rolls over to 0 at 7FFh.

Data Field

The data field may range from 0 to 1023 bytes, depending on the transfer type and the amount of data in the transaction.

CRC Fields

The CRC field is 5 bits for address and endpoint fields and 16 bits for data fields. The bits are used in error-checking. The transmitting hardware inserts the CRC bits and the receiving hardware does the required calculations; there's no need for program code to do it.

Inter-packet Delay

The USB carries data from multiple sources, in both directions, on one pair of wires. Data can travel in just one direction at a time. To ensure that the previous transmitting device has had time to switch off its driver, the bus requires a delay of a couple of bit widths between the end of one packet and the beginning of the next packet in a transaction. This delay is limited, however, to ensure that the bus doesn't waste time waiting.

A device must delay at least two bit times between packets. When a transaction requires a response in the opposite direction, the responding device may delay no more than 6.5 bit times if using a detached cable, or 7.5 bit times if using a captive cable. The host may delay no more than 7.5 bit times. These maximums apply only to the packets within a transaction.

A device waiting for a response packet must wait at least 16 bit times, but no more than 18 bit times, before invalidating the transaction. A host must wait at least 18 bit times before starting a new transaction.

These delays are handled by the hardware and require no support in code.

In Closing...

I hope you've found this book useful. Be sure to check Lakeview Research's website for updates, additions, and corrections to this book, as well as other links of use. Good luck with your projects!

Jan Axelson

Appendix A

Resources

You can find additional resources for exploring USB in the CD-ROM included with this book and at Lakeview Research's website.

About the CD-ROM

The CD-ROM that accompanies this book contains two types of information: program code and product information.

The program code includes all of the host and firmware example code presented in the book. The host software includes source and executable code for a complete Visual-Basic project. The firmware includes Cypress CY7C63001 assembly code to use with the Visual-Basic application. I've also included a variety of firmware examples provided by Cypress Semiconductor.

The product information includes documentation from Cypress Semiconductor for chips and the Starter Kit and Developer's Kit described in this book. These are provided as a convenience. They're also available from Cypress' website.

About the Website

The other resource for more about using USB is the USB Central page at Lakeview Research's website, at *www.lvr.com*. This is where I will post updates, corrections, new code samples, and links to anything I find that's relevant to developing USB products. If you have a suggestion, code, or other information that you'd like me to post or link to, let me know at *jan@lvr.com*.

Appendix B

Cypress CY7C63001 Registers

Cypress CY7C63001 Registers (sheet 1 of 2)

Bit Numbers

7	6	5	4	3	2	1	0

Port 0 Data Register (00h)

P0.7	P0.6	P0.5	P0.4	P0.3	P0.2	P0.1	P0.0
R/W	R/W	R/W	R/W	R/W	R/W	R/W	R/W

Port 1 Data Register (01h)

P1.7	P1.6	P1.5	P1.4	P1.3	P1.2	P1.1	P1.0
R/W	R/W	R/W	R/W	R/W	R/W	R/W	R/W

Port 0 Interrupt Enable (04h)

P0.7 IE	P0.6 IE	P0.5 IE	P0.4 IE	P0.3 IE	P0.2 IE	P0.1 IE	P0.0 IE
W	W	W	W	W	W	W	W

Port 1 Interrupt Enable (05h)

P17. IE	P1.6 IE	P1.5 IE	P1.4 IE	P1.3 IE	P1.2 IE	P1.1 IE	P1.0 IE
W	W	W	W	W	W	W	W

Port 0 Pull-up (08h)

Pull P0.7	Pull P0.6	Pull P0.5	Pull P0.4	Pull P0.3	Pull P0.2	Pull P0.1	Pull P0.0
W	W	W	W	W	W	W	W

Port 1 Pull-up (09h)

Pull P1.7	Pull P1.6	Pull P1.5	Pull P1.4	Pull P1.3	Pull P1.2	Pull P1.1	Pull P1.0
W	W	W	W	W	W	W	W

USB Endpoint 0 TX Configuration (10h)

EnableINs	Data1/0	Stall	Data Inval.	Count 3	Count 2	Count 1	Count 0
R/W	R/W	R/W	R/W	R/W	R/W	R/W	R/W

USB Endpoint 1 TX Configuration (11h)

EnableINs	Data1/0	Stall	EP1enable	Count 3	Count 2	Count 1	Count 0
R/W	R/W	R/W	R/W	R/W	R/W	R/W	R/W

USB Device Address (12h)

Reserved	Address6	Address5	Address4	Address3	Address2	Address1	Address0
-	R/W	R/W	R/W	R/W	R/W	R/W	R/W

USB Complete

Cypress CY7C63001 Registers (sheet 2 of 2)

Bit Numbers

7	6	5	4	3	2	1	0

USB Status and Control (13h)

Reserved	Reserved	Reserved	Enable Outs	StatusOuts	Forced J	Force Resume	Bus Activity
-	-	-	R/W	R/W	W	R/W	R/W

USB Endpoint 0 RX Status (14h)

Count 3	Count 2	Count 1	Count 0	data toggle	IN	OUT	Setup
R/W	R/W	R/W	R/W	R	R/W	R/W	R/W

Global Interrupt Enable (20h)

Wake-up	GPIO	Reserved	Endpoint 1	Endpoint 0	1.024-ms	128- μs	Reserved
R/W	R/W	R/W	R/W	R/W	R/W	R/W	R/W

Watchdog Timer (21h)

Reset 7	Reset 6	Reset 5	Reset 4	Reset 3	Reset 2	Reset 1	Reset 0
W	W	W	W	W	W	W	W

Cext Clear (22h)

Reserved	Reserved	Reserved	Reserved	Reserved	Reserved	Reserved	Cext
-	-	-	-	-	-	-	R/W

Timer (23h)

Count 7	Count 6	Count 5	Count 4	Count 3	Count 2	Count 1	Count 0
R	R	R	R	R	R	R	R

Port 0 Isink (30h–37h)

Reserved	Reserved	Reserved	Reserved	Isink3	Isink2	Isink1	Isink0
W	W	W	W	W	W	W	W

Port 1 Isink (38h–3Fh)

Reserved	Reserved	Reserved	Reserved	Isink3	Isink2	Isink1	Isink0
W	W	W	W	W	W	W	W

Status and Control (FFh)

Reserved	Watchdog Reset	USB Reset	Power-on Reset	Suspend	Reserved	Reserved	Run
W	R/W	R/W	R/W	R/W	W	W	R/W

Index

Index

USB Complete

Index